A Pilot's Guide to **Aircraft** And **Their Systems**

A Pilot's Guide
to Aircraft And
Their Systems

The more you know about your
aircraft systems, the better you fly

Dale Crane

A Focus Series Book
Aviation Supplies & Academics, Inc.
Newcastle, Washington

A Pilot's Guide to Aircraft and Their Systems
by Dale Crane

Aviation Supplies & Academics, Inc.
7005 132nd Place SE
Newcastle, Washington 98059-3153
www.asa2fly.com

© 2002 Aviation Supplies & Academics, Inc.

Published 2002 by Aviation Supplies & Academics, Inc.

Printed in the United States of America

05   04   03   02   9   8   7   6   5   4   3   2   1

ASA-ACFT-SYS
ISBN 1-56027-461-1

Photo credits: p.52, Cessna Aircraft; p.57 and cover, Lancair;
p.283, TEC Aviation Division.

Library of Congress Cataloging-in-Publication Data:

Crane, Dale.
  A pilot's guide to aircraft and their systems : the more you know
about your aircraft systems, the better you fly / by Dale Crane.
      p.   cm. — (Focus series book)
Includes index.
  ISBN 1-56027-461-1
  1. Airplanes. 2. Aeronautical instruments. 3. Aeronautics—Systems
engineering. 4. Private flying. I. Title. II. Series.

TL670 .C74 2002
629.133'34—dc21   2002153716
02

Contents

Section 5
Aircraft Fuel Systems

Section 6
Aircraft Electrical Systems

Section 7
Aircraft Instrument Systems

Section 8
Avionics Systems

Section 9
Aircraft Environmental Control Systems

Section 10
Aircraft Ice and Rain Control Systems

Section 11
Aircraft Fire Extinguishing Systems

Section 16
Aircraft Piston Engine Lubrication and Cooling Systems

Section 17
Propellers

Preface

In the early days of aviation an aviator had to be, pretty much, a mechanic as well as a pilot because the airplanes and engines were less than completely dependable. When a pilot had a forced landing away from help, it was up to him to find and fix the problem to get the airplane back into the air. Fortunately these airplanes were not complex nor complicated.

In the more than half a century since World War II, aircraft have become a vital component of our transportation system and as such, have been developed and finely tuned to become the fast, efficient, dependable, and safe machines they are today.

These technological advances have been accompanied with additional complexities and demands that the aircraft be operated in *exactly* the way the designer intended. To do this, pilots must understand what each handle or knob controls and what he or she can expect from each system. Maintenance technicians must thoroughly understand the aircraft and their systems to keep them functioning as they were designed and built to do.

This book has been prepared to furnish pilots and armchair aviators with a brief insight of *what* the aircraft, powerplant, and each of the systems do. For those whose interest has been piqued by this book and want to learn your aircraft in more depth, I recommend the ASA *Aviation Maintenance Technician Series* of books that explain *how* the aircraft and its systems work. In addition, the ASA *Dictionary of Aeronautical Terms* contains many definitions that will help you understand the complex terms used in modern aviation.

It is the sincere desire of the author and editors of *A Pilot's Guide to Aircraft and Their Systems* that this book will help you enjoy your flying and make you a safer and more efficient pilot.

—Dale Crane

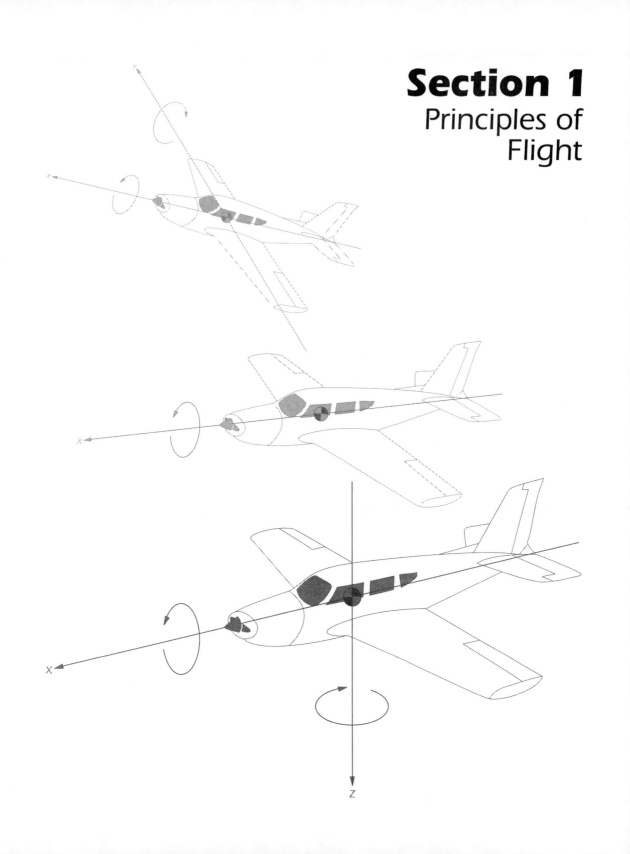

Section 1
Principles of
Flight

Chapter 1   Forces Acting on an Airplane in Flight

How Does a Heavier-Than-Air Flying Machine Defy the Law of Gravity?

A heavier-than-air craft flies by obeying a different law; Newton's third law of motion. An airplane flies by creating a downward force on a mass of air that is equal to its own weight. In return, this mass of air produces an upward force on the airplane and supports it.

Newton's third law of motion states that every action (or force) gives rise to a reaction (or opposing force) of equal strength but of opposite direction.

The wing of an airplane has a very special cross sectional shape called an airfoil section. When this airfoil moves through the air the relative wind strikes it at an angle called the angle of attack.

The air in the relative wind strikes the leading edge of the airfoil and some flows over the top and some across the bottom. The air flowing over the top finds the surface dropping away from it, and, in the same way you speed up as you run down a hill, the air speeds up. According to Bernoulli's principle, when the air speeds up, its pressure drops and the low pressure above the wing pulls the air down to the surface and as it leaves the wing it is deflected downward.

Bernoulli's principle. When the total energy in a column of moving fluid remains constant, any increase in the kinetic energy of the fluid (its velocity) results in a corresponding decrease in its potential energy (its pressure).

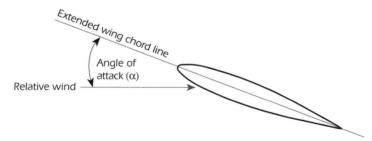

Figure 1. The angle of attack is the acute angle between the chord line of an airfoil and the relative wind.

The air flowing below the wing finds the surface rising into its path. This slows down the air and its pressure increases. As the air leaves the airfoil it is deflected downward.

When the weight of the air deflected downward equals the weight of the airplane, the air supports the airplane.

Five things affect the amount of air deflected downward:

Factors affecting lift
- Physical characteristics
  - –airfoil shape
  - –airfoil area
- Air density
  - –air temperature
  - –barometric pressure
- Pilot controlled
  - –airspeed
  - –angle of attack

1. Shape of the airfoil
2. Angle of attack
3. Area of the airfoil
4. Density of the air
5. Speed of the air

The shape and area of the airfoil are physical characteristics of the airplane. The density of the air is determined by the outside air temperature. The altitude, the speed of the air, and the angle of attack are controlled by the pilot.

Five Forces

The five forces are in equilibrium during straight and level unaccelerated flight.

In straight and level flight at a constant airspeed and altitude five forces are in balance on an airplane:

1. Thrust, acting forward, is caused by the propeller moving air rearward.
2. Lift, acting perpendicular to the relative wind, is caused by the wing deflecting air downward.
3. Weight of the aircraft, caused by gravity, acts toward the center of the Earth.
4. Drag, acting in the direction opposite to thrust, is caused by the resistance of the air as the aircraft moves through it.
5. Tail load is a downward aerodynamic force produced by the horizontal tail deflecting air upward. The amount of tail load is determined by the airspeed and it is used for longitudinal stability.

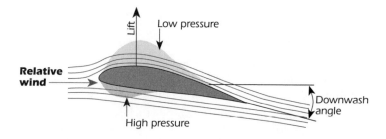

Figure 2. The shape of the airfoil causes the air through which it is passing to be deflected downward.

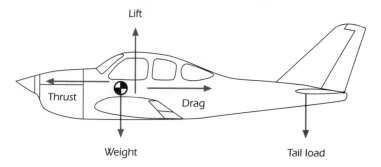

Figure 3. In straight and level, unaccelerated flight, the five forces are balanced.

Chapter 2 **Axes of an Airplane**

An airplane moves in three dimensions and is controlled by rotating it about one or more of its three axes. *See* Figure 4.

1. Longitudinal (roll) axis—Extends through the aircraft from nose to tail passing through the center of gravity. The airplane is rotated about its longitudinal axis by changing the amount of lift produced by the left or right wing. This is done by deflecting the ailerons. The ailerons are connected in such a way that as the aileron on one wing moves downward increasing the lift, the one on the opposite wing moves upward decreasing the lift, and the airplane rolls.

2. Lateral (pitch) axis—Extends across the airplane from wing tip to wing tip, passing through the center of gravity. The airplane is rotated about its lateral axis by varying the tail load. This is done by deflecting the movable horizontal tail surface. When the trailing edge of the surface moves upward the downward tail load increases and the nose rises. When the trailing edge moves downward the tail load decreases and the nose drops.

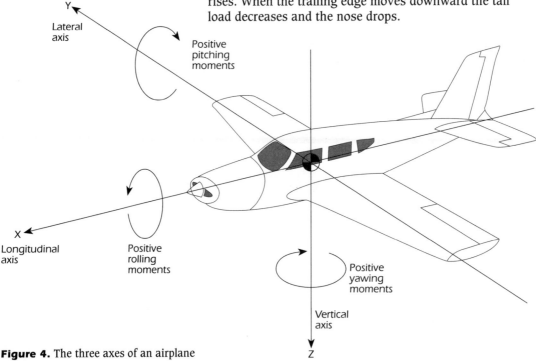

Figure 4. The three axes of an airplane

3. Vertical (yaw) axis—Extends through the airplane vertically, passing through the center of gravity. An airplane is
yawed (not turned) by changing the horizontal aerodynamic force on the vertical tail by deflecting the movable
vertical tail surface.

Control of an Airplane

An airplane is controlled by varying the forces that rotate it
about one or more of its three axes.

Pitch Control

The movable horizontal tail surfaces (elevators, stabilator, or
ruddervators) vary the tail load. When the control column or
stick is moved aft, the trailing edge of the surface rises, deflecting air upward. This increases the downward tail load and
causes the airplane to rotate nose-up about its lateral axis.
When the column is moved forward, the trailing edge moves
downward, deflecting air downward, canceling the downward
tail load and producing an upward force on the tail. The tail
moves upward and the airplane rotates nose-down about its
lateral axis.

An airplane is free to rotate about its three axes so it does
not always maintain a fixed relationship with the Earth. Because of this, the terms "up" and "down" do not necessarily
mean the same thing they mean when we are earthbound. In
normal flight, moving the control column back causes the nose
to move up (relative to the horizon). But if we are inverted,
moving the control column back causes the nose to move *down*
(relative to the horizon).

To minimize confusion, in this book the terms up and
down and right and left mean what they do when the airplane
is sitting on the ground.

Roll Control

The ailerons, the movable surfaces on the trailing edge of the
wing near the tips, vary the deflection of the air flowing over
them. They are controlled by rotating the control wheel or
moving the control stick laterally. The ailerons are rigged so
that when one moves downward, the one on the opposite wing
moves upward.

The aileron moving downward deflects air downward and
causes the wing on which it is mounted to rise. At the same
time the aileron on the opposite wing moves upward, deflect-

elevators. The horizontal movable
control surface in the tail section,
or empennage of an airplane.

stabilator. A single-piece movable
horizontal tail surface on an airplane that serves the dual purpose
of the horizontal stabilizer and the
elevators.

ruddervator. The control surfaces
on an airplane that combine the
function of the rudder and the
elevators. Ruddervators are the
movable surfaces in a V-tail
empennage.

Rotating the control wheel to the
left moves the left aileron up and
the right aileron down.

ing air upward and causes its wing to move downward. This rotates the airplane about its longitudinal axis, or causes it to roll.

Yaw Control

The movable portion of the vertical tail is called the rudder, but it is not to be confused with the rudder on a boat because it does not turn the airplane. It only causes the airplane to yaw or rotate about its vertical axis. Depressing the right rudder pedal deflects the trailing edge of the rudder to the right, deflecting air to the right, moving the tail to the left and the nose to the right. Depressing the left rudder pedal has the opposite effect.

An airplane turns when it banks, or rotates about its longitudinal axis. The lift force acts perpendicular to the lateral axis and when the airplane banks, this force has both a vertical and a horizontal component. The horizontal component pulls the nose around and the airplane turns.

yaw. A flight condition in which an airplane rotates about its vertical axis. Yawing is not the same as turning because an airplane can be yawed while continuing in straight flight.

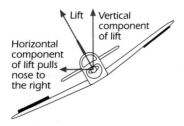

Figure 5. An airplane turns when the wings tilt giving the lift force a horizontal component that pulls the nose around.

Chapter 3 **Stability**

An airplane has two conflicting requirements: stability and controllability. Stability is the characteristic that causes an airplane to want to remain in straight and level flight or return to that condition if disturbed. Controllability is the characteristic that allows an airplane to be maneuvered (rotated about its three axes) by the pilot. An airplane with a high degree of stability may be difficult to fly, and one with very little stability is highly maneuverable. For this reason some modern fighter airplanes have almost no inherent stability and must be flown with an automatic pilot that has a faster response rate than a human pilot.

Two kinds of stability are of concern to the pilot: static and dynamic.

Static Stability

An airplane is statically stable if, when it is disturbed from straight and level flight, a force is generated that tries to restore it to its undisturbed condition.

Longitudinal Stability

When an airplane that is trimmed for straight and level flight encounters rough air that causes the nose to pitch downward, the airspeed increases and the downward tail load (an aerodynamic force that is determined by the airspeed) increases and returns the airplane to level flight. If the nose pitches upward, the airspeed and tail load decrease and the nose drops back to level flight.

"Stability" relates to maintaining the desired flight attitude with a minimum of pilot effort.

"Control" involves rotating the airplane about one or more of its three axes.

static stability. The characteristic of an aircraft that causes it to return to straight and level flight after it has been disturbed from that condition.

Static Stability
Produces restorative force when aircraft is disturbed

Dynamic Stability
Decreases restorative forces as original condition is approached

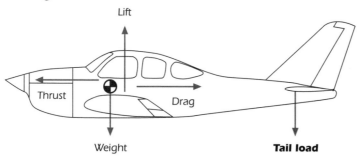

Figure 6. The downward tail load that varies with the airspeed produces static longitudinal stability.

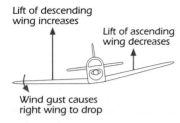

Lift of descending wing increases

Lift of ascending wing decreases

Wind gust causes right wing to drop

Figure 7. Dihedral produces lateral stability.

side slip. A flight maneuver in which an airplane is banked while the rudder keeps it on a straight heading. This crossed-control condition causes the airplane to move sideways toward the low wing.

Lateral Stability

Dihedral is the positive angle between the lateral axis of an airplane and a line which passes through the center of the wing. When a wind gust causes a wing to drop, the relative wind strikes the descending wing at a greater angle (a higher angle of attack) and the lift on that side increases. The angle of attack of the ascending wing decreases as does its lift, and the airplane returns to level flight.

Airplanes in which maneuverability is more important than stability have little or no dihedral. Some acrobatic biplanes have dihedral on the lower wing and cathedral (negative dihedral) on the upper wing.

Directional Stability

When a wing drops, the airplane side slips and the relative wind strikes the vertical tail surface at an angle. This deflects the air and produces a force that rotates the airplane about its vertical axis and returns it to straight flight so the air flows evenly around the vertical tail.

Dynamic Stability

Static stability creates a restorative force when the airplane departs from straight and level flight. Dynamic stability causes this force to diminish as the aircraft moves in the direction of returning to its original condition.

Chapter 4 **Secondary Controls and Devices**

The primary controls that rotate an aircraft about its three axes are the elevators, ailerons, and rudder. But there are important secondary controls. Flaps increase the curvature of the wing cross-section to increase both lift and drag to assist in takeoff and landing. Tabs and adjustable stabilizers trim the aircraft for steady-state, hands-off flight under varying flight conditions. Flight spoilers destroy lift and create a great deal of drag to allow an airplane to descend at a steep angle without picking up excessive airspeed. Ground spoilers destroy lift, putting the maximum amount of weight on the wheels to increase braking effectiveness on landing.

Secondary flight controls:
– Modify the amount of lift produced by the primary controls.
– Change the amount of force needed to operate the primary controls.

Flaps

There are several types of flaps ranging from the simple hinged trailing edge of the wing between the fuselage and the aileron to the complex triple-slotted flap used on many of the large jet transport aircraft. The purpose of all flaps is the same: to change the amount of air that is deflected downward by the wing.

Simple Flap

The simple flap is a hinged portion of the trailing edge of the wing between the aileron and the fuselage. Its effectiveness is quite limited. Normally with a simple flap, deflection of up to about 20° increases the lift more than the drag and it is used to allow the airplane to take off in the shortest possible distance. Deflection between 20° and 40° increases the drag more than the lift and is used for landing. Full flap deflection allows the airplane to approach at a steeper angle without building up excess speed, and to touch down at the slowest possible speed.

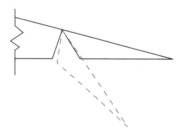

Figure 8. A simple flap has limited effectiveness and is seldom used on modern airplanes.

Fowler Flap

Fowler flaps and the similar Zap flaps are much more effective than the simple flap because they not only change the airfoil shape but since they move out of the wing trailing edge, they also increase the wing area. Fowler flaps were originally designed for large airplanes but have been effectively used on many popular small airplanes as well.

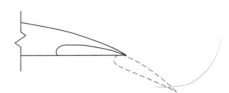

Figure 9. Fowler flaps increase the wing area as well as changing the airfoil shape.

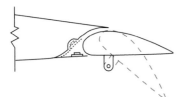

Figure 10. When a slotted flap is deflected, high-velocity air from below the wing is forced to flow over the top of the flap, producing a low pressure that prevents the air from breaking away from the upper surface.

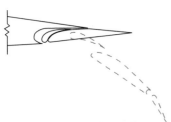

Figure 11. Triple-slotted flaps deflect the maximum amount of air. Air flowing through the slots creates a low pressure that pulls the air to the upper surface and prevents its breaking away.

critical angle of attack. The highest angle of attack at which air passes over an airfoil in a smooth flow. At angles greater than the critical angle, the air burbles or flows in a disturbed pattern and lift is lost.

Slotted Flap

When a flap is deflected beyond a certain degree, the airflow can no longer follow the upper surface but breaks away causing a loss of lift. In order to produce the maximum amount of drag without losing lift, slotted flaps are often used. When a slotted flap is lowered, a slot is opened between its leading edge and the wing structure. High-velocity air from below the wing is ducted over the top of the deflected flap lowering the pressure and pulling air down to follow the flap surface. This greatly increases the amount of air deflected by the flap.

Triple-Slotted Flap

The ultimate in flaps is the triple-slotted flap used on many of the high-performance jet transport airplanes. As the flaps are lowered they progressively unfold with slots formed between the sections to deflect air over their surfaces. Triple-slotted flaps increase the wing area and allow the pilot to select the optimum amount of flap for the existing flight condition. As the flaps extend, high-pressure air from below the wing flows through the slots creating a low pressure that pulls air down to the upper surface and prevents its breaking away.

Slots and Slats

The amount of lift produced by a wing increases with the angle of attack up to the critical angle at which the smooth flow of air over the top of the wing breaks away. This is the angle at which the wing stalls.

The critical angle of attack can be increased with an accompanying increase in lift at low speed by installing either a fixed slot or a movable slat that produces a passageway for high-pressure air from below the wing to be sprayed out at a high velocity over the upper surface. This fast moving air creates a low pressure that holds the air down on the surface until the wing reaches a much higher angle of attack than it could attain without the slot.

Fixed slots were installed in some of the older airplanes ahead of the ailerons. This allowed the inboard portion of the wing to stall before the outer portion so the ailerons could remain effective during the stall.

Some high-performance jet fighters and utility airplanes that are designed for extremely slow flight have full-span slats. These devices form the leading edge of the wings and at low angles of attack are held in place by the force of the air. At a high angle of attack, the air flows across the leading edge and the pressure over the leading edge drops. The slats automatically extend, forming the duct that causes the air to flow smoothly over the upper surface until an extremely high angle of attack is reached.

Figure 12. Slots in the leading edge of a wing duct high-energy air from below the wing and spray it out over the upper surface. The high-velocity air produces a low pressure that prevents the air above the wing from breaking away until a higher angle of attack is reached.

Stall Strips

It is important that an airplane have lateral control during a stall, and it is characteristic of a tapered wing for the stall to begin at the outboard trailing edge, just where the ailerons are located.

Small triangular stall strips, typically about a foot long, are installed on the leading edge of the wing in the root area. When the angle of attack is increased to near the stall point, air flowing over the stall strip is disturbed and the airflow breaks away over the root while the area ahead of the ailerons remains unstalled. Lateral control is thus maintained during the stall.

Trim Devices

An airplane flies hands-off when the five forces are in balance. But changing the engine thrust or the airspeed throws the forces out of balance and constant pressure must be held on the controls to maintain a desirable flight condition. To prevent the pilot from having to hold pressure on the controls, tabs may be installed on the movable surfaces to produce aerodynamic forces that hold them deflected.

Longitudinal Trim

Because the longitudinal trim determines the airspeed at which the airplane will fly level with hands off the controls, almost all airplanes have some method of adjusting the longitudinal trim. Some airplanes have an adjustable stabilizer. A jackscrew, operated by either an electric motor or by a cable controlled by a crank or a wheel in the cockpit, raises or

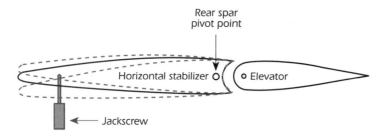

Figure 13. A jackscrew raises or lowers the leading edge of the stabilizer to vary the steady-state downward tail load as airspeed changes.

Trim tabs and adjustable stabilizers allow the pilot to trim an airplane so it will fly hands-off in any desired attitude or airspeed.

Servo tabs allow the pilot to produce an aerodynamic force that that moves the primary control surface.

Spoilers destroy lift and increase drag.

lowers the leading edge of the horizontal stabilizer. This changes the tail load and compensates for changes in airspeed for the various flight conditions.

Some airplanes have an adjustable trim tab on the trailing edge of the elevator. This is controlled from the cockpit by an electric motor, or a hand wheel or crank. When the tab is deflected upward, air over the elevator is deflected upward and the elevator moves downward, producing a nose-down trim condition. *See* Figure 14.

An improvement on the trim tab is the servo tab. It is similar to a trim tab except the jackscrew is attached to the fixed surface. As the elevator moves up or down, the servo tab moves in the opposite direction to produce an aerodynamic force that assists the pilot in moving the control surface.

The linkage between the servo tab and the jackscrew is adjustable to provide a fixed deflection to adjust the tail load for hands-off flight at the desired airspeed. *See* Figure 15.

Some airplanes have stabilators for longitudinal control. These surfaces pivot about a fixed point and are statically balanced by a weight attached to their leading edge. A long tab is hinged to the trailing edge and controlled by a jackscrew mounted inside the fuselage. *See* Figure 16A. When the control column is moved aft, the trailing edge of the stabilator moves upward and the surface area ahead of the pivot point tries to force it higher. The antiservo tab also moves upward relative to the stabilator and produces a downward aerodynamic force that tries to move the stabilator back down (Figure 16B).

When the control column is moved forward, the trailing edge of the stabilator moves downward (Figure 16C) and the antiservo tab also moves down creating an aerodynamic force that tries to bring the stabilator back to a neutral position.

The linkage between the jackscrew and the tab is adjustable to provide a steady-state trim position for any chosen airspeed.

Spoilers

Airplanes are designed to be as streamlined as possible. This is good, but it does present some problems.

When in flight at high altitude the air traffic controller may direct you to expedite a change to a lower altitude. Retarding the throttle to decrease the thrust so you can descend without

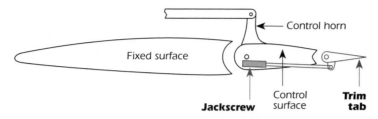

Figure 14. A trim tab is adjustable from the cockpit to produce an aerodynamic force on the elevator that holds it deflected to vary the steady-state downward tail load as airspeed changes.

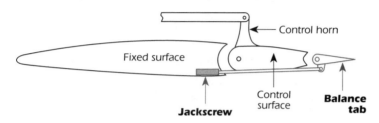

Figure 15. A servo tab moves in the direction opposite to that of the surface on which it is mounted. Servo tabs produce an aerodynamic force that aids the pilot in moving the surface.

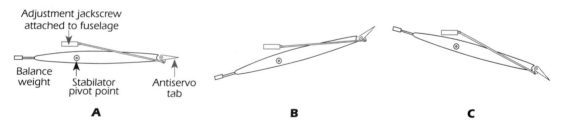

Figure 16. A stabilator has an antiservo tab on its trailing edge to make its movement less sensitive. The tab moves in the same direction as the stabilator.

exceeding safe airspeed is not a viable option because the sudden decrease in engine power will shock cool the engine and cause major damage. Airplanes in which this could happen may be equipped with spoilers. These are small surfaces that extend vertically above the wing to destroy lift and produce a large amount of drag. With spoilers deployed the airplane can maintain engine power and descend without exceeding a safe speed and without shock cooling the engine.

Some airplanes use spoilers to assist in lateral control. When the control wheel is rotated to the right, the spoiler on the right wing extends from the top of the wing and destroys lift allowing the right wing to drop and start the turn. When spoilers are used there is no adverse yaw.

Jet transport airplanes have multiple spoilers on top of the wings. Some may be deployed in flight to aid in lateral control and to produce drag to slow the airplane, others are deployed only on the ground to destroy lift and put the maximum amount of weight on the landing gear to assist in braking.

Frost on an airplane wing adds little weight, but each crystal acts as a tiny spoiler and destroys the smooth flow of air over the surface.

Never attempt a takeoff when the airplane is coated with frost. Remove it with a brush or broom.

---

adverse yaw. A flight condition at the beginning of a turn in which the nose of an airplane starts to move in the direction opposite the direction the turn is being made. Adverse yaw is caused by the induced drag produced by the downward-deflected aileron holding the wing back as it begins to rise.

Chapter 5 **Phases of Flight**

Takeoff

The tricycle landing gear is designed in such a way that the wings produce the minimum amount of drag to allow the airplane to accelerate rapidly. Deflecting the flaps to the takeoff setting changes the airfoil shape of the wing to produce the maximum lift at the minimum speed.

Fully advancing the throttle increases the engine power and the thrust produced by the propeller to accelerate the airplane along the runway. When takeoff speed is reached, a slight backward pressure on the control wheel increases the downward tail load and the airplane rotates about its main wheels. This increases the angle of attack causing the wing to deflect enough air downward for the airplane to fly.

Climb

With the airplane off the ground and accelerating, raising the flaps and retracting the landing gear decreases the drag and increases the acceleration. When the airspeed recommended for climb is reached, decreasing the engine power and adjusting the elevator trim tab or stabilizer provide just exactly the correct amount of tail load to allow the airplane to continue to climb at the desired airspeed without any force being applied to the control wheel.

Cruise

When about two hundred feet above the desired cruising altitude, reducing the power and RPM to the cruise values specified in the POH and rolling the trim tab or stabilizer slightly nose down, allow the airplane to pick up speed. By the time it has descended to the chosen altitude the tail load will have automatically adjusted to hold the airspeed and altitude at the desired values. This is called "putting the airplane on the step."

Turning Flight

An airplane is turned by tilting the lift away from vertical so it will pull the nose around. Rotating the wheel to the left lowers the aileron on the right wing and raises the one on the left wing. The airplane banks to the left and the lift pulls the nose around to the left.

On an airplane with a tricycle landing gear, the two main wheels are behind the center of gravity and the nose wheel is well ahead of the CG.

Phases of flight:
Takeoff
Climb
Cruise
Turning Flight
Stalls
Descent
Approach
Touchdown

POH. Pilot's Operating Handbook

adverse yaw. A flight condition at the beginning of a turn in which the nose of an airplane starts to move in the direction opposite the direction the turn is begin made.

One problem is that as the aileron on the right wing moves down to increase the lift, it also increases the drag which starts the nose moving to the right, the wrong direction. As soon as the bank is established, the lift pulls the nose around to the left as it should. This adverse yaw, the momentary movement of the nose in the wrong direction as a turn is started, is overcome by using pressure on the left rudder pedal to start the nose moving to the left. As soon as the lift begins to pull the nose around, the pressure may be relaxed.

Adverse yaw is minimized in the design of an airplane by the upward-deflected aileron traveling farther than the aileron that moves downward. The additional upward movement of the aileron produces drag that partially overcomes the adverse yaw. Also, most modern airplanes use Frize-type ailerons in which the leading edge protrudes below the lower surface of the wing when the aileron is deflected upward. This produces drag which pulls the downward-moving wing in the correct direction for the turn.

Stalls

stall. An aerodynamic condition in which the angle of attack becomes excessive and the air no longer flows smoothly over an airfoil. When an airfoil stalls, it no longer produces lift.

Contrary to what the term implies on the ground, an airplane stall has nothing to do with a failed engine; it is an aerodynamic term referring to the airplane's ability to continue to produce lift. An airplane stalls when the angle of attack becomes so high that the air flowing over the wing can no longer adhere to the surface and it breaks away, destroying the lift.

A normal stall, as used in training, is done by reducing the engine power and slowly raising the nose until the airflow over the wing breaks away and the nose drops. As soon as it drops, the airspeed builds up and the airplane regains normal flight.

An airplane can stall at any airspeed; this can be proven by placing it in a medium-banked turn at a speed well above the straight-and-level stall speed and pulling back sharply on the control wheel. The angle of attack increases and the wing stalls.

spin. A maneuver in which one wing is stalled while the other continues to produce lift. The airplane descends slowly in a steep nose-down rotating attitude.

A spin is a flight condition in which one wing is stalled while the other is flying. A spin is entered by raising the nose until the airplane is near its stalling attitude and depressing one of the rudder pedals. The airplane yaws and the wing that moves rearward stalls. The opposite wing continues to fly and pulls the airplane around in a spin. The nose drops because there is not enough lift to continue level flight. Most modern general aviation airplanes will recover from a spin if the controls are released. Directional stability will stop the rotation and the airflow over the stalled wing will be restored. Easing back on the wheel will bring the nose back to level flight.

Descent

If the descent is started quite a distance from the airport, adjusting the trim tab or stabilizer for a slightly nose-down attitude will increase the airspeed, and since there is no change in engine power or thrust, the airplane will descend.

The rate of descent may be controlled by either the airspeed or engine power or both. Lowering the nose without decreasing the power may result in a higher than desired airspeed, but descending by suddenly reducing the power at altitude can seriously damage the engine by shock cooling it.

shock cooling. Rapid cooling of an engine by a fast descent from altitude with the throttle closed. The cylinders cool and contract around the pistons, causing cylinder-wall scuffing.

Approach

The successful termination of a flight begins by placing the airplane in the proper position on the approach path, at the proper airspeed and altitude, and in the proper configuration.

The flaps are lowered the correct amount, the landing gear is lowered and checked to be down and locked, the longitudinal trim is adjusted to establish the desired hands-off airspeed, and the engine power is set for the proper descent rate. The powerplant controls are adjusted to allow a go-around if necessary. This means the propeller in full Low Pitch (high RPM), mixture control in Full Rich, and carburetor heat as specified in the POH.

The GUMP-CC check for an approach helps you remember the important items:
Gas (on)
Undercarriage (down and locked)
Mixture (full rich)
Prop (full RPM)
Cowl flaps (open)
Carburetor heat
    (as specified in POH)

Touchdown

The touchdown should be made at the slowest possible speed. Lowering the flaps to the full down position (or as specified in the POH) and reducing the engine power allows the airplane to descend. When just above the runway, the power is fully reduced and back pressure is applied to the control wheel to bring the nose up to increase the angle of attack. This slows the airplane and allows it to descend at the slowest rate. When the airplane touches down on the main wheels and is rolling straight down the runway, the nose is lowered and the flaps are retracted to get the maximum weight on the wheels for efficient braking.

A Pilot's Guide |

Ground Effect

Two questions occur to every pilot at one time or another: Why will an airplane sometime lift off yet refuse to climb? And why does an airplane float so far on landing before it touches down? There is one answer to both of these questions — ground effect.

ground effect. The increase in lift produced by an airfoil when flying near the ground.

As you begin the takeoff run in a tricycle-gear-airplane the angle of attack is low and there is very little lift or drag, but when you rotate, the angle of attack increases and the wing deflects air downward, producing lift. Because of the nearness to the ground, the deflected air has only a small vertical component so there is not a large increase in the induced drag. The airplane can lift off at an airspeed lower than its normal take-off speed. But if it is held at this same attitude and allowed to rise above the ground effect, the induced drag will increase and more power is needed to prevent the airplane from settling. Pulling back on the yoke at this low airspeed will increase the induced drag so much, the airplane can no longer climb. The only solution to this dangerous situation is to slightly lower the nose immediately after lift off. This allows the airspeed to build up and the lift to increase without the large increase in induced drag.

Some airplanes that have no flaps have a reputation for "floating." A power-off approach can be made using the correct airspeed and you can see the touchdown point right where it should be. But as you begin to flare, the airplane does not settle as it should and it floats beyond the touchdown point; ground effect is the culprit.

When the airplane is less than half a wing span above the surface, the downwashed air is effectively flattened out and the induced drag does not increase during the flare as it would at a greater height — the airplane continues to fly. Flaps, properly used, produce enough drag at the landing speed that floating is a minor problem.

20   Section 1 **Principles of Flight**

Chapter 6 **Basic Rotary-Wing Aerodynamics**

The concept of rotary-wing flight was proposed as early as 1500 by Leonardo da Vinci who made drawings and models of his "helix." Through the years, models of rotary-wing machines were built and flown with varying degrees of success, but the first successful man-carrying rotary-wing machines were the Autogiros built in Spain by Juan de la Cierva in 1920. These machines were designed to make flying safer by removing the danger of stalls and spins.

Cierva's first Autogiro was built from an airplane fuselage with its engine and propeller, empennage and landing gear. For lift, it had a freewheeling four-blade rotor mounted on a pylon above the fuselage. The propeller provided thrust to pull the machine across the ground until there was enough air flowing upward through the rotor to start it spinning. As it spun, it produced enough aerodynamic lift to rise into the air.

The autogiro enjoyed limited success but it could not hover except in a strong headwind. This realm of flight had to await the helicopter.

Throughout the 1920s and well into the 1930s, there were many experimental helicopters built in America and abroad with varying degrees of success, until in September of 1939 Igor Sikorsky flew his VS-300 with which he solved many of the control problems that had plagued other experimenters. The VS-300 made its first flights with a main rotor and three auxiliary control rotors, but this configuration soon gave way to one main rotor and a single tail rotor that is a standard configuration today.

Development of the helicopter was assisted to a great extent by the autogiro and many of the features of modern helicopters were first used on these aircraft that had unpowered rotors.

autogiro. A heavier-than-air rotor-wing aircraft that is sustained in the air by free-wheeling rotors turned by aerodynamic forces rather than by engine power. It has a conventional engine and propeller for forward flight.

gyroplane. The modern, generally accepted term for an autogiro.

helicopter. A heavier-than-air rotor-wing aircraft that is supported in flight by aerodynamic lift produced by an engine-driven rotor.

Aerodynamic Principles

Rotary-wing aerodynamics is more complex than fixed-wing aerodynamics because of the speed variation along the length of the rotating airfoil, the dissymmetry of lift caused by forward flight, and the problem caused by the helicopter flying in its own downwash.

Lift, or Rotor Thrust

The lift, or thrust, produced by a helicopter rotor is similar to the lift produced by the fixed wing of an airplane, and it is affected by these factors:

- The density of the air
- The square of the rotor tip speed
- The blade lift coefficient which is a function of the shape of the airfoil section and the angle of attack
- The rotor solidity (the ratio of the blade area to the rotor disk area)

Figure 17. The symmetrical airfoil of a typical helicopter rotor blade

asymmetrical airfoil. An airfoil section that is not the same on both sides of the chord line.

coning angle. The upward flapping angle formed by helicopter rotor blades as they are producing lift.

The airfoil sections used on helicopter rotors have normally been of the symmetrical type like that in Figure 17. With these airfoils, the center of pressure remains relatively constant as the angle of attack changes. This is important because as the blade rotates its angle of attack constantly changes, and when the center of pressure moves, it causes undesirable stresses and vibration. Modern structural developments have overcome some of the vibration problems and asymmetrical airfoils are used on some modern rotor blades.

The area used for computing the lift of a helicopter rotor system is more complex than that for a fixed-wing aircraft because the spinning rotor creates a lift-producing disk.

The speed of a rotor blade through the air varies from its root to its tip, and it also varies with the speed of the helicopter through the air. When the helicopter is hovering in still air, the speed of the rotor blade through the air is the same on both sides of the disk. But when it is moving through the air, the blade that is traveling in the same direction as the helicopter (the advancing blade) has a speed equal to its tip speed plus the speed of the helicopter. The blade traveling in the direction opposite to that of the helicopter (the retreating blade) has an airspeed equal to its tip speed minus the helicopter speed.

When a helicopter is parked and the rotor not turning, the rotor blades droop because of their weight, but as they begin to turn with a very low pitch angle, centrifugal force pulls them out straight because they are not producing any lift.

When the pitch angle is increased so the blades produce lift, the tips raise and the rotor assumes a coning angle. The direction of the lift produced by the rotor system is perpendicular to the tip-path plane which is the bisector of the coning angle. By tilting the coning angle, the helicopter can be made to move forward, rearward, or to either side.

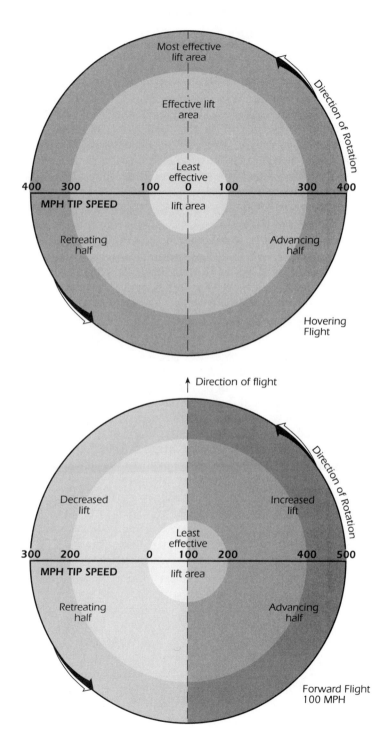

Figure 18. Production of dissymmetry of lift

advancing blade. The blade of a helicopter rotor that is moving in the same direction as the helicopter is moving.

retreating blade. The blade of a helicopter rotor that is moving in the direction opposite to the direction the helicopter is moving.

Dissymmetry of Lift

One of the problems with the first autogiros was that they would roll over when pulled forward through the air by their propeller. This rolling-over tendency was caused by dissymmetry of lift, which in turn was caused by the difference in airspeed between the advancing and retreating blades. Lift increases as the airspeed of the rotor increases, and the greater speed of the advancing blade gives the advancing half of the disk more lift than the retreating half. The most effective way to overcome dissymmetry of lift is to hinge the rotor blades so they are free to flap up and down.

The advancing blade with its greater airspeed has more lift, so it flaps upward, and as it does, its angle of attack decreases and its lift decreases. The retreating blade with its lower airspeed has less lift, so it flaps downward. This increases its angle of attack and thus its lift. Rotor blade flapping thus prevents dissymmetry of lift. *See* Figure 18 on the previous page.

Retreating Blade Stall

A rotor blade, like the wing of an airplane, stalls when its angle of attack becomes excessive. Low-speed flight of an airplane is normally limited by the stall, but the retreating blade stall of a helicopter occurs at high speed. When the helicopter is in high-speed forward flight, the advancing blade has a high airspeed and a low angle of attack, but the retreating blade has a low airspeed and a high angle of attack. When the forward speed is great enough, the angle of attack is so high that the rotor tip stalls (Figure 19). Increasing either the blade pitch or

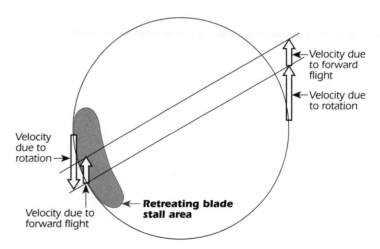

Figure 19. When a helicopter is flown at a high speed, the airspeed of the tip of the retreating blade is low and its angle of attack is high. The tip of the retreating blade stalls as is indicated by the shaded area.

helicopter forward speed causes the stall to progress inward toward the hub, and when approximately 15% of the rotor disk is stalled, the helicopter can no longer be controlled.

A retreating blade stall causes rotor roughness, erratic stick forces, and a stick shake in which the frequency is determined by the number of rotor blades.

Torque

Newton's third law of motion states that for every action there is an equal and opposite reaction. The engine mounted in the fuselage of a helicopter drives the rotor, and the torque (twisting moment) the engine imparts to the rotor has an equal but opposite reactive force that tries to rotate the fuselage. There are a number of ways the torque acting on the fuselage can be compensated for. The engine can drive two rotors, one above the other, on concentric shafts with the rotors turning in opposite directions. The torque caused by the upper rotor is balanced by the opposite torque caused by the lower rotor. Some helicopters have two rotors mounted at an angle above the cabin and intermeshing with each other so that the torque from one rotor counteracts the torque of the other. Still other helicopters have two rotors, with one mounted on the forward end of the fuselage and the other at the aft end. By far the most popular configuration of helicopters has a single rotor, and its torque is counteracted by the thrust produced by a small rotor on the aft end of the fuselage. By changing the pitch of the tail rotor blades with the foot pedals, the pilot can vary the amount of tail rotor thrust to control the yaw of the fuselage about its vertical axis.

Torque compensation:
- Two main rotors
  - Coaxial
  - Side-by-side
  - Fore-and-aft
- Single main rotor
  - Tail antitorque rotor

The pilot controls thrust produced by the tail rotor changing the pitch of the tail rotor blades with the antitorque pedals.

Autorotation

If the rotor of a helicopter is disengaged from the engine in flight it no longer forces air downward, but air begins to flow upward through the rotor. It will continue to turn and will produce lift in the same way as the rotor of an autogiro. The aerodynamic force that causes this rotation is called an autorotative force, and it operates as is shown in Figure 20 on the next page.

Lift always acts perpendicular to the relative wind, while drag acts parallel to it. When air is flowing upward through the rotor, the lift vector is tilted forward, and the resultant lift is tilted ahead of the axis of rotation. The resultant lift has a horizontal component that acts forward in the plane of rotor

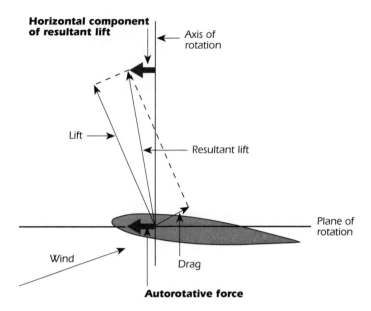

Figure 20. When air flows upward through a rotor, the resultant lift has a component that acts forward in the plane of rotation and causes the rotor to spin.

rotation and produces an autorotative force that causes the rotor to spin. The rotor increases in speed until the drag becomes great enough to bring the resultant lift in line with the axis of rotation, and the rotor stabilizes at this speed.

Ground Effect

Less power is required for an airplane to fly very near the surface than when it is flying higher up. Because of the same aerodynamic principles, a helicopter can hover near the ground with less power than it can a few feet higher. The reason for this increased efficiency near the ground is called ground effect.

ground effect. The increase in lift of a helicopter when flying near the ground.

When a helicopter is hovering at a height well above the ground, the downwash is not affected by the presence of the ground, and there is a vertical velocity of the air moving through the rotor disk. This vertical component, V_V, and the rotational velocity of the rotor, V_R, produce an angle of attack like that in Figure 21A. But when the helicopter is hovering at an altitude of less than one half of the rotor diameter, the air strikes the ground and flows outward. This decreases its vertical velocity, and the angle of attack of the blades increases as seen in Figure 21B. Increasing the angle of attack for the same rotor speed increases the lift, and because the lift always acts perpendicular to the relative wind, the lift vector tilts toward the vertical.

Since a lower blade angle is used to produce the lift needed to hover, the induced drag is decreased and less power is required for the helicopter to hover. Helicopter specifications list the hover ceiling for a helicopter both in ground effect (IGE) and out of ground effect (OGE). The hover ceiling IGE is always higher than it is OGE.

IGE. In ground effect

OGE. Out of ground effect

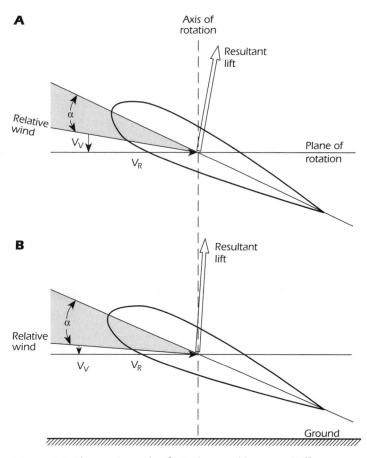

Figure 21. Changes in angle of attack caused by ground effect

Gyroscopic Precession

A gyroscope is a rapidly spinning wheel with its weight concentrated about its rim, and its spinning produces dynamic forces that are greater than the static force of gravity. One of the characteristics of a gyroscope is gyroscopic precession, which causes a force applied to the spinning wheel to be felt at a point 90° from the point of application in the direction of rotation.

The spinning rotor of a helicopter acts in the same way as a gyroscope. Increasing the pitch of the retreating blade and decreasing the pitch of the advancing blade allows precession to tilt the disk forward and moves the helicopter ahead.

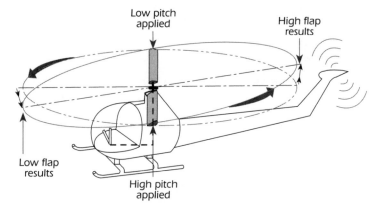

Figure 22. The rotor of a helicopter acts as a gyroscope and is affected by gyroscopic precession. If the blade pitch is increased on the left side of the rotor, the disk will tilt forward.

Chapter 7   **Rotor Systems**

The rotor systems have been the subject of most of the research and development in rotary wing aviation because these are the most complex and critical components of a helicopter. To minimize vibration and allow the pilot to control the attitude of the helicopter, the blades must be free to flap, drag, and feather.

The blades flap up and down as they rotate to counteract dissymmetry of lift. This is done on some two-blade rotors by mounting the rotor on a teetering hinge. When one blade flaps upward, the blade on the opposite side flaps down. On rotors with three or more blades, each blade usually has a flapping hinge at the point it attaches to the hub so it is free to flap up or down as the aerodynamic forces change.

Dynamic forces place a tremendous strain on the rotor blades in their plane of rotation. The advancing blade tries to speed up while the retreating blade tends to slow down. To relieve this strain, some rotor blades have a lead-lag, or drag, hinge and a damper that gives the blades limited movement in the plane of rotation.

The amount of the lift is controlled by changing the pitch angle of the blades. This is done by mounting the blades to the hub in a feathering bearing that allows the pilot to change the pitch angle of the blades.

The three basic types of rotor systems used by modern helicopters are the semirigid, fully articulated, and rigid rotors.

A semirigid rotor has two blades. Each blade is free to feather with the pitch angle controlled by the pilot. The rotor is mounted on the mast with a teetering hinge which allows it to tilt to compensate for dissymmetry of lift.

A fully articulated rotor system has more than two blades, and each blade is free to flap, drag, and feather.

A rigid rotor has many advantages in its lack of moving parts, and has become popular only since the development of new technologies and materials. The blades have a feathering bearing, but the flapping and dragging are done by the flexing of components in the hub and by the blades themselves.

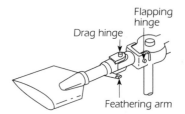

Fully articulated rotor blades are free to flap, drag, and feather.

Blades of semirigid rotor are free to feather, and blades flap as rotor rocks back and forth as a unit.

Blades of rigid rotor are free to feather, but are not hinged to flap or drag.

Figure 23. Three basic types of rotor systems

Chapter 8 **Helicopter Flight Controls**

The basic flight controls of a single-main-rotor helicopter are the collective pitch control, the cyclic pitch control, and the antitorque pedals.

Collective Pitch Control

collective pitch control. The helicopter control that allows the pilot to change the pitch of all the rotor blades at the same time. Engine power is coordinated with this control to increase or decrease lift.

The collective pitch lever is located by the left side of the pilot's seat and is operated with the left hand. As this lever is moved up and down it changes the pitch of all the rotor blades at the same time. Raising the collective control increases the blade pitch, the angle of attack, and the thrust, or lift, produced by the rotor disk. Increasing the angle of attack also increases the drag, and the rotor would slow down if engine power were not increased. For this reason, the engine power is coordinated with the collective pitch control to increase the power when the collective pitch is increased.

Cyclic Pitch Control

cyclic pitch control. The control that allows the pilot to change the pitch of the rotor blades individually, at a specific point in their rotation. The pilot can then tilt the plane of rotation of the rotor disk to change the direction of lift produced by the rotor.

The cyclic pitch control moved by the pilot's right hand changes the pitch of the individual blades at a specific point in their rotation. This tilts the plane of the rotor disk, which gives the lift a horizontal component and pulls the helicopter in the direction the rotor is tilted.

Because of gyroscopic precession, the blade pitch is actually changed 90° of blade rotation before the change is desired. For example, to tilt the rotor forward, the pitch is decreased on the advancing blade when it is at right angles to the fuselage.

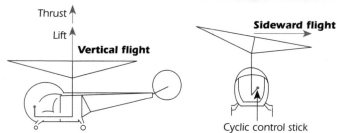
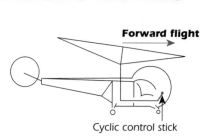

Figure 24. Moving the cyclic control changes the pitch of the main rotor blades at a point in their rotation. This tilts the rotor disk and creates a horizontal component of lift that moves the helicopter in the direction the disk is tilted.

On the opposite side of the helicopter, the pitch of the retreating blade is increased. These pitch changes cause the front of the rotor disk to lower and the rear of the disk to raise. *See* Figure 22 on Page 28.

Horizontal Stabilizer

Some helicopters have either a fixed or movable horizontal stabilizer near the tail, like the one in Figure 25, to hold the fuselage level in forward flight. When the cyclic pitch control is moved forward, the rotor tilts forward and the fuselage tries to follow it. Fixed horizontal stabilizers are set so that they provide the required downward force at cruise speed to keep the fuselage level and minimize the drag. Movable horizontal stabilizers are controlled by the pilot to allow the tail to rise on takeoff so the maximum amount of thrust can be used to increase the airspeed.

Antitorque Pedals

The rotor on most single-rotor helicopters rotates to the left as viewed from above. The torque reaction to this rotation causes the fuselage to rotate to the right. This torque force is compensated by thrust from the tail rotor that keeps the fuselage from rotating. The tail rotor thrust is controlled by the pilot changing the pitch of the tail rotor blades with the antitorque pedals. *See* Figure 26 on the next page.

When the pedals are in their neutral position, the tail rotor has a medium positive pitch, and the thrust from the tail rotor is approximately equal to the torque of the main rotor during cruising flight. This allows the helicopter to maintain a constant heading in level flight.

When the left pedal is moved forward, the pitch of the tail rotor increases and produces additional thrust that rotates the nose to the left. When the right pedal is moved forward, the pitch is decreased until the tail rotor has a negative pitch. This assists the torque in rotating the nose to the right.

Sideways thrust from the tail rotor tends to pull the helicopter to the right, or causes it to drift. To counteract this tendency, the rotor mast of some helicopters is offset to the left so that the tip-plane path has a built-in tilt that produces enough side thrust to the left to counteract the drift.

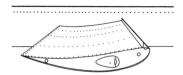

Figure 25. A horizontal stabilizer on a helicopter provides a downward aerodynamic force to hold the tail down in forward flight.

antitorque pedals. Foot pedals used by the pilot to control the pitch of the antitorque rotor on the tail of a single-rotor helicopter.

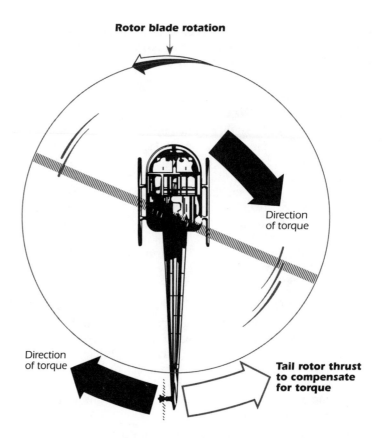

Figure 26. Torque of the engine driving the main rotor tries to rotate the fuselage to the right. This rotation is prevented by tail rotor thrust.

Chapter 9 **Stabilization Systems**

A helicopter is statically stable, but dynamically unstable. This means that when it is disturbed from a condition of level flight, a force is set up that tries to restore it. But this restorative force, instead of decreasing with time, increases and causes the helicopter to develop divergent oscillation.

divergent oscillation.
Oscillations whose amplitude increases with time.

Several types of stabilization systems have been developed to prevent this from happening. Two of the commonly used systems are the stabilizer bar and the offset flapping hinge.

Stabilizer Bar

One popular method of stabilizing a helicopter with a two-blade rotor is the stabilizer bar shown in Figure 27. Two long arms with weighted ends are mounted on a center bar so they rotate with the rotor mast. The bar is perpendicular to the rotor blades and is free to pivot with respect to the rotor mast. The weighted bar acts as a gyroscope and remains rigid in space as the helicopter pitches or rolls.

Rigidity in space causes the stabilizer bar to continue rotating in its original plane when the helicopter pitches or rolls. The angular difference between the stabilizer bar and the rotor mast moves the pitch-change linkage in the correct direction to change the pitch of the blades and bring the helicopter back to a level flight attitude.

Offset Flapping Hinge

By moving the flapping hinge of a fully articulated rotor away from the rotor mast, as is shown in Figure 28 on the next page, stabilizing forces are generated when the helicopter pitches or rolls. The angle of attack of the descending blade is increased and a restorative force is produced, which acts from the offset hinge and restores the helicopter to level flight.

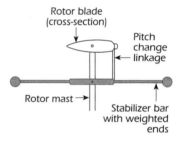

Figure 27. Stabilization with a stabilizer bar

Offsetting the flapping hinge from the center of the mast increases the corrective action produced by the flapping rotor.

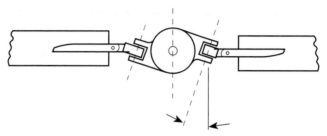

Angling the flapping hinge increases the stabilizing effect.

Figure 28. Stabilization with offset and angled flapping hinges

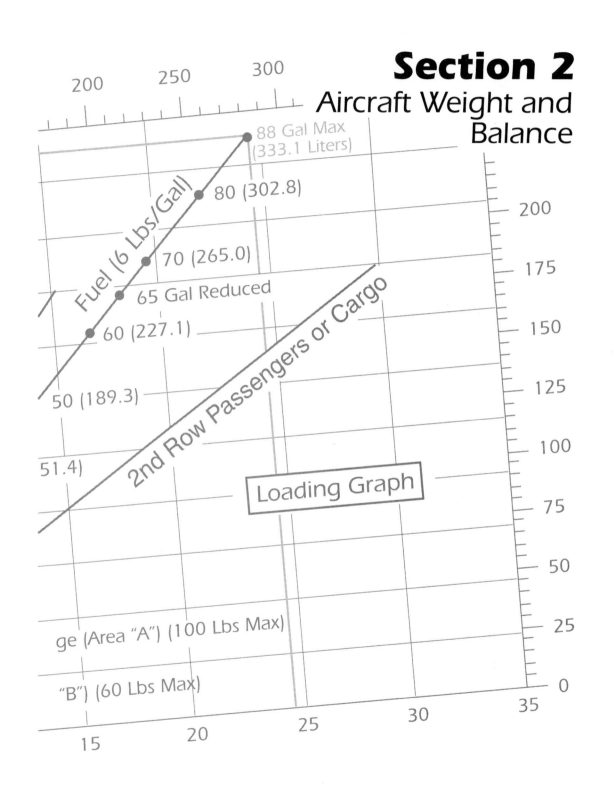

200   250   300

88 Gal Max
(333.1 Liters)

80 (302.8)

Fuel (6 Lbs/Gal)

70 (265.0)

65 Gal Reduced

2nd Row Passengers or Cargo

60 (227.1)

50 (189.3)

51.4)

Loading Graph

ge (Area "A") (100 Lbs Max)

"B") (60 Lbs Max)

200

175

150

125

100

75

50

25

0

15   20   25   30   35

Chapter 10 **Determining the Loaded Weight and Center of Gravity**

While it is not a system of an aircraft, weight and balance is so important and so all encompassing with regards to safety and efficiency of flight, that an overview of the basics should come next.

Modern general aviation aircraft are designed and built so they can lift the maximum weight and carry it the greatest distance at the highest practical speed. These highly efficient aircraft must be operated "by the numbers." It is the responsibility of the pilot-in-command to determine on the preflight inspection that the aircraft is loaded in such away that its total weight and CG are within the allowable limits.

Too much weight can cause these types of problems:

- The aircraft needs a higher takeoff speed which requires a longer takeoff run.

- Reduction of both the rate and angle of climb.

- Reduction of the cruising speed and cruising range.

- The aircraft requires a longer landing roll because of the higher landing speed.

The CG outside of the allowable limits can cause:

- Decreased longitudinal stability.

- Decreased elevator authority.

When an airplane is certificated by the FAA, the pertinent weight and balance data is furnished in the Type Certificate Data Sheets (TCDS) and in the Pilot's Operating Handbook or the Airplane Flight Manual (POH/AFM). Typical weight and balance data is shown in Figure 29 on the next page. It is the responsibility of the AMT who maintains and inspects the aircraft to determine that the most recent and correct data is included in the aircraft records.

Therefore, an important part of preflight planning is determining that the airplane is loaded so that its weight and CG location are within the allowable limits. We will examine three popular ways of determining the weight and balance status, that use two different sets of data: the computational method

CG. Center of gravity. The point at which all of the weight in an object is considered to be concentrated.

If the aircraft weight is too great, or if the center of gravity falls outside the allowable limits, the aircraft is not safe to fly.

AMT. Aviation Maintenance Technician

datum. An imaginary vertical reference plane or line chosen by the aircraft manufacturer from which all arms used for weight and balance computation are measured.

reference datum. An imaginary vertical reference plane chosen by the aircraft manufacturer from which all measurements are made to determine the arm of an object in a weight and balance computation.

arm. The horizontal distance, in inches from the reference datum, to the center of gravity (CG) of an item. A positive (+) arm is behind the datum and a negative (–) arm is ahead of the datum.

moment. The product of the weight of an item in pounds multiplied by its arm in inches. Moment is stated in pound-inches (lb.-in.).

and the electronic flight computer method using weights and arms, and the loading graph method using weights and moment indexes.

Airplane basic empty weight	1,874.0 lbs, EWCG +36.1
CG range	(+40.9) to (+46.0) at 3,100 lbs (+33.0) to (+46.0) at 2,250 lbs or less Straight line variation between points given
Empty weight CG range	None
Maximum weight	3,100 lbs takeoff/flight 2,950 lbs landing
No. of seats	4 (2 front at +37.0) (2 rear at +74.0)
Maximum baggage	160 lbs Area A (100 lbs at +97.0) Area B (60 lbs at +116.0)
Fuel capacity	92 gal (88 gal usable); two 46 gal integral tanks in wings at +46.6 See NOTE 1 for data on unusable fuel.
Oil capacity	12 qt (–15)

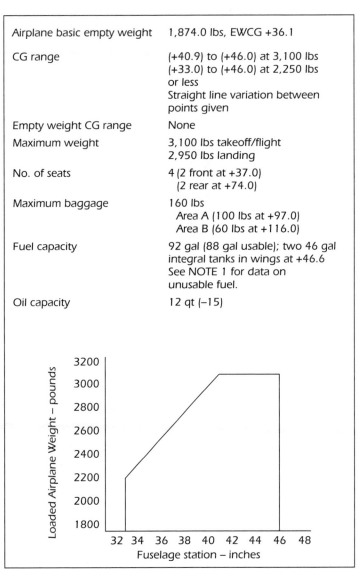

Figure 29. Weight and balance data needed to determine proper loading

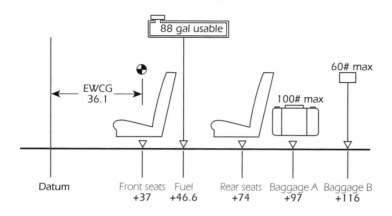

Datum   Front seats   Fuel   Rear seats   Baggage A   Baggage B
              +37   +46.6   +74   +97   +116

Figure 30. Airplane loading diagram

The Computational Method

Use the data from the POH/AFM as shown in Figure 29 to make a worksheet like the one in Figure 31. This worksheet provides space for all pertinent data and has the airplane empty weight and EWCG, and the arms for the baggage areas, seats, and fuel.

EWCG (Empty Weight Center of Gravity). The center of gravity of an aircraft when it contains only the items specified in the aircraft empty weight.

A typical flight will have you load the airplane in this way:

Pilot .... 120 lbs
Front seat passenger .... 180 lbs
Rear seat passengers .... 175 lbs
Fuel 88 gallons .... 528 lbs
Baggage A .... 100 lbs
Baggage B................................. 50 lbs

Item	Weight (3,100 max.)	Arm (inches)	Moment (lb-in)	CG (in/datum)
Airplane (BEW)	1,874		67,651.4	+ 36.1
Front seats		37		
Rear seats		74		
Fuel (88 gal usable)		46.6		
Baggage A (100 max.)		97		
Baggage B (60 max.)		116		

Figure 31. Blank weight and balance worksheet

Weight x Arm = Moment

Moment/Weight = CG

Find the moment of each item by multiplying its weight by its arm. Enter these values in the worksheet, Figure 32. Aviation gasoline has a nominal weight of 6.0 pounds per gallon.

Add all the weights and the moments, then divide the total moment by the total weight to find the CG location in inches from the datum.

The loaded weight of the airplane is 3,027 pounds which is less than the maximum allowable weight of 3,100 pounds. The loaded CG is 43.54 inches behind the datum.

Refer to the envelope in Figure 29. Draw a horizontal line to the right from the weight of 3,027 pounds and a line vertically upward from 43.54 inches. These lines cross within the envelope confirming that the loaded weight and CG location are within the allowable limits.

The Electronic Flight Computer Method

An electronic flight computer such as the CX-2 Pathfinder in Figure 33 can find the loaded weight and CG location with a few keystrokes.

Using the same data as in the previous example, enter the figures into the computer following these steps:

1. Press the ON button, followed by the WT/BAL button. Select the #1 menu, and enter the number of items (6) and 1 for the reduction factor. Press BACK then choose the Wt/Arm Entry menu.

2. Enter the airplane empty weight (1,874) and press ENTER.

3. Enter the arm of the empty airplane (36.1) and press ENTER.

4. The computer returns to the top menu. Enter 2 for the Item #.

Item	Weight (3,100 max.)	Arm (inches)	Moment (lb-in)	CG (in/datum)
Airplane (BEW)	1,874		67,651.4	+ 36.1
Front seats	300	37	11,100	
Rear seats	175	74	12,950	
Fuel (88 gal usable)	528	46.6	24,604.8	
Baggage A (100 max.)	100	97	9,700	
Baggage B (60 max.)	50	116	5,800	
	3,027		131,806.2	+ 43.54

Figure 32. Completed weight and balance worksheet.

5. Enter the weight of the front seat occupants (300) and press ENTER.

6. Enter the arm of the front seats (37) and press ENTER.

7. Enter 3 for the item number, then enter the weight of the rear seat occupants (175) and press ENTER.

8. Enter the arm of the rear seats (74) and press ENTER.

9. Enter 4 for the item number, then enter the weight of the fuel (88 x 6 = 528) and press ENTER.

10. Enter the arm of the fuel (46.6) and press ENTER.

11. Enter 5 for the item number, then enter the weight of the baggage in space A (100) and press ENTER.

12. Enter the arm of the space A baggage (97) and press ENTER.

13. Enter 6 for the item number, then enter the weight of the baggage in space B (50) and press ENTER.

14. Enter the arm of the space B baggage (116) and press ENTER.

15. Press BACK then choose the Wt/Bal Total menu.

The loaded weight of 3027 shows in the Wt row, 131806 shows in the Mom row, and the center of gravity of 43.54 inches shows in the CG row.

Figure 33. Dedicated electronic flight computers are programmed to solve weight and balance problems.

The Loading Graph Method

Because of its speed and simplicity, many manufacturers have included a loading graph and a CG moment envelope in the POH to assist in determining the loaded weight and loaded CG.

Moment Indexes

Moments found by multiplying the weight of each component by its arm result in large numbers that are awkward to handle and can become a source of mathematical error. To eliminate these large numbers, moment indexes are used. The moment is divided by a reduction factor such as 100 or 1,000 to get the moment index. The loading graph provides the moment index for each component so you can avoid mathematical calculation. The CG envelope uses moment indexes rather than arms and moments.

moment index. The moment (weight x arm) divided by a reduction factor such as 100 or 1,000 to make the number smaller and reduce the number of digits.

reduction factor. A number, usually 100 or 1,000 by which a moment is divided to produce a smaller number that is less likely to cause mathematical errors when computing the center of gravity.

A graph of load weight and load moment indexes shows diagonal lines for each item, which relate the weight to the moment index without the need to use mathematics.

Loading Graph

Figure 34 is a typical loading graph taken from the POH of a modern four-place general aviation airplane. To compute the weight and balance, using the loading graph in Figure 34, make a loading schedule chart like the one in Figure 35.

In Figure 34, follow the horizontal line for 300 pounds load weight to the right until it intersects the diagonal line for pilot and front passenger. From this point, drop a line vertically to the load moment index along the bottom to find the load moment for the front seat occupants. This is 11.1 pound-inches/1,000. Record it in the loading schedule chart.

Find the load moment for the 175 pounds of rear seat occupants along the diagonal for second row passengers or cargo. This is 12.9; record it in the loading schedule chart.

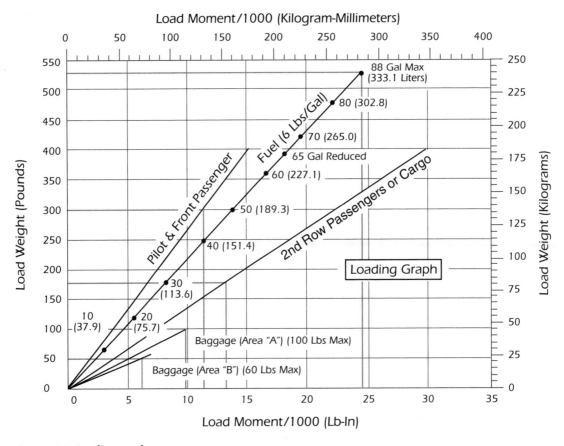

Figure 34. Loading graph

Find the load moment for the fuel and the baggage in areas A and B in the same way and enter them in the loading schedule chart. The maximum fuel is marked on the diagonal line for fuel in terms of gallons and liters. The maximum is 88 gallons of usable fuel. The total capacity is 92 gallons, but four gallons are unusable and have already been included in the empty weight of the aircraft. The weight of 88 gallons of gasoline is 528 pounds, and its moment index is 24.6. The 100 pounds of baggage in area A has a moment index of 9.7, and the 50 pounds in area B has an index of 5.8. Enter these weights and moment indexes in the loading schedule chart, then add all of the weights and moment indexes to find the totals. The total weight is 3,027 pounds and the total moment index is 131.8 lb.-in./1,000. Plot these values in the CG Moment Envelope in Figure 36 on the next page.

Draw a line vertically upward from 131.8 on the horizontal index at the bottom of the chart and a horizontal line from 3,027 pounds in the left-hand vertical index. These lines intersect within the dashed area, which shows that the aircraft is loaded properly for takeoff but is too heavy for landing.

If you must return for landing, you would have to fly long enough to burn off 77 pounds (slightly less than 13 gallons) of fuel to reduce the aircraft weight to that allowed for landing.

loading schedule. A method and procedure used to show that an aircraft is properly loaded and will not exceed approved weight and balance limitations during operation.

Item	Weight	Moment/1,000
Airplane (BEW)	1,874	67.7
Front seat	300	11.1
Rear seat	175	12.9
Fuel	528	24.6
Baggage A	100	9.7
Baggage B	50	5.8
Total	3,027	131.8

Figure 35. Loading schedule chart

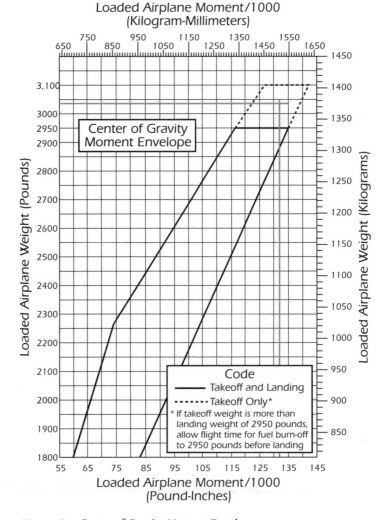

Figure 36. Center of Gravity Moment Envelope

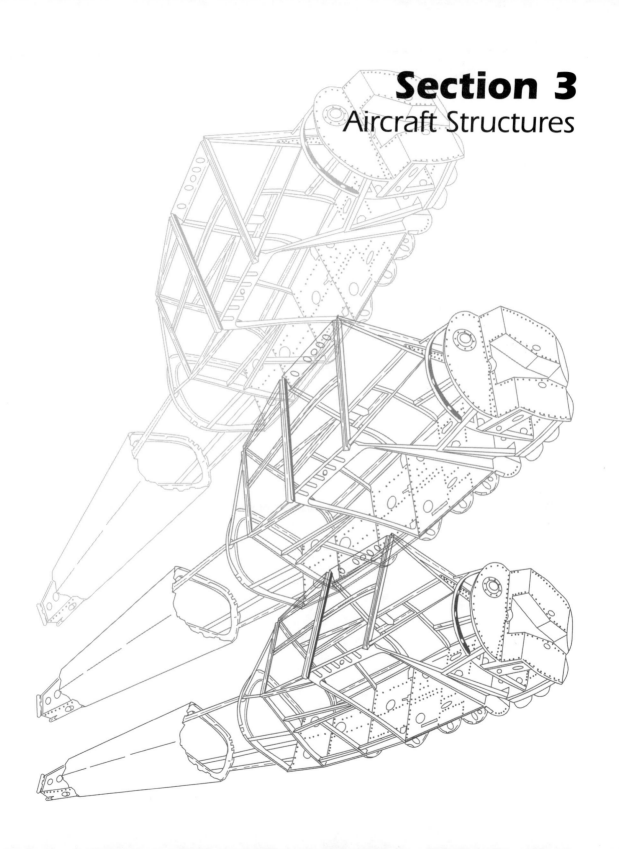

Section 3
Aircraft Structures

Chapter 11 **Types of Structures**

Aircraft structures have undergone about as much progress as have powerplants and instrumentation. The modern aircraft has the strongest and lightest weight structure of all transportation devices.

Truss Structures

Before efficient engines were developed, airplanes flew quite slowly and required wings with large areas. The aerodynamic loads were low and the structure was, by modern standards, flimsy. Up through World War I almost all airplanes were built with a wood truss structure covered with cotton or linen fabric. The wings were braced by struts or wires.

The simplest training and personal airplanes for decades after World War II had a truss-type wing like that in Figure 37. Wood or extruded aluminum alloy spars are separated by steel tubular compression struts and the truss is made rigid with strong steel drag and antidrag wires. Ribs having the correct airfoil shape are attached to the spars and aluminum alloy leading and trailing edges are attached to the ribs. A wingtip bow completes the structure and the entire structure is covered with fabric that is shrunk to drum-head tautness to give the wing its smooth surface and proper aerodynamic shape.

A Pratt truss structure, normally used for wings, is made up of longitudinal beams and cross braces. Compression loads between the main beams are carried by rigid cross braces called compression struts. Tension loads are carried by stays, or wires, that go from one main beam to the other and cross between the compression struts.

A Warren truss, normally used for welded steel fuselages has rigid cross members that carry both compression and tension loads.

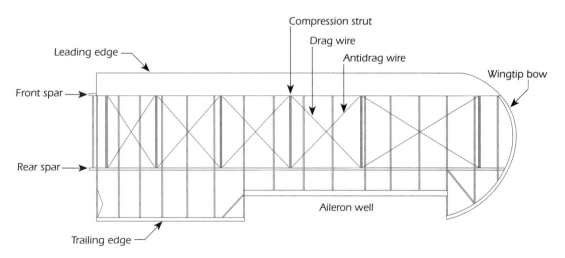

Figure 37. A truss-type wing

superstructure. The framework of formers and stringers attached to the main truss of a truss-type aircraft fuselage to give it its streamline and attractive shape.

Truss-type fuselages have a rectangular or triangular cross-section. To minimize wind resistance and give them a pleasing shape, they normally have a superstructure of wood or light metal formers and stringers. The entire structure is covered with fabric.

Until the end of World War I most fuselage trusses were made of wood, but thin-wall steel tubing has almost completely replaced the wood beams and braces.

Monocoque Structure

monocoque structure. A single-shell type of aircraft structure in which all flight loads are carried in its outer skin. The skins are formed into compound curves and fastened together into a structure resembling an eggshell.

semimonocoque structure. A form of stressed-skin aircraft structure in which the outer skin is supported by a substructure of formers and stringers that gives the skin its shape and increases its rigidity.

One major breakthrough in aircraft structure was the monocoque, or stressed-skin structure. Thin plywood, and later thin sheets of aluminum alloy are formed into compound curved skins which are joined to form a structure similar to that of an eggshell. Today all airplanes with the exception of special purpose airplanes and some amateur-built airplanes have either a monocoque or semimonocoque structure.

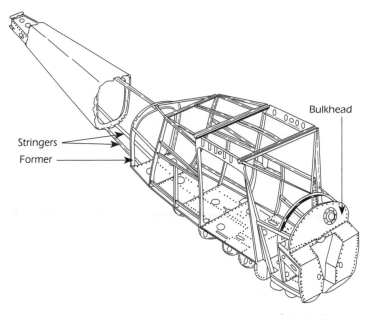

Bulkhead

Stringers

Former

Figure 38. A semimonocoque structure carries most of the load in its external skin but its formers, stringers, and longerons carry some of the load to give the structure rigidity.

Chapter 12 **Structural Loads**

Airplane designers and engineers are continually faced with compromises. An aircraft structure must be as light as it can be, consistent with the forces to which it will be subjected. There are five basic forms of stress: tension, compression, torsion, shear, and bending. Tension and compression are the basic stresses and the others are combinations of these two.

Tension

Tension (or tensile) stresses try to pull an object apart. When a nut is tightened onto a bolt to hold two components together, the bolt is stretched (strained) by a tensile stress.

The strength of aircraft metals is rated in terms of pounds per square inch (psi) of tensile stress they will withstand without deformation. For example, the aluminum alloy of which most aircraft structure is made is rated at 53,000 psi. A one-inch square bar will withstand a pull of 26.5 tons before it begins to stretch, and 67,000 pounds before it breaks. Some aircraft-quality steels have a tensile strength of up to 262,000 psi.

Compression

Compression (or compressive stresses) tries to squeeze an object together. The thousands of rivets in an aircraft structure have been installed by subjecting them to a compressive stress that causes them to expand to tightly fill the hole in the skins and form a shop head that holds the skins tightly together.

Torsion

Torsion is the stress in a propeller shaft or a helicopter rotor mast that tends to twist it. Torsion is a composite force made up of a tensile stress acting at 45° to the object and a compressive stress acting at 90° to the tensile stress.

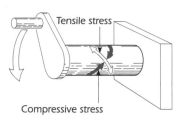

stress. A force within an object that tries to prevent an outside force from changing its shape.

strain. A deformation, or physical change, in a material caused by a stress.

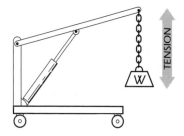

Figure 39. Tension, or a tensile load, tries to pull an object apart.

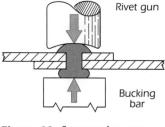

Figure 40. Compression, or a compressive stress, tries to push an object together. When a rivet is driven with a compressive force on its ends, it swells up to tightly fill the hole.

Figure 41. A torsional stress is a combination of tension and compression. These two stresses act at right angles to each other and at 45° to the axis of the shaft.

Bending

Wings are subjected to a bending stress. In flight the wing tends to bend upward. The bottom skin is under a tensile stress and the top skin is under a compressive stress. On landing, the stresses reverse.

Shear

A shear stress is a special type of tensile stress that tries to slide an object apart. The clevis bolt that attaches a cable to a structural component is subjected to a shear stress. When this stress becomes too great, the clevis bolt will shear, or be cut as it would be with a pair of scissors.

Figure 42. Bending stresses try to stretch the lower skin while compressing the upper skin.

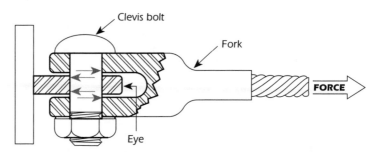

Figure 43. Shear stresses try to cause an object to slide apart.

Chapter 13 **Structural Materials**

The two main classifications of aircraft materials are metallic and nonmetallic. Since most modern aircraft are made of metal, we will begin with it.

Metallic Materials

Aircraft metals may be divided into two classifications: ferrous and nonferrous.

Ferrous Metals

Ferrous metals are those which contain iron. Steel, an alloy of iron that contains carbon and other elements, is the most widely used ferrous metal in aircraft structures.

Most of the high-strength steel used in aircraft structures contains chromium and molybdenum. This is called chrome-moly steel and is identified by a four-digit number that begins with 41, such as 4130.

Most of the bolts and nuts used in an aircraft are made of steel alloyed with nickel.

Most ferrous metals rust when exposed to air and moisture and must be protected. Nuts, bolts, and many fittings are kept from rusting by plating them with a thin coating of cadmium, a dull, silvery metal.

Corrosion-resistant steel, sometimes called stainless steel, is iron alloyed with chromium, nickel, and manganese. Some series of corrosion-resistant steel are nonmagnetic and cannot be hardened by heat treatment. Others can be heat treated and are magnetic.

Aircraft firewalls are normally made of corrosion-resistant steel. Hardware that is exposed to an especially corrosive environment is made of this type of steel.

A ferrous metal is any metal that contains iron and has magnetic characteristics, which include the ability to be magnetized and to be attracted by a magnet.

Nonferrous Metals

Aluminum and magnesium alloys have made all-metal aircraft possible and titanium alloys find wide use in modern high performance aircraft. Aluminum is the third most abundant element on the Earth's surface and is found in a clay called Bauxite. The metal aluminum was first used in jewelry and art because its cost was between that of gold and silver, but in the late 1880s an economical way was discovered to extract it from

Aluminum is called aluminium in the United Kingdom, and the generic name for structural aluminum alloys is dural, taken from the trade name Duralumin, an alloy first used in Germany for the construction of the Zeppelins of World War I.

Aluminum is lightweight, malleable, ductile, a good conductor of heat and electricity, and a good reflector of heat and light. Pure aluminum is highly resistant to corrosion.

aluminum alloy. Aluminum to which has been added one or more other chemical elements. These alloying elements increase the hardness, toughness, resistance to fatigue, or durability of the aluminum.

Rivets made of 2017 or 2024 aluminum alloy are called icebox rivets. After removal from the heat-treating oven they are quenched in water and stored at a sub-freezing temperature; they remain soft until driven, and then attain their full strength.

its ore. Pure aluminum is soft and weak, but is resistant to corrosion. When alloyed with copper and other elements it becomes very strong, but unfortunately susceptible to corrosion.

The alloys of aluminum that are most widely used in aircraft structure are identified by a four-digit number. They are:

1100—Commercially pure aluminum. Used only for nonstructural applications such as fairings.

2024—Alloyed with copper, manganese and magnesium. Can be heat treated and is the most widely used structural alloy.

2117—Alloyed with copper and magnesium. This is the alloy used for most aircraft rivets.

5052—Alloyed with magnesium and chromium. This non-heat-treatable alloy is used for tubing to carry fluids in the aircraft.

7075—Alloyed with zinc, copper, magnesium, and chromium. This high-strength heat-treatable alloy is used for the primary structure of many modern high-performance aircraft.

Aluminum alloy is generally corrosive but pure aluminum is not. Sheets of aluminum alloy must be protected from corrosion by preventing air or moisture from reaching their surfaces. A very thin coating of pure aluminum is rolled onto sheets of aluminum alloy to protect it and provide a shiny and attractive surface. Aluminum alloy thus treated is called clad aluminum.

Figure 44. The structure of most modern commercially built airplanes is predominantly aluminum alloy.

For applications where a shiny surface is not needed, the alloy is coated with an electrolytically-deposited oxide film. This film is so dense that air or moisture cannot reach the metal. This type of treatment is called Anodizing.

Magnesium is only about 2/3 the weight of aluminum and is used in applications where weight is critical. Thin sheets of magnesium are used for covering control surfaces, and cast magnesium is used for some engine components.

Magnesium has two serious problems: it is brittle and cracks when it is subject to vibration, and it is highly susceptible to corrosion.

Titanium is a vital structural metal because it is lightweight and corrosion resistant and most importantly, it retains its strength to a high temperature. It is used in turbine-engine powered aircraft in the areas near the engines.

Corrosion

The lightweight reactive metals of which aircraft structure is made are highly susceptible to damage from corrosion and must be protected.

Corrosion is an electrochemical action that occurs when electrons are drawn away from a metal. Some of the metal is changed into a salt that has no physical strength.

There are a number of types of corrosion that attack an aircraft. Failure to recognize it and to properly treat the corroded area can result in extremely expensive damage to the aircraft. When you find corrosion on your airplane, consult with an AMT to determine the extent of the damage and to recommend ways of removing the corrosion deposits and preventing further damage.

Oxidation

Oxidation occurs in a metal when oxygen unites with the metal to form an oxide on the surface.

Iron oxide, better known as rust, is a reddish-brown, porous surface that forms on unprotected iron or steel. Oxygen and moisture can penetrate the surface and reach the metal and continue to convert it into rust until the metal is completely destroyed.

Iron and steel surfaces may be temporarily protected from rust by coating them with grease or oil, and permanently protected by covering them with a film that does not allow oxygen

corrosion. An electrochemical action that takes place inside a metal or on its surface. The metal reacts with an electrolyte, and part of the metal is changed into a salt, which is the corrosion. Corrosion is dry and powdery and has no physical strength.

Corrosion protection

- Ferrous metals
  - Temporary—oil or grease
  - Permanent—paint; nickel,
    zinc, cadmium, or chrome
    plating
- Nonferrous metals
  - Corrosion inhibiting primer
  - Airtight oxide film
  - Cladding

Oxide films:

- electrolytically deposited—
  called Anodizing
- chemically deposited—
  called Alodizing

Cladding is done when sheet
metal is formed by rolling a thin
layer of pure aluminum on the
surface of a sheet of aluminum
alloy.

or air to reach the metal. Paint forms a protective film, and
plating the metal with nickel, zinc, cadmium, or chromium
provides a rust-free surface.

Any time a steel aircraft part has been scratched or abraded
enough to remove the protective film, it should be treated to
prevent oxygen and moisture from reaching the steel. A coating of oil gives temporary protection and an AMT can recommend more permanent protection such as coating the area with
primer from a spray can.

Aluminum reacts with oxygen in the air to form a rough
white oxide on the surface. Aluminum oxide differs from iron
oxide in that it forms an airtight film that prevents oxygen
reaching the metal. Once the oxide forms, the action slows and
almost stops.

Aluminum alloys are highly susceptible to corrosion and
the surface must be protected to exclude all oxygen and moisture. Surfaces that are to remain bright and shiny are covered
with a thin coating of pure aluminum that protects the metal
by forming an impenetrable oxide on the surface which prevents oxygen from reaching the alloy.

Aluminum alloys that are to be painted are treated in the
factory with an electrolytic process that forms an oxide film on
the surface which prevents oxygen from reaching the metal. If
either the clad surface or the oxide film is scratched through to
the metal, corrosion is likely to form and the metal must be
protected. An AMT can repair a damaged surface with a chemical treatment that forms a new protective oxide film.

Copper acts much like aluminum. When exposed to oxygen,
it forms a dull green protective film that excludes the oxygen
from the metal and prevents further oxidation.

Surface Corrosion

When an airplane sits out in the open and is exposed to air
containing salt or industrial contaminants, the surface of any
unprotected aluminum or magnesium alloy will form a dull
surface. If the airplane is allowed to remain in this environment, small pits or bubbles will form under the cladding or
paint film. When these bubbles are picked with the sharp point
of a knife you will see that they, like the pits, are filled with a
powdery salt which is the product of corrosion.

All traces of the corrosion must be removed, preferably
with a nylon scrubber, to prevent damage to the metal and the
surface must then be protected to prevent further corrosion. Be

sure to consult with an AMT to determine the extent of the damage and to recommend the correct type of protection.

Galvanic Corrosion

When dissimilar metals are covered with an electrolyte, a chemical action takes place in which one of the metals is changed into a salt, and it corrodes. This shows up generally where steel screws are used to hold an inspection plate in an aluminum alloy skin, or where steel bolts attach a component to an aluminum casting. Galvanic corrosion can often be cleaned out and treated by an AMT to prevent further damage.

Intergranular Corrosion

Not all corrosion is visible on the surface. Intergranular corrosion attacks the metal along the grain boundaries inside the metal and is not apparent on the surface until it has severely weakened the structure. Pick the top off any "pimples" on the surface of the metal, and if the corrosion cannot be cleaned out to a smooth surface with a nylon scrubber, have an AMT examine it—because it may be intergranular.

Stress corrosion is a type of intergranular corrosion that forms in castings around pressed-in bushings. Any evidence of corrosion around fittings attached to a casting should be referred to an AMT who determines the extent of the damage with dye penetrant or an eddy-current detector.

Some angles and channels are made of extruded aluminum alloy. This material has been squeezed through dies in much the same way as toothpaste is squeezed from a tube. It comes through the dies with a layer-like structure that is susceptible to intergranular corrosion. If the surface of an extruded angle or channel bulges or is puffy, refer it to an AMT. Normally by the time this type of corrosion is visible, the part is beyond repair and must be replaced.

Concentration Cell Corrosion

The edges of sheets of aluminum or magnesium alloy in the joints of the skin have the least protection from corrosion. They should be checked carefully for indication of a white or gray powder. This can normally be removed with a nylon scrubber and the area protected by spraying the joint with a water-displacing lubricant such as WD-40.

Corrosion of this type can also form under decals and on aluminum fluid lines under the end fittings. If the corrosion

Types of corrosion—all are bad
- Surface
- Galvanic
- Intergranular
- Stress
- Concentration Cell
- Filiform

Dye penetrant inspection is a method of nondestructive inspection used to detect surface defects in metal or plastic parts. The part to be inspected is soaked in a penetrating liquid for a specified period of time, and then all the penetrant is washed from its surface. The surface is then covered with a developing powder that pulls the penetrant from any defects that extend to the surface of the part. The penetrant plainly shows up on the powder-covered surface, outlining the defect.

deposits are accessible, remove them with a nylon scrubber but if they are under the fitting on a fluid line, check with an AMT for complete removal.

Filiform Corrosion

One form of surface corrosion that can cause expensive damage forms under a dense paint film on a surface which has been improperly primed. If a painted surface has little lines where the paint is puffy, there is a possibility that this thread-like corrosion has formed. Be sure to have the surface inspected because the corrosion can cause severe damage if it is not checked, and this usually requires removing all the paint and treating the bare metal.

Nonmetallic Materials

The earliest airplane structure was made of wood and the surfaces were covered with cotton or linen fabric. Some monocoque structures were made of plies of wood shaped in a mold and bonded together with casein (milk) glue. Until well after World War II small personal airplanes and trainers had wood wing spars and were covered with cotton fabric.

Cotton fabric which was shrunk with nitrate or butyrate dope has been replaced with a much stronger and longer-lived polyester fabric that is shrunk on the structure with heat and then finished with nontautening dope.

The space age has introduced many new materials that have replaced metal in numerous applications ranging from amateur-built aircraft, jet-transport airplanes, and high-performance military aircraft.

Composite Structures

Composite materials are becoming increasingly popular in aircraft construction. They were first used for nonstructural applications such as wheel speed fairings and wing tips. Then as more research has been done, composite materials have replaced metal in many of the highly-stressed areas of modern military and transport aircraft. Composite materials will continue to account for greater percentages of aircraft structure as new materials and new fabrication techniques are developed.

A composite material has two components: the reinforcing material and the matrix.

primer. A component in a finishing system that provides a good bond between the surface and the material used for the topcoats.

composite structure. A type of aircraft structure made of plastic resins reinforced with strong, lightweight filaments. Fiberglass, carbon, Kevlar, and boron are materials used for composite structure. Composite materials combine high strength and rigidity with light weight.

Figure 45. The Lancair Columbia 300. This modern aircraft gets its strength and beauty from its composite structure.

Reinforcing Materials

Most of the early composite structure was made of a resin reinforced with glass fibers. This is still used in some amateur-built aircraft but stronger, stiffer, and tougher reinforcing fibers are available.

Kevlar® is an aramid fiber that is extremely flexible and tough and has excellent resistance to chemicals. Its strength is similar to that of metal but is much lighter in weight.

Graphite (carbon) fibers are woven into a black fabric that is extremely strong for its weight and is extremely stiff. It is used for primary structure where strength and rigidity are the prime considerations.

Hybrid fabrics are composed of different types of fibers woven together to take advantage of the special characteristics of each material. A popular hybrid fabric is made of Kevlar® and graphite.

Because the fibers of a reinforcing material are all unidirectional in their strength, they are made into fabric having different weaves that allow the strength to be tailored to their particular application.

Kevlar is to a great extent replacing fiberglass as a reinforcing fabric for composite construction.

unidirectional fabric. Fabric in which all of the threads run in the same direction. These threads are often bound with a few fibers run at right angles, just enough to hold the yarns together and prevent their bunching.

Unidirectional fabric has all the fibers oriented in the same direction and held together by small cross threads. By orienting the fibers in each ply in a different direction, the final lay up of material can have the strength or stiffness the designer desires.

Bidirectional fabrics are woven with the threads in the warp (threads that run the length of the material) and fill (threads that cross the warp threads) interlacing. There are a number of weaves that allow the fabric to be draped over complex shapes with a high degree of smoothness.

Matrix Material

matrix. The material used in composite construction to bond the fibers together and to transmit the forces into the fibers. Resins are the most widely used matrix materials.

Two of the more popular matrix materials are polyester and epoxy.

Polyester resins were the first developed and have been used extensively with fiberglass. Although low in cost and easy to use, they do not have the strength of other types of resins.

autoclave. A pressure vessel used to apply heat and pressure to cure composite materials.

There are a number of types of epoxy resins used as matrix materials. Some cure at room temperature while others are cured with heat and pressure in an autoclave. Some epoxy resins are very rigid and others are flexible when cured.

Transparent Components

Windshields and side windows are critical components of an aircraft because of the importance of the pilot being able to see with a minimum of distortion.

The windows and windshields of smaller general aviation aircraft are made of transparent acrylic resins. These materials are thermoplastic resins, meaning that they are formed with heat; when reheated they soften.

Acrylic materials are relatively light weight and strong, but they are soft and must be protected from scratching and uneven heating which occurs when an aircraft is parked outside in the hot summer sun.

Never wipe or clean the windshield and windows with a dry rag. Instead, use plenty of water and then your hand or soft cloth. This will eliminate scratches.

When cleaning an acrylic windshield, use plenty of clean water to wash the dust and dirt from the surface, then use your hand or a clean, soft cloth to remove stubborn grime. Use only cleaners specifically approved for acrylic plastics because some cleaners will cause damage. Especially never wipe a plastic windshield with a dry rag because it will scratch the soft material. Minor scratches can be removed with the special polishing materials called Micro-Mesh®. After all the scratches have been removed, it is a good idea to protect the windshield with a coating of good-quality wax.

Larger aircraft that fly into known icing conditions are normally equipped with heated windshields. These thick and extremely expensive windshields are made of three glass sections separated by layers of vinyl compound. The inside surface of the outer glass is coated with an electrically-conductive material. An electronically controlled current flows through this coating and heats the glass enough to prevent ice from forming on it. Heated windshields are used for preventing the formation of ice and do not get hot enough to melt ice that has been allowed to form over them.

The windshield heat should be turned on prior to entering known icing conditions, because these systems are only strong enough to prevent ice—not remove it.

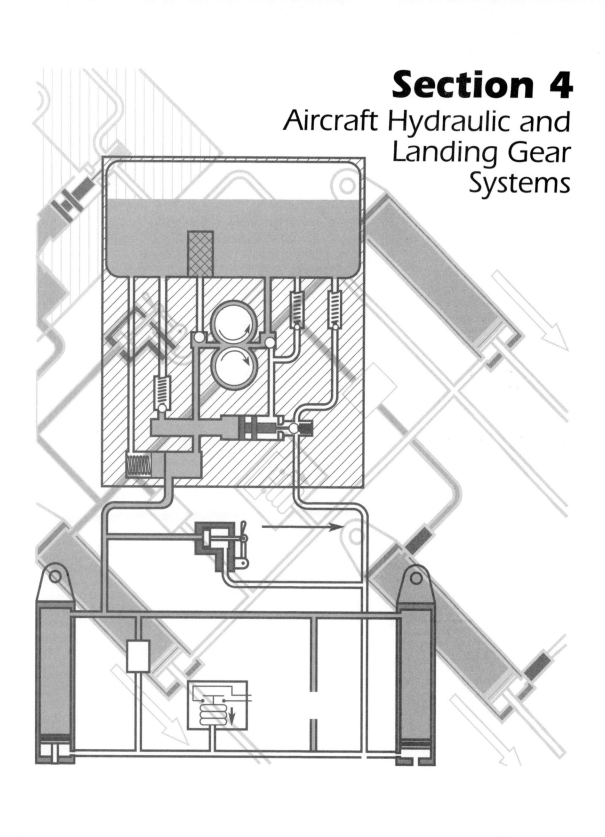

Section 4
Aircraft Hydraulic and Landing Gear Systems

Chapter 14 **Hydraulic Principles**

Hydraulic systems are ideally suited for use in aircraft because they allow you to multiply a force and transmit the force to any location on the aircraft without the weight and expense of a mechanical system.

Hydraulic brakes have become standard on almost all aircraft, and hydraulic systems are used on many aircraft for retractable landing gear and powered flight controls.

Hydraulic systems work on a simple principle that has been with us for centuries: When the pressure on a confined volume of fluid is increased at any point, this increase is transmitted undiminished to all points of the enclosing vessel and acts at right angles to the walls of the vessel. This is illustrated by Figure 46.

A hydraulic system allows you to gain a mechanical advantage. For example, in Figure 46 a 10-pound weight pushing downward on a piston having an area of one square inch produces a pressure of 10 pounds per square inch (psi). This pressure is spread equally throughout the system and pushes upward on the large piston which has an area of 10 square inches. A force of 10 pounds acts on each square inch of piston area allowing the large piston to support 100 pounds.

A hydraulic system does not gain any work; the small piston has a 10-pound force applied and it moves 1 inch. Ten inch-pounds of work has been done on the small piston. The large piston exerts a force of 100 pounds but moves only one tenth of an inch, which is also ten inch-pounds of work.

hydraulic system. A fluid power system that transmits a force from one location to another through an incompressible fluid. A pneumatic system does the same thing but uses a compressible fluid such as air.

work. The product of force times distance. When one pound of force causes an object to move one foot, one foot-pound of work has been done.

Figure 46. The increase in pressure caused by the 10-pound weight is transmitted into the large cylinder where it supports a 100-pound weight.

Chapter 15 **Hydraulic Fluid**

Theoretically any liquid can be used in a hydraulic system but only a few fluids are practical. There are three basic types of fluids used in aircraft hydraulic systems, and it is extremely important that only the proper fluid be used. The wrong fluid can damage the seals and cause a system to fail. It is vital when servicing a hydraulic system to check the aircraft service manual, use only the correct fluid, and be sure the fluid is fresh and uncontaminated.

If a system Is serviced with the wrong type of fluid, all the fluid must be drained, the system flushed with the proper solvent, and all the seals in the system changed. An approved solvent must be used to flush the system because the normal hydraulic fluid is too viscous to do a good job of cleaning out the system.

Vegetable Base Fluid

MIL-H-7644 hydraulic fluid was used in the past for simple brake systems that used natural rubber seals. It is essentially castor oil and alcohol and is dyed blue. Systems using this fluid can be flushed with alcohol.

Mineral Base Fluid

MIL-H-5606 hydraulic fluid is the most widely used fluid in general aviation aircraft. It is a kerosine-type fluid with additives that inhibit foaming and keep it from reacting with metals to form corrosion. It is dyed red and systems using it can be flushed with varsol or Stoddard solvent.

Systems using MIL-H-5606 fluid have synthetic rubber seals and hoses. If any of it is spilled on a tire, it may be removed by washing it with soap and water.

Phosphate Ester Fluid

Jet aircraft that have high-pressure hydraulic systems with some lines routed in areas near the hot engine use a fire-resistant phosphate ester hydraulic fluid known as Skydrol 500B. This fluid is dyed purple and is used in systems using butyl, silicone rubber, or Teflon seals and hoses. These systems may be flushed with trichlorethylene or other solvents especially approved for them. If it is spilled on a painted surface it will damage the finish.

Chapter 16 **Aircraft Hydraulic Systems**

Many general aviation airplanes with hydraulically retractable landing gear have a very simple hydraulic system, usually a power pack system in which the reservoir, pump, selector valve and auxiliary valves are in one easily serviced unit. Figures 47 and 48 on the next two pages show a typical power pack system when the landing gear is being raised and when it is being lowered. Aircraft that use this type of system have hydraulic brakes that are not connected to this system.

When the landing gear switch is placed in the GEAR UP position, the electrically operated gear type pump turns in the direction shown. Fluid is taken in through the filter and is carried around the outside of the gears inside the pump and down through the gear-up check valve which moves to the left allowing the fluid to unseat the ball and flow into the gear-up side of the cylinders. This pulls the pistons inward, raising the gear. Fluid from the opposite side of the pistons returns to the reservoir.

There are no mechanical up locks in this system, but the landing gear is held in its retracted position by hydraulic pressure. When all three gears are fully retracted, the pressure continues to build up until it reaches a value that turns the pressure switch OFF and stops the hydraulic pump motor. If the pressure in the system leaks to a specified value, the pressure switch turns ON and allows the pump to restore the pressure to its cutout value.

To lower the gear, the landing gear switch is placed in the GEAR DOWN position as shown in Figure 48 on Page 67.

The direction of the pump reverses and fluid flows down to the left side of the gear-up check valve forcing it to the right, unseating the ball so return fluid can flow back into the reservoir. The fluid continues down and moves the shuttle valve to the left and flows into the down side of the actuating cylinders, moving the pistons outward and lowering the landing gear. As each gear reaches its down-and-locked position, the pressure in the gear down line builds up and fluid is bypassed back into the reservoir through the low-pressure control valve. When all three gears are down and locked, limit switches turn the pump motor OFF.

The hydraulic power pack was developed to make hydraulic systems lightweight and easy to service. A power pack typically contains the reservoir, pump, high-pressure relief valve, low-pressure control valve, and a shuttle valve all in one unit.

In the event of an electrical power failure that prevents the use of the hydraulic pump, opening the free-fall valve bypasses fluid from the up side of the cylinders to the down side and the weight of the landing gear will cause it to free fall to the down and locked position.

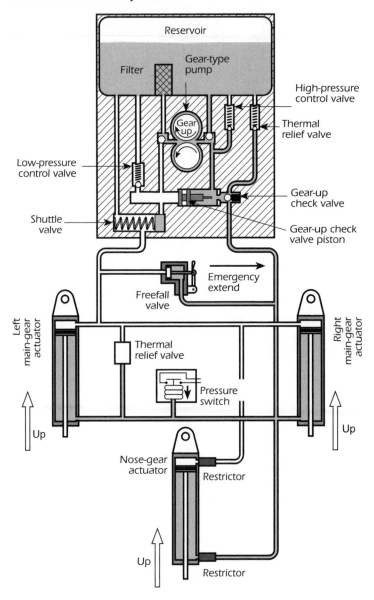

Figure 47. Hydraulic power pack system while the landing gear is being raised

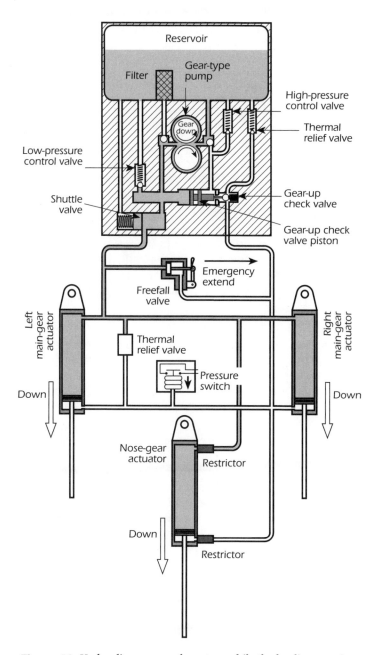

Figure 48. Hydraulic power pack system while the landing gear is being lowered.

Chapter 17   **Hydraulic Brakes**

Aircraft brakes are an excellent example of the superiority of hydraulics over electricity or mechanics. The systems are lightweight and the amount of force that can be applied is unlimited.

Large aircraft use brakes that are actuated by pressure from the main hydraulic systems and when the pilot depresses the brake pedal, pressure is metered to the brakes proportionate to the force applied to the pedal.

Antiskid brakes are used on all large aircraft. The pilot applies the brakes and if any wheel begins to lock up as it would in a skid, pressure is automatically removed from that brake until the wheel begins to rotate and then it is reapplied. Below a speed of 15 to 20 miles per hour the system deactivates to allow the pilot control for taxiing and parking.

Brake Master Cylinder

Many small general aviation airplanes use a simple master cylinder, such as the one in Figure 49 that is operated when the pilot depresses the brake pedal which is mounted on the rudder pedal. In other airplanes the brake master cylinder is actuated by a hand lever, or by pressure on heel pedals. Regardless of the type, the principle is the same.

When the piston rod is depressed, the compensator port, a passage between the line to the brakes and the reservoir, is closed off and pressure in the line to the brakes is increased. When the brake pedal is released the return spring forces the piston and piston rod up, releasing the pressure to the brakes and opening the compensator port. Expanded fluid caused by heat will flow back into the reservoir rather than being trapped in the brake lines and causing the brakes to drag.

Brake Wheel Units

There have been many types of hydraulic brakes used on airplanes but the most popular one is the Cleveland brake that uses a steel disk bolted to the inboard wheel half so it turns with the wheel. *See* Figure 50.

The torque plate of the brake assembly bolts to the landing gear around the axle. The composition brake linings are riveted to the back plate and the pressure plate and the wheel disk rides between them. *See* Figure 51.

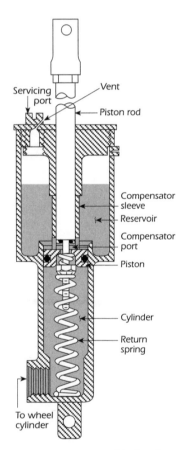

Figure 49. A typical hydraulic brake master cylinder, mounted on the rudder pedal and actuated by movement of the top half of the pedal.

Figure 50. The Cleveland brake has a steel disk bolted to the inboard wheel half so it rotates with the wheel.

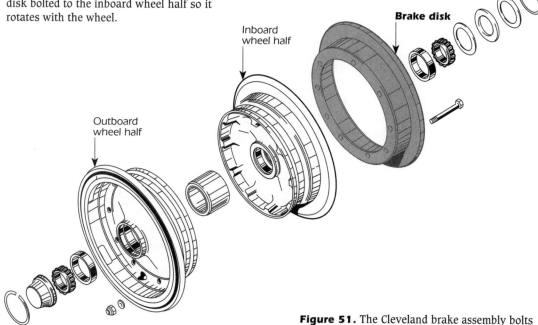

Inboard wheel half

Brake disk

Outboard wheel half

Figure 51. The Cleveland brake assembly bolts to the landing gear and the disk on the wheel rides between the linings.

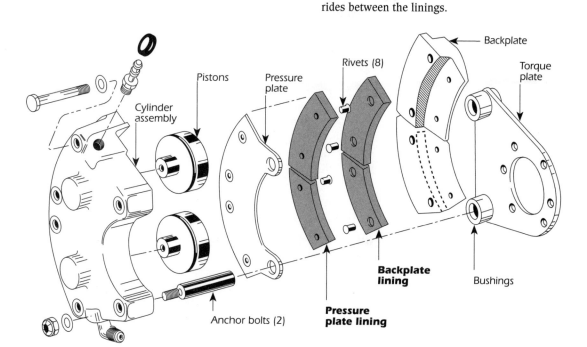

Pistons

Pressure plate

Rivets (8)

Backplate

Torque plate

Cylinder assembly

Anchor bolts (2)

Pressure plate lining

Backplate lining

Bushings

The cylinder assembly consists of a housing with two cylinders machined in it. Pistons fit in these cylinders and when fluid from the brake master cylinder flows into the cylinders it forces the pistons out against the pressure plate. The pressure plate moves over and squeezes the brake disk between the two linings, creating enough friction to slow and stop the airplane.

The cylinder assembly has two anchor bolts that ride in bushings in the torque plate. These bolts allow the cylinder assembly and pressure plate to move back and forth enough to compensate for the change in thickness of the brake linings as they wear.

Brake Servicing

The brakes are such a vital part of an airplane that all pilots should be able to recognize any problems and troubleshoot the cause. When servicing the brakes with fluid, be sure to use only the fluid specified in the service manual for the airplane.

Some of the most common problems are:

The brake pedal feels normal, but the braking action is not adequate.

The cause is possibly worn out brake linings. It is possible to see the linings where they contact the disk. Replacement of the linings is a simple matter for an AMT.

If the linings look good, have a technician disassemble the brake and check it for freedom of movement. Rust, corrosion or hardened grease may keep the brake assembly from moving in and out as it should

When the pedal is depressed and held, it slowly goes all the way down.

If it goes all the way down with no opposition, it could mean that there is no fluid in the reservoir or badly damaged seals. When it goes down slowly under sustained pressure, a piston seal or a compensator port seal may be allowing the fluid to leak past. Replacing the seals requires the disassembly of the master cylinder and is a job for an AMT.

When the brakes feel spongy.

This is one of the more common problems and is caused by air in the brake system. An AMT can bleed the brakes by connecting a tube to the servicing port at the top of the reservoir and attaching a pressure pot of clean fluid to the bleeder port on the wheel cylinder and forcing fluid through the system until it flows out of the reservoir without any trace of bubbles.

bleeding of the brakes. The maintenance procedure of removing air entrapped in hydraulic fluid in the brakes. Fluid is bled from the brake system until fluid with no bubbles flows out.

Chapter 18 **Landing Gear**

Aircraft shock absorbers have evolved from the bungee cords that were popular up through the Piper Cub and Super Cub days to the spring steel gears used on many of the high wing Cessnas and the oleo shock absorbers that are almost universally used on low wing and some high wing airplanes. Even airplanes with spring steel main gear have oleo struts for the nose wheel.

bungee cord. An elastic cord made up of a series of small strips of rubber or rubber bands encased in a loosely braided cloth cover.

Oleo Strut

An oleo, or air-oil shock strut is a relatively simple shock absorber that has been used for many years and is extremely dependable.

The cylinder attaches to the airframe and the wheel is mounted in a fork on the piston. A pair of torque links, commonly called scissors, or nut crackers, holds the piston and wheel aligned with the cylinder while allowing the piston to move up and down in the cylinder to absorb landing and taxi shocks.

An oleo strut absorbs the landing impact by transferring hydraulic fluid from inside the piston to the inside of the cylinder through a metering orifice. A tapered metering pin moves up into the orifice to progressively restrict the flow of fluid as the strut compresses. This progressive restriction results in a smooth absorption of the shock. Taxi shocks are taken up by compressed air or nitrogen in the cylinder above the oil.

Shock struts differ in their detail. The one in Figure 53 on the next page has a snubber tube and flapper valve to restrict the flow of fluid back into the piston, in order to prevent rebound.

Shock Strut Servicing

Oleo struts must be serviced with oil and air.

To service the strut with oil, the AMT carefully removes the filler plug and air valve from the top of the strut. This requires caution because the strut contains high-pressure compressed air or nitrogen. As the air bleeds out of the strut it collapses and when it is fully collapsed with the piston all of the way into the cylinder the strut is completely filled with the type of hydraulic fluid specified in the aircraft service manual. This is

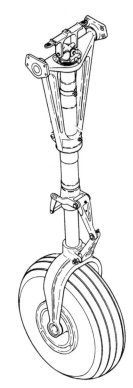

Figure 52. The piston of the oleo nose wheel strut is held in the cylinder by the torque links.

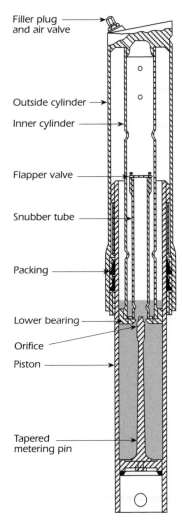

Filler plug and air valve

Outside cylinder

Inner cylinder

Flapper valve

Snubber tube

Packing

Lower bearing

Orifice

Piston

Tapered metering pin

Figure 53. An oleo shock strut in its fully extended position

shimmy. Abnormal and often violent vibration of the nose wheel of an airplane.

a simple procedure for the nose-wheel strut of a small general aviation airplane, but for the main gear struts of large aircraft the procedure is more complex. While filling the strut with oil the piston is moved up and down inside the cylinder with an exerciser jack to assure that the cylinder is completely filled. After the cylinder is full of oil, the filler plug/air valve is reinstalled.

To service the main struts on large aircraft with air, the airplane is taken off of the exerciser jack and with the weight of the airplane on the wheels, high pressure compressed air or nitrogen is put into the cylinder through the air valve. Enough air is put into the strut to extend the piston out for a specified distance. While the air is being put into the strut the airplane is rocked from side to side to prevent the piston sticking in the cylinder and causing improper inflation.

Airing the nose gear shock struts on small airplanes is simple. The tail of the airplane is depressed to allow the shock strut to fully extend and a specified pressure of compressed air, normally less than 100 psi, is put into the strut through the air valve.

Shimmy Dampers

A loose or unrestrained nose gear can shimmy enough to cause structural damage. To prevent this, a shimmy damper is installed between the piston and the cylinder of the oleo strut. The cylinder of the shimmy damper is attached to the piston of the oleo strut and the shimmy damper piston is connected to a stationary part of the strut. The piston is free to move back and forth inside the cylinder, allowing the nose gear to be steered, but is restrained by the fluid having to pass from one side of the piston to the other through a small orifice.

Nose Wheel Centering Mechanism

It is important that a retractable nose wheel be aligned straight ahead when it is pulled up into its nose-wheel well. A centering cam inside the oleo strut straightens the wheel when the weight is off the nose wheel and the oleo strut extends to its limit.

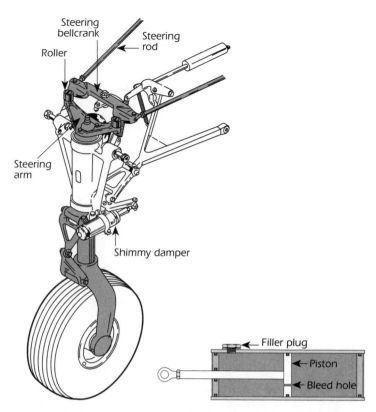

squat switch. A safety switch on one of the main landing gear shock struts actuated by the torque links when weight is on the landing gear. A squat switch may be used to prevent the landing gear handle from being moved to the UP position when weight is on the landing gear, or to prevent the cabin from being pressurized when on the ground.

Figure 54. Retractable nose gear showing the steering mechanism and shimmy damper. A shimmy damper is a small hydraulic cylinder with the piston movement restricted by allowing the fluid to pass from one side to the other through a small bleed hole.

Chapter 19 **Aircraft Wheels**

Because aircraft wheels take such a tremendous beating on landing they must be made extremely strong and at the same time they must be light weight. Almost all aircraft wheels are made of cast aluminum alloy.

Most modern aircraft wheels are of the two piece type and since they are designed for use with tubeless tires the two halves are sealed airtight with an O-ring.

An airplane wheel with an inflated tire is potentially lethal. If you should have to remove the wheel from the airplane, it is always a good idea, after the wheel is raised off the ground with a jack, to deflate the tire before removing the axle nut. By doing this, if the through bolts should be broken, the wheel will not explode in your face.

When the wheels are removed for an inspection, the bearings must be cleaned and repacked with grease.

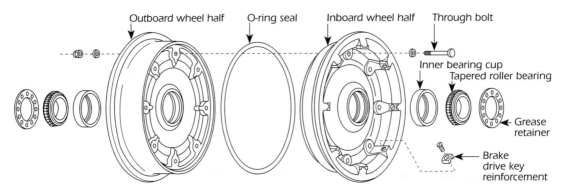

Figure 55. Exploded view of a typical two-piece wheel for a light airplane.

Chapter 20 **Aircraft Tires**

Practically all modern airplane tires are tubeless, and their bead forms an airtight seal with the bead seat area of the wheel. The carcass, or body, of the tire is made of plies of rubberized fabric that are oriented so their main strength crosses each adjacent layer at a 45° angle. This gives the tire the maximum strength for the landing impact loads to which the tire is subjected.

The tread of the tire is the design of the grooves that are cut across the outside periphery. The tread design that has become almost universal is the rib tread which is a series of straight grooves around the periphery of the tire.

Modern tires are made with ply fabric of aramid fibers which are far stronger than nylon or fiberglass. The strength of a tire is specified by its ply rating which is not the actual number of plies, but is the number of plies of cotton fabric needed to produce a tire of the same strength.

There are still some tube-type tires, and the difference between a tube-type and a tubeless tire is the inner liner. The inner liner of a tubeless tire is made of an impermeable material so it will hold air, the liner of a tube-type tire is made extra smooth so it will not chafe and wear the tube.

Tire Maintenance

The most important maintenance a pilot can perform on a tire is to be sure that it is properly inflated. Over or under inflation can cause abnormal wear on the tread and shorten the life of the tire.

Fixed-gear airplanes that enclose the wheel in a streamline fairing, or wheel pant, make it difficult to inspect the tire on a preflight walk around inspection, but it is important to take the trouble to examine the condition of the tread. *See* Figure 56 on the next page.

When a tire has been worn until the tread grooves are just about gone, the tire should be removed. It can be retreaded by a facility that is FAA-approved for this type of operation. If the tread is worn until the ply fabric shows through, it must be replaced because it is too far gone to be retreaded.

tire bead. The high-strength carbon-steel wire bundles that give an aircraft tire its strength and stiffness where it mounts on the wheel. The beads are encased in rubber-impregnated fabric.

When the tread is worn more in the center than on the shoulders, the tire has been operated in an overinflated condition. If the tread is worn more on the shoulders than in the center, it has been operated in an underinflated condition.

retread. The replacement of the tread rubber on an aircraft tire.

A Normally worn tread. Tire should be removed and retreaded.

B Excessively worn tread. Worn down to the plies and too far gone for safe operation or retreading.

C Tire operated while overinflated. Center of tread worn more than on shoulders.

Figure 56. The tread wear of a tire is an indicator of its condition.

D Tire operated while underinflated. Shoulders of tread are worn more than in center.

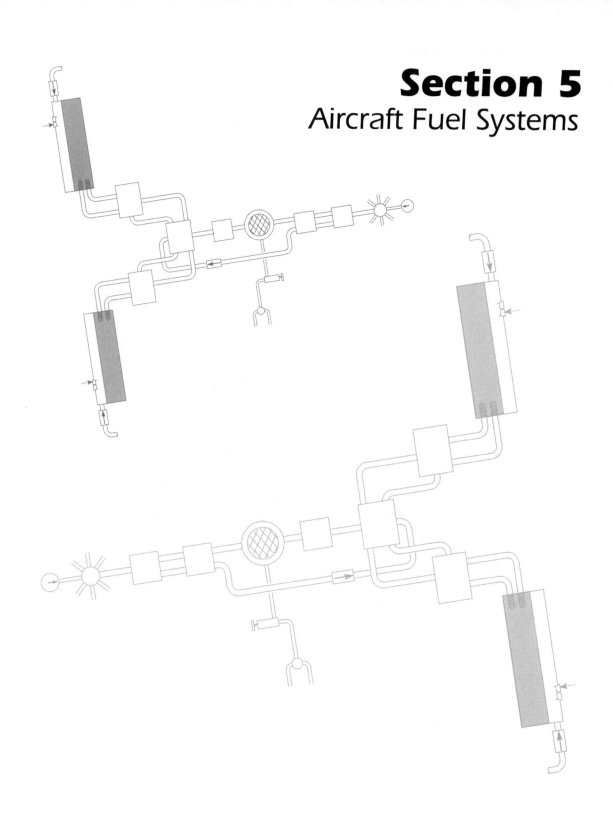

Section 5
Aircraft Fuel Systems

Chapter 21 **Aircraft Fuel**

Aviation fuel has gone through a number of changes since the phenomenal increase in turbine-engine powered aircraft. Many of the post World War II light airplane engines were designed to operate on 80-octane aviation gasoline, but since this fuel amounted to such a small percentage of the total amount of petroleum fuel sold, it was phased out in favor of 100-low lead (100LL) gasoline that has more lead than these engines were designed to accommodate. One-hundred octane fuel was also phased out and large engines that were designed to operate on it were forced to use 100LL that contains less lead than they are designed to use.

A recent survey shows that in the last year reported, the American petroleum industry produced 120 billion (120,000,000,000) gallons of automobile gasoline, 23 billion gallons of Jet-A fuel, and only 250 million (250,000,000) gallons of 100LL aviation gasoline. From this report it is understandable that the petroleum industry wants to rid itself of having to refine, market, distribute, and be legally responsible for a product that represents only about two-tenths of a percent of their production.

There are two alternatives for 100LL that may be used by the operator of a small general aviation airplane. A fuel known as 82UL gasoline is available that is essentially automobile gasoline and because it does not require special refining it costs only a bit more than half that of 100LL. The other alternative is to use automobile gasoline under the authorization of a Supplementary Type Certificate (STC) that is approved for certain models of airplanes under specified conditions.

The Correct Fuel is Essential

In the early days of flying, engine power was limited by the fuel used. If too much power (cylinder pressure) was demanded of an engine, the fuel-air mixture inside the cylinder was compressed so much that it exploded rather than burning smoothly as it should. This is called detonation.

During the 1930s it was found that if a small amount of tetraethyl lead (TEL), a poisonous chemical, was added to the fuel, then much more power could be produced by the engine before detonation occurred. Leaded fuel was the norm until it

aviation gasoline (Avgas).
A highly refined hydrocarbon fuel obtained by fractional distillation of crude petroleum.

detonation. *An explosion, or uncontrolled burning, of the fuel inside an engine cylinder when the fuel-air mixture reaches its critical pressure and/or temperature.*

was determined that the exhaust gases from this fuel contained compounds that were harmful to the ecology and low-lead or unleaded fuel took over.

The design of an aircraft engine is such that some lead or an appropriate substitute is needed. If a fuel is burned that contains too much lead, spark plugs will be fouled and valves can stick in their guides. If a fuel is burned that has too little lead there is not enough lubrication of the valves and undue wear will result.

Aviation gasoline is rated by a number that pertains to its ability to resist detonation. This is sometimes referred to as its octane rating.

An engine designed to operate on Grade-80 gasoline can use Grade-100, but additional additives may be required to scavenge some of the lead products to prevent fouling the spark plugs. An engine designed to operate on Grade-100 gasoline must *not* be fueled with Grade-80 as it will cause detonation when the maximum power is demanded of the engine. It is so important that only the proper grade of fuel be used that the FAA requires that a placard be positioned adjacent to the fuel tank filler that specifies "Avgas" and the minimum grade of fuel required.

octane rating. A rating of the antidetonation characteristics of a reciprocating engine fuel, based on the performance of the fuel in a special test engine. The higher the number the better the fuel resists detonation.

Grade 80 was formerly known as 80/87.

Grade 100 was formerly known as 100/130.

It is extremely important that jet fuel never be used with a piston engine as it will quickly and definitely cause destructive detonation.

The grade of aviation gasoline can be identified by its color.

Grade	Color
80	Red
82UL	Purple
100	Green
100LL	Blue
Jet fuel	Colorless

Aircraft fuel tester and fuel testing cup

Clean Fuel is Vital

It is important that not only the correct grade of fuel be used but that this fuel be delivered to the fuel metering system free of contaminates.

The two most prevalent types of contaminants are solids and water. Solid contaminants are normally in the form of rust or dirt that comes from contaminated storage containers, especially when the fuel is drawn from the bottom. When there is any question that the fuel being put into an airplane is contaminated, drain it through a chamois filter or other type of filter that will pass gasoline but will stop any water or solid contaminants.

Water may be found in fuel tanks even when the fuel has been pumped from a clean storage tank through clean hoses. If a fuel tank is left partially full when the aircraft is tied down out in the weather for a period of a week or so, moist air will enter the tank through the tank vent, and as the temperature changes, water will condense out of this air and settle in the bottom of the tank. Water can also enter the tank if rain water collects in the scupper around the filler neck. Be sure there is no water there before removing the filler cap.

A vital part of any preflight inspection is a check for water in the fuel. Drain a generous sample from the sumps of every tank and from the main fuel strainer into a transparent fuel tester or container. Aircraft that have a sump drain selector in the cockpit allow you to drain the tank sumps from inside the aircraft. This is not a good method of checking for water unless someone catches samples from each tank and examines them.

Water, being heavier than avgas, will sink to the bottom of the tester where it is visible. If water is present, drain fuel until it comes out with no trace of water. It is a good idea when following this procedure to rock the aircraft to be sure that any water in the tank will flow over the valve and be drained out. Some airplanes are notorious for accumulating water in the tanks that is not easy to drain out through the tank sumps. Be sure to read and follow the instructions in the POH to be sure that all of the water has been removed from these tanks.

Chapter 22 **Refueling Safety**

When gasoline flows through a rubber hose, enough static electricity may be generated to cause a spark to jump and ignite the fuel vapors that are rising out of the tank opening when it is being filled.

It is extremely important that the airplane be electrically grounded to the fuel tanker or fuel pump and that the nozzle be grounded to a bare spot on the aircraft structure near the filler opening. Be sure the grounding is in place before beginning the refueling operation and remains in place until the fueling is completed.

Important: Ground the airplane and fuel nozzle before and during the fueling process. Be sure that the aircraft and the fueling hose are electrically connected to prevent static electricity from causing a spark that could ignite the fuel vapors.

Aircraft Fuel Systems

It is imperative that the fuel system of an aircraft supply the engine with the correct amount of fuel under all conditions of flight, and that the pilot have a positive means of knowing the quantity of fuel available and be able to select fuel from any of the tanks he or she chooses.

There are two basic types of fuel systems used in general aviation airplanes: gravity-feed systems such as those used on high-wing airplanes, and pump-fed systems as used by most low-wing airplanes.

Gravity-Feed Systems

The simplest fuel system in an airplane is the gravity-feed system that is used with a float carburetor. Such a system is shown in Figure 57.

The two tanks in the wings are interconnected and feed through a common valve that has only two positions, ON and OFF. The space above the fuel in the two tanks is also interconnected and vented overboard through a vent line from the top of the left tank.

The fuel flows through a sediment bowl and strainer and on into the float carburetor. Fuel for starting the engine is taken from the strainer by a hand-operated primer pump and sprayed into the induction system near the intake valve.

There are coarse-mesh fuel strainers in the fuel line fittings inside the tanks that prevent large contaminants from blocking the flow of fuel. The fine-mesh main fuel strainer prevents small contaminants and water from getting to the carburetor.

Fuel-injected engines have a more complex fuel system than those used with a float carburetor. Figure 58 on the next page shows a typical gravity-feed fuel system used on an engine equipped with a Teledyne-Continental fuel injection system.

Fuel flows from the wing tanks into fuel reservoir tanks located inside the fuselage. These tanks connect to the fuel selector valve that has three positions: OFF, LEFT ON and RIGHT ON. From the selector valve the fuel flows to a two-speed electric auxiliary fuel pump to supply fuel to the fuel injection system under a positive pressure. This pump has a LOW and a HIGH position. From the auxiliary pump the fuel flows through the fine-mesh main strainer and to the engine-driven fuel pump which is part of the injection system.

The engine-driven pump produces a pressure that is proportional to the speed of the engine. More fuel than is needed is sent to the fuel injection control unit, and the excess is sent back by the mixture control through the fuel pump and a fuel return check valve to the selector valve and back into the selected tank.

The hand-operated primer pump takes fuel for starting the engine from the main strainer and sprays it into the intake manifold near the intake valves.

The weight of the fuel is a large percentage of an aircraft's total weight, and the balance of the aircraft in flight changes as the fuel is used. These conditions add to the complexity of the design of an aircraft fuel system. In small aircraft the fuel tanks are located near the center of gravity so the balance changes very little as the fuel is used.

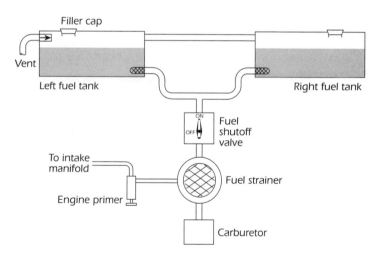

Figure 57. Gravity-feed fuel system for a high-wing training airplane

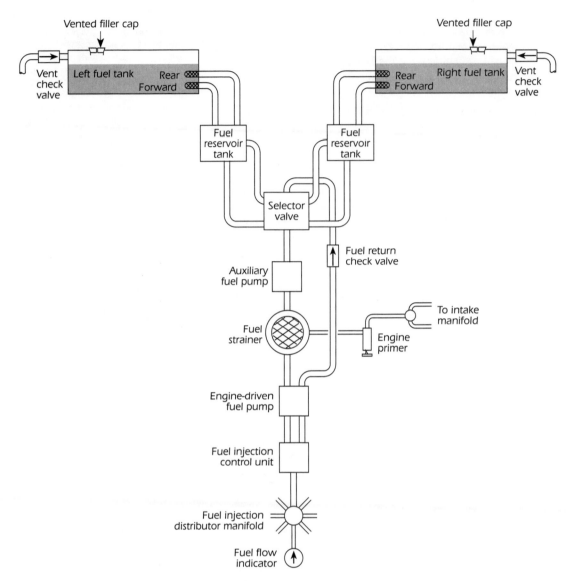

Figure 58. Gravity-feed fuel system for a single-engine high-wing airplane equipped with a fuel-injected engine

Pump-Fed Systems

Low-wing airplanes cannot depend upon gravity to supply fuel to the carburetor so an auxiliary and an engine-driven fuel pump are used. Figure 59 shows the fuel system of a typical single-engine low-wing airplane.

Fuel flows by gravity from the tanks through a selector valve that allows the pilot to select LEFT TANK, RIGHT TANK, or OFF. It passes through the fuel strainer located at the lowest point in the system to the plunger-type electric fuel pump and the diaphragm-type engine-driven fuel pump. These pumps are connected in parallel so either of them can supply the fuel to the engine. From the pumps, the fuel goes to the carburetor, and from the carburetor, a small line connects to the fuel pressure gage.

A hand-operated primer takes fuel from the main fuel strainer and sprays it out into the induction system for starting.

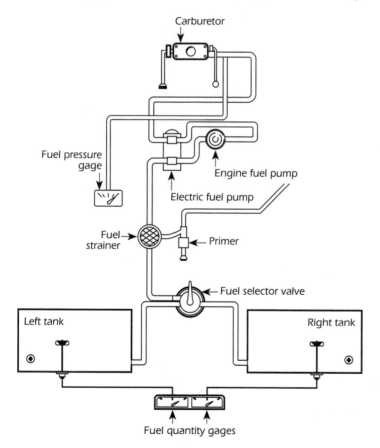

Figure 59. Pump-fed fuel system for a single-engine low-wing airplane equipped with a float carburetor

The electric pump is used to supply fuel to the carburetor until the engine pump is operating. It is also used as a safety feature for takeoff and to replace the engine-driven pump in the event it fails.

Multi-engine airplanes have a more complex fuel system. Figure 60 shows a typical low-wing multi-engine airplane that uses Teledyne-Continental (TCM) fuel injection systems.

The tip tanks are the main tanks for this airplane and each tank has an electric-motor-driven, submerged centrifugal boost pump that supplies fuel to a combination selector valve and filter. Fuel also flows across the airplane to supply fuel to the opposite engine in case of fuel exhaustion or pump failure on one side. Right and left auxiliary tanks supply fuel to the selector valves through electric in-line plunger-type auxiliary

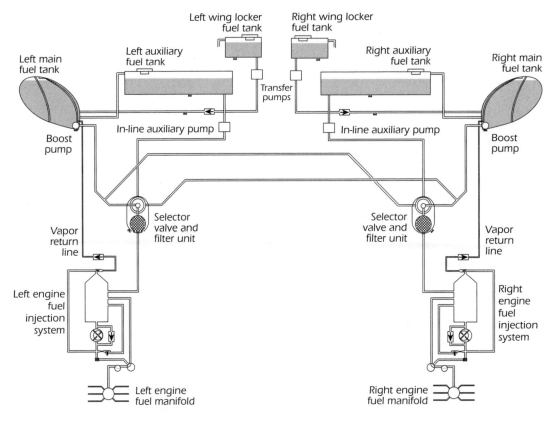

Figure 60. Pump-fed fuel system for a twin-engine low-wing airplane equipped with a fuel injection system

pumps. Fuel from left and right wing locker fuel tanks can be transferred to their respective main fuel tanks by plunger-type transfer pumps.

The fuel selector valve for the left engine has these positions: LEFT MAIN, RIGHT MAIN, LEFT AUXILIARY and OFF. The selector valve for the right engine has these positions: RIGHT MAIN, LEFT MAIN, RIGHT AUXILIARY and OFF.

From the selector valve, the fuel flows to the vapor separator portion of the engine-driven pump (which is part of the TCM fuel injection system) then through the vane-type pump to the fuel control and to the fuel manifold atop the engine. The mixture control sends only the needed fuel to the cylinders and the excess is routed back through the vapor separator portion of the fuel pump where it picks up any vapor that has been released from the fuel and carries it back into the top of the main fuel tank.

The boost pumps in the main fuel tanks have three functions: priming, purging, and backing up the engine-driven pump for takeoff and landing. For priming, the auxiliary pump operates at high speed and when the mixture control is placed in the RICH position, fuel flows from the injector nozzles for starting the engine. If the engine has been shut down while hot, vapors form in the fuel lines and prevent liquid fuel from reaching the nozzles. The auxiliary fuel pump switch may be placed in its LOW position, so the pump can operate at a low speed to circulate cool fuel through the pump and back to the main fuel tank to purge the vapors. *See* Figure 60. For takeoff and landing, the auxiliary pump backs up the engine-driven pump. If the engine-driven pump should fail, the auxiliary pump will automatically shift to high speed to supply the needed fuel. When the switch is in the OFF position, the auxiliary pump does not operate.

Priming System

Aircraft engines do not choke off the air to provide a rich mixture for starting as is done with automobile engines; instead, a small hand pump is used to draw fuel from the main fuel strainer and spray it into the intake manifold near the cylinder head. (*See* Figures 57, 58, and 59 on the previous pages).

Many fuel injected engines do not have a separate priming system, but produce the rich mixture for starting by turning on the boost pump and moving the mixture control to the RICH position until there is an indication of flow on the fuel flowmeter.

primer. A small, hand-operated pump, used to spray gasoline into the induction system for starting the engine.

Fuel Quantity Measuring Systems

All certificated aircraft are required to have a means of indicating to the pilot the quantity of fuel in each tank. These systems range from extremely simple floats riding on the surface of the fuel to electronic systems that compensate for fuel temperature and indicate the number of pounds of fuel on board the aircraft.

Each fuel quantity indicator is calibrated so it reads zero in level flight when the quantity of the fuel remaining in the tank is equal to the amount of unusable fuel.

Direct-Reading Fuel Gages

The simplest direct-reading fuel quantity indicator consists of a cork float with a wire sticking through a hole in the fuel tank cap. The higher the wire protrudes from the tank, the more fuel there is. This type of system does not give an accurate indication of the amount of fuel in the tank, but only a relative indication.

Electrical Resistance-Type Fuel Quantity Indicating System

For many years the most widely-used fuel quantity measuring system was the electrical resistance-type system. These systems use a sender, or transmitter, which consists of a variable resistor mounted on the outside of the fuel tank and operated by an arm connected to a float that rides on the surface of the fuel in the tank. Movement of the arm is transmitted through a metal bellows-type seal to operate the wiper of the resistor.

The indicator used with this system is a current-measuring instrument calibrated in fuel quantity. When the tank is empty, the float is on the bottom and the resistance is maximum. This drives the indicator pointer to the EMPTY mark on the dial. When the tank is full, the float is near the top of the tank, the resistance is minimum, and the pointer is driven to the FULL mark.

Capacitance-Type Electronic Fuel Quantity Measuring System

The electronic (capacitor-type) fuel quantity indicating system has no moving parts inside the tank and it is more accurate than other types of systems used for measuring fuel quantity.

These systems use several capacitor-type probes extending across each tank from top to bottom. When the attitude of the aircraft changes, fuel rises in some probes and lowers in others, and the total capacitance of all probes remains constant. This makes the fuel-quantity indication independent of attitude changes.

The fuel's dielectric constant (k) changes with its temperature which affects the fuel density. Because of this, the system measures the weight, actually the mass, of the fuel rather than its volume. Cold fuel is more dense than warm fuel, and there are more pounds in one gallon of cold fuel than in a gallon of warm fuel. Knowing the number of pounds of fuel available is more important than knowing the number of gallons, because the power produced by an aircraft engine is determined by the pounds, not gallons, of fuel burned.

By measuring the total capacitance of all the probes in all the fuel tanks, a totalizing system can indicate on one instrument the total number of pounds of fuel on board the aircraft.

The components in electronic (capacitance-type) fuel-quantity measuring systems are:

- Capacitor probes mounted in the fuel tanks.

- An electrical bridge circuit to measure the capacitance of the probes.

- An amplifier to increase the amplitude of the signal from the bridge circuit to a value high enough to drive the indicator.

- An indicator mounted in the instrument panel to show the amount of fuel in the tanks.

A capacitor is an electrical component made up of two conductors, called plates, separated by a dielectric, or insulator. It has the ability to store an electrical charge, and the amount of charge it can store is determined by the dielectric constant, or characteristic, of the material between the plates.

Probes like those in Figure 61 extend across the fuel tanks from top to bottom. These probes are made of concentric thin metal tubes that act as the plates. The dielectric is the fuel or air inside the tank. Air has a dielectric constant (or k) of 1, and the fuel has a k of approximately 2, depending upon its temperature. When the tank is full, fuel is the dielectric and the probe has a given amount of capacity. As the fuel is used, the dielectric becomes less fuel and more air, and the capacitance of the probe decreases.

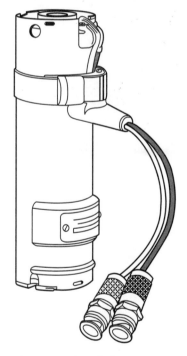

Figure 61. A typical capacitance probe mounted inside the fuel tank to measure the number of pounds of fuel in the tank.

Several probes can be installed in a fuel tank to measure the quantity of fuel in odd-shaped tanks. These capacitors are electrically connected in parallel and their total capacitance is the sum of the individual capacitances. The probes are connected into an electrical bridge-type circuit and the indicator is servo-driven to make the bridge self-balancing and provide a continuous indication of the amount of fuel remaining in the tanks.

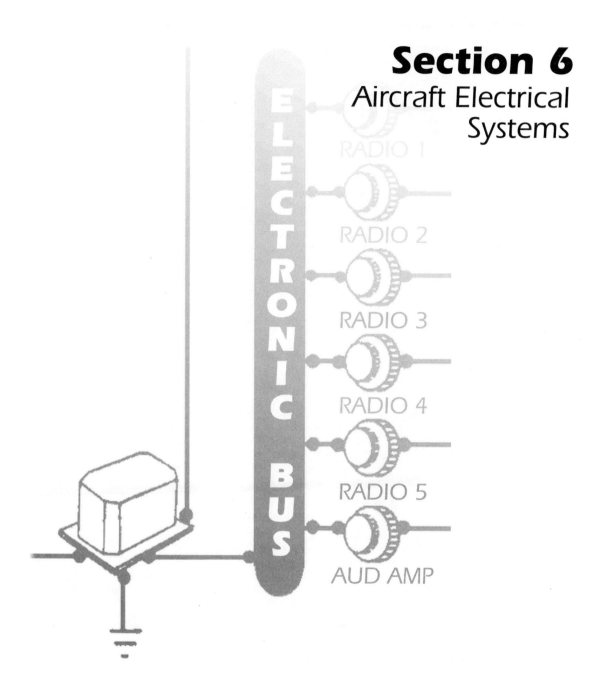

Section 6
Aircraft Electrical
Systems

ELECTRONIC BUS

RADIO 1

RADIO 2

RADIO 3

RADIO 4

RADIO 5

AUD AMP

Chapter 23 Electricity and the Aircraft

Through World War I an aircraft electrical system consisted of no more than a magneto or battery to supply a spark to ignite the fuel-air mixture inside the engine cylinders.

During the golden age of aviation, the years between the two world wars, electrical systems grew in importance and complexity. Magnetos still supplied the spark to the engines, but 14- or 28-volt direct-current generators supplied current to operate the navigation and landing lights, the radios, and in some airplanes, the retractable landing gear. Generators kept the batteries charged to operate the electric motor used to start the engines.

As the twentieth century ended, electrical systems have become just about equal in importance with the engines. General aviation aircraft still use direct current systems to provide a method of storing energy to start the engine, but the electrical loads have increased tremendously. Electricity is used to operate gyro instruments, automatic pilots, engine and flight instruments, and the all-important electronic navigation and communication systems that make the airplane such a vital transportation vehicle. Jet airliners have extremely complex electrical systems and use alternating current as the primary source of electricity. Batteries are used for emergency and backup operations and for some special applications.

Electrical Principles

"Electricity" consists of the movement of extremely tiny components of an atom called electrons. These are far too small to see, but they are a part of every physical thing that exists.

To understand how electricity works, think of a simple circuit that consists of a battery and a bulb as in Figure 62. All complete circuits must have a power source, a load to use the electricity, and conductors through which the electrons can move between the source and the load, and back to the source.

A power source is a two-terminal device that produces an excess of electrons at one terminal and a deficiency of electrons at the other. The alternator in an airplane and the battery in a watch are both power sources—they do the same thing, they move electrons in a circuit.

current. The flow of electrons. Current is measured in amperes (amps).

voltage. The electrical pressure that forces electrons to flow in a circuit. This pressure is measured in volts.

power. The ability of an electrical system to do work. Power is measured in watts, and is the product of current and voltage (power = current x voltage).

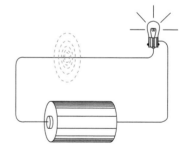

Figure 62. A complete circuit consists of a power source, a device to use the power, and conductors to join the two.

direct current (DC). Electricity in which the electrons move through the system in one direction only.

alternating current (AC). Electricity in which the electrons continually change their amount of flow and periodically reverse their direction of flow.

resistance. The friction caused when electrons move in a circuit. Resistance is measured in ohms.

transformer. An electrical device that changes the values of current and voltage in an AC circuit. When voltage is increased, current is decreased in the same proportion.

rectifier. An electrical device that allows electrons to travel in one direction but blocks their travel in the opposite direction.

Any time electrons move in a circuit, two things happen: a magnetic field surrounds the conductor and heat is generated. Figure 62 shows the invisible lines of magnetism that surround the conductor. The lamp produces light when the electrons moving through the filament produce so much heat that it glows white hot.

There are two kinds of electricity: direct current (DC) and alternating current (AC).

In DC, the electrons always flow in the same direction in a circuit. General aviation airplanes have a DC alternator that takes some of the mechanical energy from the engine and changes it into electricity to operate the various motors, lights, and radios. Most importantly, it keeps the 12- or 24-volt battery charged to store electrical energy for starting the engine.

Large jet transport airplanes use three-phase 115-volt AC as their primary electrical power. AC has the advantage that when a large amount of electrical power is needed, the voltage can be increased and the current decreased. It is current that causes heat in a conductor, and with less current smaller wires can be used, thus saving weight.

Any time a lower voltage is needed to operate some component, the AC is passed through a transformer which decreases the voltage and increases the available current. When DC is needed, AC may be passed through a rectifier which changes it into DC.

Chapter 24 DC Generation Systems

Some older airplanes still flying have generators to supply electrical power, but most modern airplanes use alternators. Both devices do exactly the same thing: they convert mechanical energy from the engine into electricity. The difference between the two is the much higher efficiency of the alternator.

Generators and alternators produce electricity in the same way by moving a conductor through a magnetic field. This forces current to flow. The amount of current is determined by:

- The strength of the magnetic field
- The speed with which the conductor moves through the field or the speed with which the magnetic field changes
- The number of turns of wire in the conductor.

The rotor of an alternator is a rotating electromagnet that is driven by the engine either by a belt or directly with gears. The typical rotor has between four and seven pairs of poles, and as the rotor turns the polarity of the magnetic field reverses. The number of pairs of poles determines the number of magnetic reversals each revolution. The strength of the magnetic field is determined by the amount of current supplied to its coil by the voltage regulator.

An alternator is turned OFF by turning off (opening) the alternator side of the split-rocker master switch. This stops the flow of field current from the battery through the coil in the rotor and the rotor poles lose their magnetism.

Surrounding the rotor is a stator which has several coils of heavy copper wire wound in slots in a laminated soft iron frame. When the rotor turns, current is produced in these coils which are joined in such a way that they act as three separate phases, or generators, connected together. The current generated in these coils goes to a rectifier made of six solid-state diodes, which blocks the flow in one direction while allowing it to flow in the opposite direction. The output is DC, the voltage of which is controlled by the voltage regulator.

The voltage regulator is often a solid-state device which senses the alternator output voltage. If, for any reason, it drops below the value set by the regulator the field current to the rotor is increased, strengthening the magnetic field and

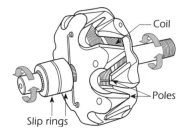

Figure 63. The rotor of a DC alternator is a multipole electromagnet

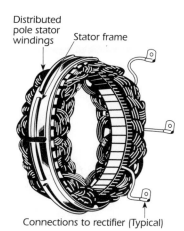

Figure 64. The stator of a DC alternator is made of several coils of heavy copper wire wound in slots in a laminated iron frame inside of which the rotor turns.

increasing the output voltage. If the voltage rises too high, the regulator decreases the field current and the voltage drops.

Some electrical systems have an overvoltage protector that stops all field current if the alternator should malfunction and produce an excessively high voltage.

Large jet transport aircraft use 115-volt, 400-hertz, three-phase AC electrical systems. The large engines in these aircraft normally have air starters and do not depend upon electrical power for starting, but there are some applications that require DC. For these, a transformer-rectifier reduces the voltage and changes the AC into DC.

transformer-rectifier. An electrical device that reduces the value of the AC to that suitable for the battery and changes the AC into DC to keep the aircraft batteries charged.

Chapter 25 **Aircraft Electrical Systems**

The typical general aviation airplane has a 24-volt DC electrical system similar to the one shown by the pictorial diagram in Figure 65 on the next page.

Airplanes use a single-wire electrical system. The negative (–) terminal of the battery and the G terminal of the alternator are connected to the metal aircraft structure so all of the return current from any operating component returns to the battery or alternator through the metal structure. This is shown on an electrical system diagram by the ground symbol, a triangular series of horizontal lines.

 **ground symbol**

The Alternator Circuit

The A+, or output, terminal of the alternator is connected to the alternator bus through a high-current circuit breaker. A wire from the alternator bus carries current to the primary bus to supply current to all of the components attached to it.

The output voltage of the alternator is controlled by the voltage regulator. This regulator supplies current to the alternator rotor field coil from the alternator bus through:

1. the alternator field circuit breaker;
2. the alternator side of the master switch;
3. the S terminal of the voltage regulator; and
4. through the regulator to its F terminal; then
5. to the alternator F terminal.

The alternator may be turned off by stopping the flow of field current by turning off the alternator side of the split-rocker master switch.

circuit breaker. An electrical component that automatically opens the circuit any time an excess of current flows. Most popped circuit breakers can be closed in flight to restore an opened circuit.

bus. A common point in an aircraft electrical system from which power from the alternator and battery supply current to all of the components in the electrical system.

The Battery Circuit

The negative terminal of the battery is connected to the ground, and the positive terminal connects to the battery contactor. When the battery side of the split-rocker master switch is turned ON, current flows from the battery through the magnetic coil inside the contactor to ground. This produces a magnetic field that closes the heavy contacts connecting the battery to the alternator bus through the ammeter. (*See* Figure 65 on the next page.)

battery contactor. A heavy-duty magnetically operated switch that carries current from the battery to the alternator bus. The contactor is controlled by current from the battery half of the split-rocker master switch.

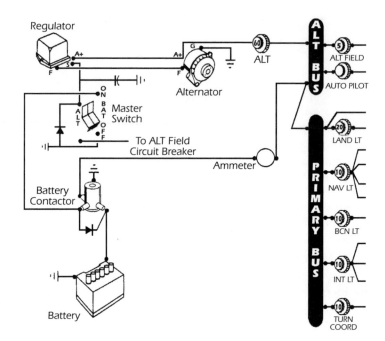

Figure 65. The alternator and battery circuit of a typical single-engine general aviation airplane.

The Electronic Bus

Any time current flows in a conductor a magnetic field surrounds the conductor, and when the current stops flowing, this field collapses and produces a spike of high voltage in the conductor. This high voltage can damage any operating electronic equipment, so it is extremely important that all electronic equipment be turned off when the engine is being started.

To prevent damage from spikes of high voltage caused by the starter, turn off all electronic equipment before starting the engine.

The split-bus contactor in Figure 66 does this automatically. Current from the alternator bus flows to the electronics bus through a normally ON, magnetically operated split-bus contactor. When the ignition/starter switch is turned to the start position, or when a power cart is connected to the ground service receptacle, current flows to the coil in the contactor and shuts off all current from the alternator bus to the electronics bus, turning off all the radios.

The diodes between the ignition/starter switch and the ground service receptacle and the split-bus contactor allow normal current to flow to the contactor but block the high-voltage spike caused by the starter or the ground power source.

The Starter Circuit

The starter is a heavy-duty electric motor that uses a large amount of current. It is controlled by the ignition/starter switch which supplies a small amount of current to turn on the starter contactor so the current can flow from the battery or ground service plug to the starter. *See* Figure 66.

When an electrical circuit is opened it is turned OFF, when it is closed it is turned ON.

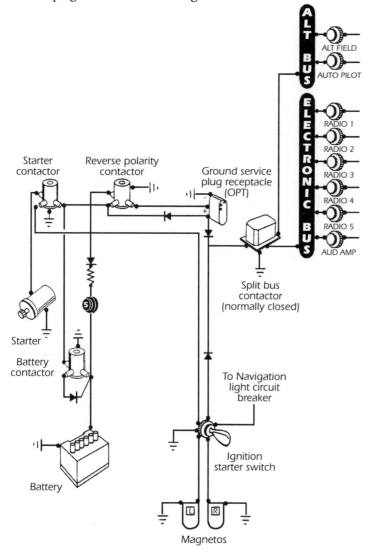

Figure 66. Electrical power is shut off to the electronic bus when the ignition/starter switch is in the start position or when the ground power is supplied to the aircraft.

ground symbol. A symbol in the diagram of a single-wire electrical system that shows where the device is grounded (connected to the aircraft or engine structure). ⏚

Ground Service Power Circuit

Aircraft batteries are small and are easily discharged when trying to start a stubborn engine in cold weather. A ground service receptacle is installed on the outside of the airplane so a battery cart or generator can supply current to the aircraft electrical system for starting.

When the ground service plug is inserted into the receptacle, current flows to the reverse-polarity contactor through the diode. If the polarity of the ground power source is correct, its + terminal going to the + terminal of the aircraft system, the reverse-polarity contactor turns ON, connecting the ground power to the aircraft battery. But if the – terminal of the ground power source is connected to the + terminal of the aircraft system, the diode blocks current to the coil of the reverse polarity contactor and it will not connect the ground power source to the aircraft electrical system. *See* Figure 66.

diode. An electronic component that acts as an electron check valve. Current can flow through it in one direction but is blocked in the opposite direction. ▶├─

The Primary Bus

Most of the electrical devices in the aircraft get their power from the primary bus through circuit breakers.

Notice that more than one circuit can be connected to a circuit breaker so when troubleshooting an electrical problem, consult the Pilot's Operating Handbook to see which circuit breaker provides current to the circuit under consideration. For example, the ignition/starter switch gets its current from the circuit breaker marked "Nav Light." *See* Figure 67.

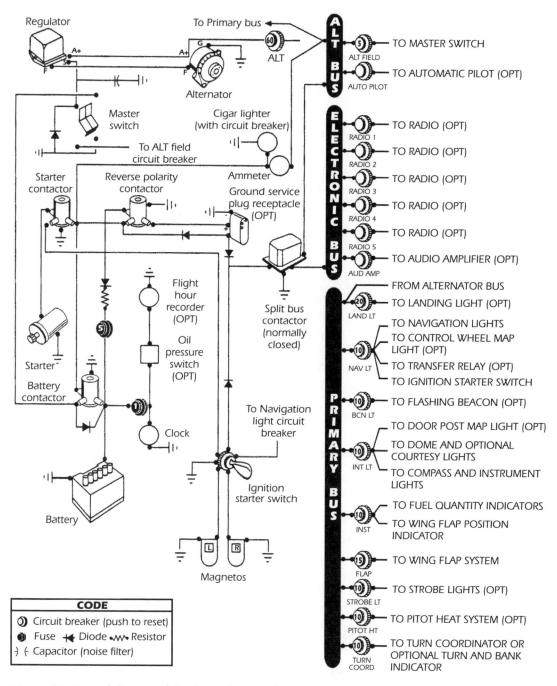

Figure 67. Pictorial diagram of the electrical system from the POH of a typical single-engine general aviation airplane.

Chapter 26 **Electrical System Troubleshooting**

The electrical system is such a vital system in an airplane that every pilot should understand it well enough to describe to the AMT all the pertinent factors when something doesn't work as it should.

The first and most important aspect of electrical system troubleshooting is to understand the electrical diagram of your system. The pictorial diagram of a general aviation airplane electrical system in Figure 6.6 is typical of those found in the POH. Know your system and go after the simplest solutions first. Here are some examples of ways to determine what is wrong:

Study the POH so you can trouble-shoot and/or describe electrical problems to your AMT.

Situation: After a careful preflight inspection you are ready to start the engine, but when the ignition/starter switch is placed in the start position, you hear a series of heavy clicking sounds and nothing else happens.

Assumption: The battery is discharged.

Action to take:

1. Turn on the dome light. It will probably be dim.

2. Move the ignition/starter switch to the start position. You hear the clicking and the dome light dims out completely.

The problem: The battery is discharged. The heavy clicking sound is the starter contactor trying to connect the starter to the battery but there is not enough current to hold it engaged.

The solution: Have the battery recharged or use a ground power unit. When the engine starts the alternator will recharge the battery.

Situation: The engine starts and runs properly, but the ammeter shows a discharge.

Assumption: The alternator is not working and the battery is supplying all of the current.

Action to take:

1. Check the alternator side of the master switch. If it is on, turn it off and back on. If the ammeter still shows a discharge—

2. Check the alternator and the alternator field circuit breakers.

The problem: The alternator is apparently not getting field current.

The solution: Have an AMT check for the presence of field current and replace the defective component.

Situation: When the master switch is in the ON position, the instruments come alive and the radio works, but when the ignition/starter switch is moved to the start position, nothing happens.

Assumption:

1. The switch may be defective.

2. The starter contactor may be defective.

3. A wire in the starter contactor circuit may be broken.

Action to take:

Try the simple solution first:

1. Turn on the navigation lights. If they do not come on, the problem is with the navigation light circuit breaker. Reset it.

The problem: If the navigation lights turn on, the problem is with the ignition/start switch or the starter contactor.

The solution: Have an AMT check the ignition/starter switch and the starter contactor, and then replace the defective component.

Alternator Failure in Flight

One of the very worst times for an alternator to fail is on a night IFR flight. When this happens it is imperative that you know the electrical system and the things you can do to ensure a safe completion of the flight.

The first indication of an alternator failure would be the low-voltage warning light if one is installed, or the ammeter showing discharge. Quickly check the alternator and alternator field circuit breakers. If they are of the type that can be pulled to turn the circuit off, pull them, then reset them.

If the circuit breakers are in, turn the alternator side of the master switch off and then back on. If the alternator does not come back online turn the alternator side off and leave it off to prevent the alternator field from discharging the battery.

With the alternator no longer supplying current to the alternator bus, the flight will have to continue on battery power alone. This will not affect the engine ignition as it is supplied by independent magnetos, but all other electrical equipment must be judiciously used.

Turn off all radios and lights that are not absolutely necessary for the safe continuation of the flight. If the aircraft has electrically actuated flaps and landing gear, be prepared to lower the landing gear manually—consider the possibility, and plan for a flaps-up landing.

Chapter 27 **Aircraft Batteries**

A battery is a device that converts electrical energy from the alternator into chemical energy and stores it until needed. There are two kinds of batteries used in aircraft electrical systems: lead-acid and nickel cadmium (ni-cad).

Battery Terms

Voltage—The electrical pressure produced by a battery, expressed in volts. Voltage is determined by the number of cells, not the physical size of a battery. A lead-acid battery has an open circuit (no load) voltage of about 2.1 volts per cell and a ni-cad cell has a voltage of 1.28 volts.

A 12-volt lead-acid battery has six cells and a 24-volt battery has 12 cells. A 24-volt ni-cad battery may have either 19 or 20 cells.

Specific gravity—The ratio of the density of the electrolyte to the density of pure water. Specific gravity indicates the state of charge of a lead-acid battery. The electrolyte, when the battery is fully charged, has a specific gravity of about 1.285, and when discharged it is down to about 1.150.

The chemistry of a ni-cad battery is such that the specific gravity of the electrolyte does not change with its state of charge.

Capacity—The total amount of current available in a battery, expressed in ampere hours. Capacity is determined by the size of the cells.

The ampere-hour capacity of a battery is affected by the rate at which it is discharged. The rating is based on the battery being discharged in 5 hours. A 25-ampere hour battery will supply 5 amps of current for 5 hours, but if it is discharged in 20 minutes its capacity is down to 16 ampere hours. At a 5-minute discharge rate (the approximate discharge rate caused by a starter) the capacity is down to less than 12 ampere-hours.

Lead-Acid Batteries

Lead-acid batteries are by far the most widely used battery for general aviation aircraft. They differ from automobile batteries in that they are subject to greater demands while cranking a cold engine, and they must be lighter in weight.

battery. An electrochemical device, normally made of a number of individual cells. Electrical energy is stored in a battery by changing it into chemical energy. Chemical energy in the battery causes a potential difference between the negative and the positive terminals, and when a conductor joins the two terminals, electrons flow from the negative terminal to the positive terminal.

Batteries are made of cells that contain intermeshing lead plates. Half of the plates are made of pure lead and the others are made of a framework containing lead dioxide. These plates are immersed in a solution of sulfuric acid and water, and the cells are permanently connected together by lead straps.

As the battery discharges the sulfuric acid changes some of the lead into lead sulfate and dilutes the electrolyte with water. Its specific gravity drops, indicating the state of charge of the battery.

When the battery is charged by connecting it to a voltage greater than its own voltage, the charging current changes the lead sulfate back to its original lead, some of the water is changed into sulfuric acid and its specific gravity rises.

Another characteristic of a lead-acid battery is that its voltage drops as it discharges. As the lead changes into lead sulfate, the internal resistance increases and voltage is dropped across it so the electrical load does not get the full voltage.

Check the electrical system section of the POH to determine the type of battery installed in the aircraft and to note any specific operating instructions for the battery.

Nickel-Cadmium Batteries

Turbine engine starters require much more current than the starter for a piston engine so ni-cad batteries became popular for these airplanes. The plates in a ni-cad battery are made of nickel hydroxide and cadmium hydroxide. The electrolyte is a solution of potassium hydroxide and water.

The specific gravity of the electrolyte does not change as the state of charge changes, and during discharge, the voltage remains essentially constant until the battery is almost totally discharged.

Ni-cad batteries are made of individual cells that may be removed from the battery case. They are connected together with stainless steel conductor strips and the entire battery of 19 or 20 cells is assembled in a steel or fiberglass case.

The low internal resistance of ni-cad cells allows them to be charged at such a high rate that the middle cells get hot and there is no way for them to dissipate this heat. As they heat up, their resistance drops and they accept more current and continue to get hotter until they destroy themselves and can cause a fire. This is called thermal runaway. Overcurrent or temperature sensors are installed with ni-cad batteries to alert the flight crew so the battery can be isolated from the electrical system.

Battery Care

Batteries are the source of many headaches for pilots of general aviation airplanes, so a few pointers on the care of lead-acid batteries are appropriate.

It is extremely important that the top of the battery be kept clean and dry as any moisture will conduct current between the terminals and discharge the battery. When cleaning the battery, be careful not to get any acid on your clothes because it will eat holes in them. Wash the top of the battery with a solution of sodium bicarbonate (baking soda) and water, being careful that none of it gets into the cells. Rinse it with fresh water and dry it thoroughly.

Corrosion is a major cause of battery related problems when it forms on the cable terminals and causes a high-resistance connection that prevents sufficient current reaching the starter.

When removing the cables from a battery, always remove the ground (–) cable first. If the "hot" (+) cable were removed first, the wrench might touch some metal part of the airplane and cause a large spark. This could cause damage and perhaps personal injury. When replacing the cables, replace the "hot" cable first, then the ground.

Remove the cables from the battery and soak all the corrosion off with a solution of sodium bicarbonate and water. Scrape or brush the battery and cable terminals, and with the metal clean and bright, connect the cable to the battery and tighten the nut. Then cover the connection with a rubber boot or a light coating of grease.

Battery Charging

An aircraft battery is lightweight and has a relatively small capacity. The alternator keeps it charged because its voltage is higher than that of the battery. When the battery is removed from the aircraft for charging, remove the caps from the cells and check the water level. Use only distilled water and fill each cell to the level specified by the battery manufacturer. Overfilling the cell will cause some of it to spew out the vent in the caps. Leave the caps loose while the battery is being charged to allow the gases to escape.

When a lead-acid battery is being charged, hydrogen and oxygen gases are released. These gases form a combustible mixture, so it is important that every precaution be taken to prevent sparks near batteries that are being charged.

Some maintenance shops have computer-controlled constant-current chargers but most aircraft owners have access to constant-voltage chargers. Check the electrolyte level and adjust it to the level of the indicator in each cell with distilled water. Be sure the charger is turned off and connect the + lead to the + terminal of the battery and the – lead to the – terminal. Set the charger for 14 or 28 volts as appropriate and turn it on. Since the battery is discharged it will initially take a large amount of current, but as it becomes charged, the current will decrease. Allow the battery to remain connected to the charger until the specific gravity of the electrolyte rises to about 1.285.

While the battery is removed from the aircraft, check the battery box for corrosion. Remove all traces, dry the box thoroughly and paint the inside with an acid-proof paint.

Nickel-Cadmium Battery Reconditioning

Ni-cad batteries are normally installed in aircraft that do not lend themselves to pilot-maintenance, but it is important to understand the difference between ni-cad and lead-acid batteries.

The chemistry of the two types of batteries is totally different and, to prevent contamination, tools used on one type must not be used on the other. The specific gravity of the electrolyte is not an indication of the battery's state of charge.

When a ni-cad battery begins to lose some of its capacity it can be restored by reconditioning, or deep-cycling, it. This is done in a shop that is equipped for this function. The battery is disassembled, cleaned, and completely discharged. It is then reassembled and charged by a computer-controlled charger to 140% of its five-hour discharge ampere-hour capacity.

Section 7
Aircraft Instrument Systems

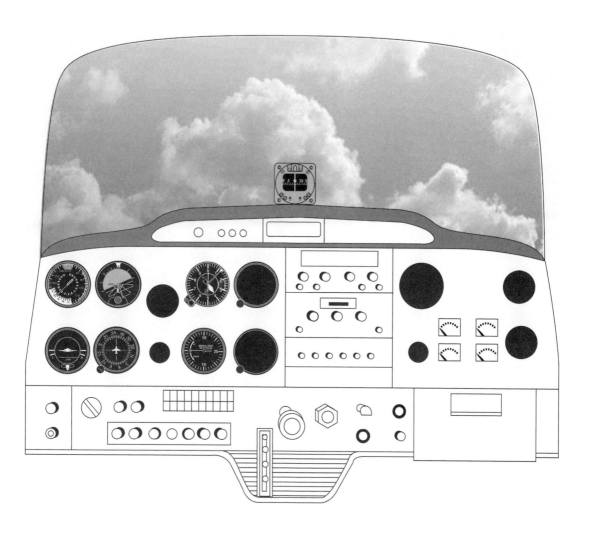

Chapter 28 **Flight Instruments**

The instruments are some of the more visible components in an airplane as they are the devices that stare back at us all the time we are flying. They tell us where we are, what we are doing, and how well we are doing it. Some of them have built-in errors, and for others, their indications must be manipulated.

The flight instruments are those that show the attitude and the progress of the aircraft in flight.

Magnetic Compass

The magnetic compass is the oldest instrument in the field of transportation and has changed very little since the days of the sailing ships. Its importance is still recognized as the FAA requires a magnetic compass of some type be installed in all aircraft for both IFR and VFR flying.

Two small bar magnets are soldered to the bottom of a hollow brass float that rides inside a housing filled with compass fluid. The compass fluid is a highly refined petroleum product, much like kerosine. A graduated card is mounted around the outside of the float in such a way that it is visible through the glass lens in the front of the housing. Across the center of the lens is a thin bar called a lubber line. The compass heading, in degrees clockwise from north, is the number read on the dial opposite the lubber line. A bellows or diaphragm allows the fluid to expand or contract with changes in the temperature.

The basic flight instruments required for VFR operations are: airspeed indicator, altimeter, magnetic direction indicator. In addition to these, IFR operations require: rate-of-turn indicator, slip-skid indicator (these two are combined in both the turn-and-slip indicator and turn coordinator), sensitive altimeter, clock, artificial horizon, and heading indicator or equivalent.

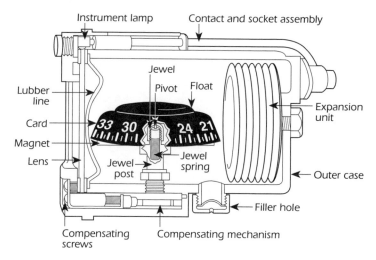

Figure 68. A cutaway view of a direct-reading magnetic compass

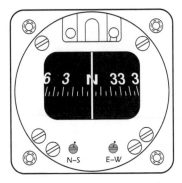

Figure 69. The numbers on the card of a magnetic compass appear to be on the wrong side.

Figure 70. The vertical-card magnetic compass minimizes the error of turning in the wrong direction to reach the desired heading.

The compass card is marked with letters N, E, S, and W representing the four cardinal headings: north, east, south, and west. Long marks are used for each 10° and short marks for each 5°. Every third long mark has the number of degrees it represents with the last digit omitted, for example, the number 3 on the card means 30°, 12 is 120° and 33 is 330°.

One problem with this type of compass is that the graduated card is viewed from the back and the numbers appear to be in the wrong direction. Look at the compass card in Figure 69. The airplane in which this compass is mounted is headed North. West is to the left, but 3, representing 30°, *east* of north, is on the left side of N.

The error of turning in the wrong direction has been minimized by using the vertical-card magnetic compass in Figure 70. The line on the nose of the symbolic airplane is the lubber line and the numbers on the card are on the correct side.

Compass Errors

A magnetic compass has four basic errors of which the pilot must be aware: variation, deviation, turning error, and acceleration error.

Variation

The molten metals in the center of the Earth cause it to act like a huge magnet with a north pole and a south pole. The magnetic field leaves the Earth perpendicular to the surface at the poles and becomes horizontal at the magnetic equator. The magnets in the compass are attracted by and align themselves with this magnetic field.

The Earth spins in space about an axis that passes through the north and south *geographic* poles, and all navigational charts are laid out according to these poles that do not change their location. Directions measured from geographic north are called true directions.

The magnetic poles are not colocated with the geographic poles, but are located several hundred miles away from them. To further complicate matters, they continually move about. Directions measured from magnetic north are called magnetic directions. The error caused by the compass pointing to magnetic north and the aeronautical charts being oriented to true north is called variation error and is corrected by information given on aeronautical charts.

An irregular line passing through both the geographic and magnetic north poles and roughly through Chicago, IL and Savannah, GA is called the agonic (no angle) line. There is no variation error when flying in the vicinity of this line. When flying in an area east of the agonic line, the compass points to a location that is west of true north and the variation must be added to the true direction to find the magnetic direction. When flying in an area west of the agonic line, the compass points to a location east of true north. The amount of variation is shown on the aeronautical charts with dashed magenta lines called isogonic lines (lines of equal variation) that specify the number of degrees east or west. These lines are continually changing and are updated on each printing of the charts.

variation. The compass error caused by the difference in the physical locations of the magnetic north pole and the geographic north pole.

If you are flying in the vicinity of Washington, DC where the variation is 10° west, and want to fly due west (270° true) you would have to fly a magnetic course of 280° because the compass points 10° west of true north.

When going from true direction to magnetic direction:

+ Add westerly variation
– Subtract easterly variation

Mnemonic aid for calculating magnetic course: East is least (subtract variation from true course), west is best (add variation to true course).

The variation error is determined by your location on the surface of the Earth and does not change with the heading of the airplane. Radio navigation aids such as VORs automatically take care of variation error as their directions are oriented to magnetic north.

Deviation

The magnets in the compass align with any magnetic field. The steel structural members in the airplane and wires carrying electrical current all attract the compass magnets.

deviation. A magnetic compass error caused by local magnetic fields within the aircraft. Deviation error is different on each heading.

The compass in an airplane must be compensated by an AMT and a compass correction card mounted in plain sight near the compass. This card is marked off in thirty-degree increments for the desired heading and with each heading is the compass correction that must be applied. Note in Figure 71 on the next page that when you want to fly a magnetic heading of 060° with the radios on, you would have to maintain a compass heading of 062°.

Deviation error is not affected by the location of the airplane over the Earth's surface, but is affected by the heading of the airplane.

If the compass appears to have an error of more than 10° when checked against the known runway direction, an AMT should check the deviation error by calibrating the compass.

Runway designator numbers are the nearest whole number to the magnetic direction of the runway centerline with the last digit omitted. For example, a runway with a magnetic direction of 093° is runway 09.

FOR STEER	000	030	060	090	120	150
RDO. ON	001	032	062	095	123	155
RDO. OFF	002	031	064	094	125	157

FOR STEER	180	210	240	270	300	330
RDO. ON	176	210	243	271	296	325
RDO. OFF	174	210	240	273	298	327

Figure 71. A compass correction card

Dip Errors

The Earth's magnetic field leaves the surface vertically at the north pole and re-enters vertically at the south pole. At the magnetic equator, the field is horizontal and the needle remains level. In the higher latitudes the field tilts and since the compass magnets are balanced on a pivot the compass card tilts with the field. This is called magnetic dip and causes two types of compass errors: turning errors and acceleration error.

Turning Errors

The forces that act on an airplane also act on the compass float assembly. When the aircraft is banked, the float also banks.

lags or leads. When starting a turn from a northerly heading, the compass lags behind the turn. When starting a turn from a southerly heading, the compass leads the turn.

The center of gravity of the float is lower than its pivot point and as the airplane turns, the magnetic field pulls on the north-seeking end of the float. If you are flying on a northerly heading and turn to either the east or west, the compass indication will lag behind the airplane and at the beginning of the turn, may temporarily start in the opposite direction. This error will decrease as the turn progresses, and will disappear at a heading of east or west.

If you start a turn from a southerly heading, the card will initially indicate a much greater rate of turn than you are making, but it will read accurately as you pass through east or west.

If you make a turn to the north from either an easterly or westerly heading, the compass indication will lag behind the airplane so you should stop the turn before you reach the desired heading. This error becomes more pronounced the closer you are to the poles. A handy rule of thumb to correct for northerly turning error is to stop the turn 15 degrees plus half of the latitude before you reach your desired heading. For example, if you are flying on an easterly heading in the vicinity of New York City where the latitude is approximately 40°N and you want to turn to a heading of 010°, stop the turn at 045° (010° + 15 + 20 = 045°). When the airplane is back in level flight, the compass will swing around to 010°.

When a turn is started to a southerly heading, the compass indication will lead the turn. The rollout should not be started until the compass has indicated that the desired heading has been passed.

In the Southern Hemisphere the errors are reversed.

Turning to the north, the compass lags
Turning to the south, the compass leads

Acceleration Error

Turning errors show up on turns to the north or south heading, but acceleration error shows up only when flying on an east or west heading.

The compass card is mounted like a pendulum. When the airplane accelerates on either an east or west heading, the side of the card nearest the pilot tilts upward and the vertical component of the Earth's field causes the card to rotate in a direction that indicates a turn toward the north. When decelerating, the side nearest the pilot tilts downward and the magnetic pull causes the card to indicate a turn to the south.

The mnemonic, "**ANDS**" (Acceleration–North/Deceleration–South) will help you remember the proper correction for acceleration error.

Pitot-Static System

Three very important flight instruments operate on pressures taken from the pitot-static system. These are the pressure altimeter, airspeed indicator, and vertical speed indicator.

Flight instruments depend upon accurate sampling of the ambient atmospheric pressure to determine the height and speed of movement of the aircraft through the air, both horizontally and vertically. This pressure is sampled at two or more locations outside the aircraft by the pitot-static system.

The pressure of the static, or still, air is measured at a flush port on the side of the fuselage or the vertical fin in an area proven by flight tests to be in undisturbed air. These ports are normally paired, one on either side of the aircraft to prevent lateral movement of the aircraft from giving erroneous static pressure indications. The areas around the static ports on some aircraft are heated with electric heater elements to prevent ice forming over the port and blocking the entry of the static air.

Pitot, or impact air, pressure is taken in through an open-end tube pointed directly into the relative wind flowing around the aircraft. These tubes are normally mounted on the nose of multi-engine aircraft or below the wing leading edge of single-engine aircraft, and are protected from ice with built-in electric heaters.

The pitot tube connects to the airspeed indicator, and the static ports deliver their pressure to the airspeed indicator, altimeter, and vertical-speed indicator. If the static ports should ice over, or in any other way become obstructed, a static-system alternate source valve may be opened to take in static air pressure from a location inside the aircraft. This type of arrangement is shown in Figure 72.

When the alternate source valve is open, the static-system instruments will read incorrectly. The POH includes a chart showing the amount of error caused when the alternate source is used.

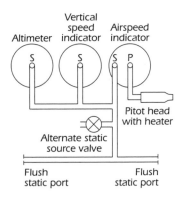

Figure 72. A typical pitot-static system for a single-engine airplane

Position Error

The airplane manufacturer has located the static ports in a position where the air at their surface is as undisturbed as possible. But under some flight conditions, particularly at a high angle of attack with the landing gear and flaps down, the air around the static port may be disturbed to the extent that it can cause an error in the indication of the altimeter and airspeed indicator. Part of the certification tests for an airplane is a check of position error in the static system. If, at any speed, the difference is greater than that allowed by FAA regulations, a new location is chosen for the static ports and when the final location is selected the static system is calibrated. A note is included in the POH of any corrections that must be applied to the airspeed for the various configurations of flaps and landing gear.

Required Inspections

14 CFR §91.411 requires that no person may operate an aircraft in controlled airspace under IFR unless within the preceding 24 calendar months the static pressure system has been tested and inspected and found to comply with Appendix E of 14 CFR Part 43. This is a four-part inspection that can be conducted by an AMT with the appropriate test equipment:

IFR. Instrument flight rules

1. The static system must be free from entrapped moisture and restrictions.

2. The static system of an unpressurized aircraft must be evacuated to a pressure of 1 in. Hg. (an indication of 1,000 feet on the altimeter), and there must not be leakage of more than 100 feet in 1 minute.

3. The static-port heater must function properly.

4. There must be no alterations or deformation of the airframe surface that could affect the relationship between the static pressure system and the true ambient static air pressure for any flight condition.

Altimeter

A pressure altimeter is an absolute pressure gage, similar to a barometer in which the dial is calibrated in feet.

Types of Altitude

The word "altitude" is meaningless unless it is qualified by the reference level from which it is measured. There are five types of altitude that are of importance to a pilot: indicated altitude, pressure altitude, density altitude, true altitude, and absolute altitude. *See* Figure 73.

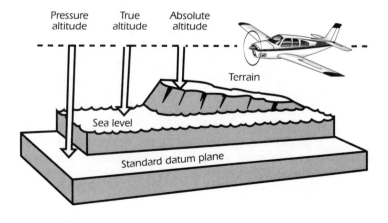

Figure 73. Types of altitude

Indicated Altitude

When flying below 18,000 feet, the height above the surface is important to the flight crew. Because the local barometric pressure is constantly changing, the pilot must have a reference pressure from which the altimeter can measure the altitude. This reference, called the altimeter setting, is the barometric pressure at a reporting station, corrected to the pressure it would have if the barometer were at the same location, but at sea level.

altimeter setting. Station barometric pressure corrected for the height of the station above mean sea level.

The standard sea-level barometric pressure is the pressure that will support a column of mercury 29.92 inches (760 millimeters) high, and is equal to 14.69 psi, or 1013.2 millibars. This is called a pressure of one atmosphere.

FSS. Flight service station

If the barometric pressure at the flight service station is 27.60 in. Hg, and the surveyed elevation of the FSS is 1,000 feet MSL (above mean sea level), the barometric pressure corrected to sea level would be 28.60. This is based on the standard pressure lapse rate of 1 in. Hg for each 1,000 feet. In this instance, the pressure at sea level is 1 in. Hg greater than that existing at the FSS. The altimeter setting, transmitted to all aircraft operating within the geographic area of the FSS, would therefore be 28.60 in. Hg.

MSL. The elevation above mean sea level.

When the barometric scale on the altimeter is adjusted to the altimeter setting, the pointers of the altimeter indicate the height of the aircraft above MSL. This is extremely important in maintaining vertical separation from other aircraft when flying below 18,000 feet and for terrain clearance, because the elevations on the aeronautical charts are measured in feet MSL.

14 CFR §91.121 requires that each person operating an aircraft shall maintain the cruising altitude of that aircraft by reference to an altimeter that is set, when operating below 18,000 feet MSL, to the current reported altimeter setting of a station along the route and within 100 nautical miles of the aircraft.

If there is no station within the area prescribed, the current reported altimeter setting of an appropriate available station or in the case of an aircraft not equipped with a radio, the elevation of the departure airport or an appropriate altimeter setting available before departure.

Pressure Altitude

When the barometric scale of an altimeter is set to the standard sea-level pressure, 29.92 in. Hg. or 1013.2 millibars, the altimeter shows pressure altitude, or the altitude measured from the standard reference pressure level. This is not an actual height above sea level or above the ground, but is a flight level, or a level of constant barometric pressure. Pressure altitude is used as a basis for determining aircraft and engine performance, and for ensuring vertical separation when flying at or above 18,000 feet. When a flight level is specified, it is a pressure altitude in units of hundreds of feet. For example, FL260 is a pressure altitude of 26,000 feet.

pressure altitude. Altitude above the standard reference plane of 29.92" Hg or 1013.2 mb.

When operating at or above 18,000 feet MSL, 14 CFR §91.121 requires that the flight level be maintained by reference to an altimeter that is set to 29.92 in. Hg.

Density Altitude

The performance of an aircraft and its engines is determined by the density of the air in which they operate. This density, which is affected by both the pressure and the temperature of the air, also affects the indication of the altimeter.

density altitude. Pressure altitude corrected for nonstandard temperature. Density altitude is used for computing the performance of an aircraft and its engines.

At the lower elevations in the International Standard Atmosphere (ISA), the temperature lapse rate, or the rate at which the temperature of the air decreases with altitude, is 2°C (3.6°F) per thousand feet until the stratosphere is reached at approximately 36,000 feet. Here the temperature stabilizes at -56.5°C (-69.7°F). Air density increases as the temperature decreases.

The pressure of the air decreases with altitude. In the lower levels it decreases at a rate of approximately 1 in. Hg. per 1,000 feet. The pressure continues to drop, but at a lesser rate, even after the temperature stabilizes.

Because aircraft and engine performance is affected by the density of the air, the pilot must know the density altitude, or the altitude in standard air at which the density is the same as that of the existing air.

Density altitude is found by using a flight computer or chart to correct pressure altitude for nonstandard air temperature. For example, if a takeoff is to be made from an airport with a pressure altitude of 6,000 feet on an afternoon when the temperature is 98°F (37°C), the density altitude, as shown on a flight computer, would be just a little less than 10,000 feet, and the aircraft and engine performance would be that which you should expect at 10,000 feet.

True Altitude

True altitude is the actual vertical distance of an aircraft above mean sea level, or its height MSL. Airport, terrain, and obstacle elevations are expressed in terms of their height MSL. True altitude is not shown on the altimeter, but may be calculated with a flight computer, taking into consideration the pressure altitude and the actual outside air temperature.

Absolute Altitude

absolute pressure. Pressure measured from zero pressure, or a vacuum.

The absolute altitude is the height of an aircraft above the surface of the terrain. Aircraft may be equipped with radar or radio altimeters that transmit a pulse of electrical energy directly downward. The time required for the pulse to reach the surface and bounce back to the aircraft is measured and converted inside the instrument to display the height in feet of the aircraft above the surface.

Pressure Altimeter

A pressure altimeter is an aneroid barometer that measures absolute ambient pressure. The dial is calibrated from 1 through 9 with four short lines between each number. The standard three-pointer altimeter, like the one in Figure 74, has a long pointer that makes one revolution of the dial for each 1,000-foot change in altitude. Each number represents 100 feet, and there are marks between the numbers for each 20 feet. The short pointer makes one revolution for 10,000 feet, with each number representing 1,000 feet. The third pointer is actually a portion of a disk which shows around the outside edge of the dial with a very thin arm holding a triangle. Each number read opposite this triangle is multiplied by 10,000 feet. As this third pointer moves, the disk portion progressively covers a barber-pole-striped segment of the dial. Below 10,000 feet, the entire striped segment is visible, but above this altitude, a mask begins to cover it, and above 15,000 feet, all of the stripes are covered.

Principle of Operation

The sensitive element in a pressure altimeter is a stack of evacuated, corrugated bronze aneroid capsules like those in Figure 74. The air pressure acting on these capsules tries to compress them against their natural springiness which tries to expand them. The result is that their thickness changes as the air pressure changes. Stacking several capsules increases the dimension change as the pressure varies over the usable range of the instrument, usually from -1,000 feet to 20,000 or 50,000 feet.

Another configuration of altimeter is the drum-type, like the one in Figure 75. Drum altimeters have only one pointer which makes one revolution for each 1,000 feet. Each number represents 100 feet and each mark, 20 feet. A drum is geared to the mechanism that drives the pointer and is marked in thousands of feet. To read this type altimeter, first look at the drum to get the thousands of feet and then at the pointer to get the feet and hundreds of feet.

Figure 75. Drum-type altimeter

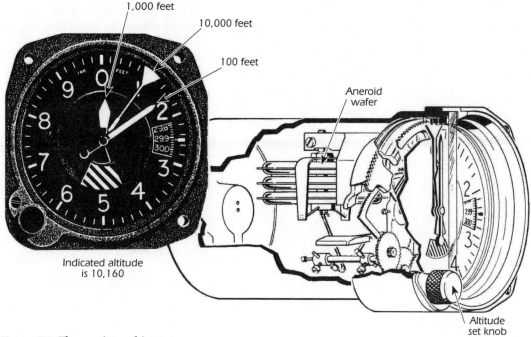

Figure 74. Three-pointer altimeter

Kollsman window. A barometric scale window of a sensitive altimeter used to adjust the altitude for the altimeter setting.

bezel. The rim around an instrument case that holds the glass cover.

Sensitive altimeters have an adjustable barometric scale that allows the pilot to set in the reference pressure from which the altitude is measured. This scale is visible in a small window in the dial, and is adjusted by a knob on the instrument bezel. The range of the scale is from 28.00 to 31.00 in. Hg. (948 to 1050 millibars) which includes the extremes in barometric change at sea level.

Rotating the knob changes both the barometric scale and the altimeter pointers in such a way that a change in the barometric scale of 1 in. Hg. changes the pointer indication by 1,000 feet. This is the standard pressure lapse rate below 5,000 feet. When the barometric scale is adjusted to 29.92 in. Hg, or 1013.2 millibars, the pointers indicate the pressure altitude. To display indicated altitude, adjust the barometric scale to the local altimeter setting. The instrument then indicates the height above the existing sea-level pressure.

Altimeter Errors

A pressure altimeter is designed to indicate standard changes from standard conditions, but most flying involves nonstandard conditions, and the pilot must be able to modify the indications to correct for these conditions. There are two types of errors: mechanical errors and inherent errors.

Mechanical Errors

An altimeter is a delicate instrument whose indications may become erroneous due to age, vibration, or mechanical damage. 14 CFR §91.411 requires that no airplane or helicopter may be operated in controlled airspace under IFR, unless within the preceding 24 calendar months the altimeter has been tested and found to comply with the provisions of Appendix E of 14 CFR Part 43.

This appendix requires that the altimeter be tested by an appropriately rated, FAA-approved repair station for the following errors and found to be within the tolerances allowed.

Scale error. The error that causes the instrument indication to be different from the master instrument indication.

Hysteresis. The error that causes the indication at the various test points to be different when the pressure is decreasing and when it is increasing.

After effect. The error that causes the instrument indication, after the series of tests is completed, to be different from the indication before the tests were started.

Friction. The error caused by friction within the instrument. It causes the indications to be different before and after the instrument is vibrated.

Case leak. This error is caused by the case leaking when the opening for the static line is sealed off.

Barometric scale error. This is an error in which the relationship between the barometric scale indication and the altitude shown by the pointers is out of limits.

A preflight check to determine the condition of an altimeter consists of setting the barometric scale to the altimeter setting transmitted by the local FSS. The altimeter pointers should indicate the surveyed elevation of the airport. If the indication differs more than 75 feet from the surveyed elevation, the instrument should be referred to an FAA-certificated instrument repair station for recalibration.

Inherent Errors

When an altimeter is operating properly and has passed all the tests required by 14 CFR §91.411, it will still show an erroneous indication when the ambient temperature or pressure differs from standard.

Nonstandard Temperature

Figure 76 on the next page shows the way nonstandard temperature affects an altimeter. When the airplane is flying in air that is warmer than standard, the air is less dense and the pressure levels are farther apart. When the airplane is flying at an indicated altitude of 5,000 feet, the pressure level for that altitude is higher than it would be in air at standard temperature, and the airplane will be higher than it would be if the air were cooler.

"When flying from hot to cold or from a high to a low, look out below." The aircraft is lower than the altimeter indicates.

If the air is colder than standard, it is denser, and the pressure levels are closer together. When the airplane is flying at an indicated altitude of 5,000 feet, its true altitude is lower than it would be if the air were warmer.

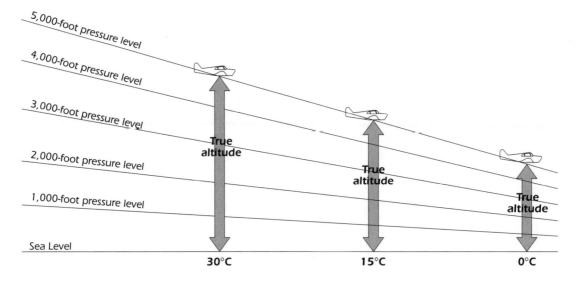

Figure 76. Effects of nonstandard temperature on an altimeter

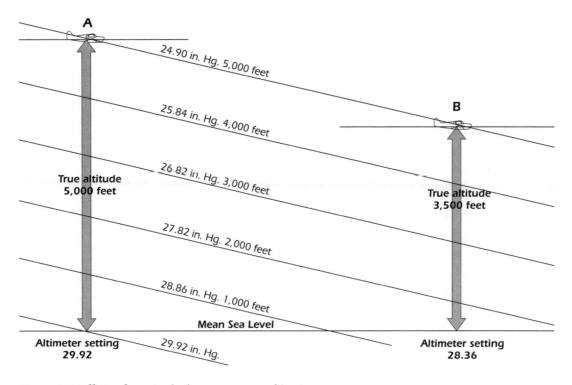

Figure 77. Effects of nonstandard pressure on an altimeter

Nonstandard Pressure

Any time the barometric pressure lapse rate differs from the standard of 1 in. Hg per thousand feet in the lower elevations, the indicated altitude will be different from the true altitude. For example, Figure 77 shows an airplane at point A flying in air in which conditions are standard—the altimeter setting is 29.92. When the altimeter indicates 5,000 feet, the true altitude is also 5,000 feet.

The airplane then flies to point B, where the pressure is lower than standard and the altimeter setting is 28.36, but the pilot does not change the altimeter to this new altimeter setting. When the altimeter shows an indicated altitude of 5,000 feet, the true altitude, or the height above mean sea level, is really only 3,500 feet. This gives rise to the memory aid "When flying from hot to cold, or from a high to a low, look out below." You are lower than your instruments indicate.

Encoding Altimeter

It is not enough for only the pilot to have an indication of the airplane's altitude; the air traffic controller on the ground also needs to know the altitude of the airplane. To provide this information, the airplane may be equipped with an encoding altimeter.

When the ATC transponder is set to Mode C, the encoding altimeter supplies the transponder with a series of pulses that identifies the flight level, in increments of 100 feet, at which the airplane is flying. This series of pulses is transmitted to the ground radar where they appear on the controller's scope as an alphanumeric display around the return for the airplane. The transponder allows the ground controller to identify the aircraft under his or her control and to know the pressure altitude at which each is flying.

A computer inside the encoding altimeter measures the pressure referenced from 29.92 in. Hg. and delivers this data to the transponder. When the pilot adjusts the barometric scale to the local altimeter setting, the data sent to the transponder is not affected. 14 CFR §91.217 requires that the altitude transmitted by the transponder be within 125 feet of the altitude indicated on the instrument used to maintain flight altitude.

Absolute Altimeter

The absolute altimeter, also called a radar or radio altimeter, measures the height of the aircraft above the terrain. It does this by transmitting a radio signal, either a frequency-

encoding altimeter. A sensitive altimeter that sends signals to the ATC transponder, showing the pressure altitude the aircraft is flying.

ATC. Air traffic control

transponder. The airborne portion of the ATC radar beacon system.

modulated continuous-wave or a pulse, to the ground, and accurately measuring the time used by the signal to travel from the aircraft to the ground and return. This transit time is modified with a time delay and is converted inside the indicator to distance in feet.

Most absolute altimeters have a provision for setting in a decision height (DH) or a minimum descent altitude (MDA) so that when the aircraft reaches that height above ground, a light will illuminate or an aural warning will sound.

Absolute altimeters are incorporated into ground proximity warning systems (GPWS) and into some flight directors. They are particularly useful for monitoring height for the last few feet of an instrument approach.

Airspeed Indicator

An airspeed indicator (ASI) is a differential pressure gage that measures the difference between the ambient static air pressure and the total, or ram, pressure caused by the motion of the aircraft through the air. These two pressures are taken from the pitot-static system.

The mechanism of the airspeed indicator in Figure 78 consists of a thin, corrugated phosphor-bronze capsule, or diaphragm, that receives its pressure from the pitot tube. The instrument case is sealed and is connected to the static ports. As the pitot pressure increases, or the static pressure decreases, the diaphragm expands, and this dimensional change is measured by a rocking shaft and a set of gears that drives a pointer across the instrument dial. Most modern airspeed indicators are calibrated in knots (nautical miles per hour) while some of the older instruments show statute miles per hour, and some instruments show both.

Just as there are several types of altitude, there are also different types of airspeed: indicated airspeed (IAS), calibrated airspeed (CAS), equivalent airspeed (EAS), and true airspeed (TAS).

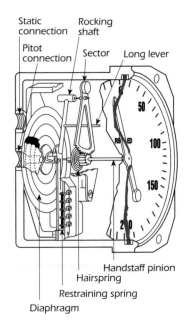

Figure 78. Mechanism of an airspeed indicator

Indicated Airspeed

IAS is the airspeed indication shown on the dial of the instrument. It is uncorrected for instrument or system errors and is based on the standard atmospheric conditions and lapse rate.

Calibrated Airspeed

CAS is the speed the aircraft is moving through the air, which is found by correcting IAS for instrument and position errors. The POH has a chart or graph to help correct IAS for these errors and provide the correct CAS for the various flap and landing gear configurations.

Equivalent Airspeed

EAS is CAS corrected for compression of the air inside the pitot tube. EAS is the same as CAS in standard atmosphere at sea level. As the airspeed and pressure altitude increase, the CAS becomes higher than it should be and a correction for compression must be subtracted from the CAS. EAS is important for high-speed aircraft but is generally ignored for smaller general aviation aircraft.

True Airspeed

TAS is the most important type of airspeed; it is CAS corrected for nonstandard pressure and temperature. TAS and CAS are the same in standard atmosphere at sea level. But under nonstandard conditions, TAS may be found by applying a correction for pressure altitude and temperature to the CAS using a flight computer.

Some aircraft are equipped with true airspeed indicators that have a temperature-compensated aneroid bellows inside the instrument case. This bellows modifies the movement of the rocking shaft inside the instrument case so the pointer shows the actual TAS.

There is a series of airspeed indicators for general aviation aircraft called True Speed indicators. These instruments have the conventional airspeed mechanism, with an added subdial visible through cutouts in the regular dial. A knob on the instrument bezel allows you to rotate the subdial to align an indication of the outside air temperature with the pressure altitude being flown. This alignment causes the instrument pointer to indicate the true airspeed on the subdial. *See* Figure 79.

Figure 79. A True Speed indicator allows the pilot to correct indicated airspeed for nonstandard temperature and pressure, for an indication of true airspeed.

Mach Number

As aircraft speed increases, the problems associated with compressibility and the formation of shock waves on the surface assume increasing importance. The indicated airspeed at which these conditions occur changes with temperature. Because of this, airspeed is not entirely adequate to warn the pilot of the impending problems. Mach number is more useful. Mach num-

shock wave. A pressure wave formed when an aircraft passes through the air at a speed greater than the speed of sound.

transonic flight. Flight in which an aircraft transitions from subsonic to supersonic flight. Some air flowing over the aircraft is slower than the speed of sound and other is supersonic.

A Machmeter shows the ratio of the speed of sound to the true airspeed the aircraft is flying.

ber is the ratio of the airplane's true airspeed to the speed of sound in the same atmospheric conditions. An airplane flying at the speed of sound is flying at Mach 1.0.

As an airplane approaches the speed of sound, the air flowing over certain areas of its surface speeds up until it reaches the speed of sound, when shock waves form causing a sudden increase in drag. If the airplane is not properly designed for transonic flight, the shock waves can cause serious control problems.

Most jet airliners and high-speed corporate airplanes are limited to the maximum Mach number they can safely fly. For example, when an airplane is flying at Mach .83 at 30,000 feet where the speed of sound under standard conditions is 589.5 knots, the airspeed is 489.1 knots. The speed of sound varies with the air temperature, and if the airplane were flying at Mach .83 at 10,000 feet where the air is much warmer, its airspeed would be 529.8 knots.

A machmeter uses an airspeed indicator mechanism whose pointer movement is modified by an altimeter aneroid. The dial is calibrated in Mach numbers, and the pointer shows at a glance the relationship between the speed of the aircraft and the speed of sound.

A maximum allowable airspeed indicator has two pointers. One is a normal airspeed pointer and the other pointer is actuated by a temperature-compensated altimeter aneroid. It is either colored red or is checkered, and it indicates the safe airspeed for the existing altitude to prevent the pilot from exceeding the allowable Mach number.

Airspeed Color Codes

The dial of an airspeed indicator is color-coded to alert you at a glance of the significance of the speed at which the aircraft is flying. These colors and their meaning are shown in Figure 80.

White arc	Flap operating range
Bottom	Flaps-down stall speed
Top	Maximum airspeed for flaps-down flight
Green arc	Normal operating range
Bottom	Flaps-up stall speed
Top	Maximum airspeed for rough air
Blue radial line	Airspeed for best single-engine rate of climb
Yellow arc	Structural warning area
Bottom	Maximum airspeed for rough air
Top	Never-exceed airspeed
Red radial line	Never-exceed airspeed

Figure 80. Color codes for an airspeed indicator

Vertical-Speed Indicators

The vertical-speed indicator (VSI) in Figure 81 on the next page is also called a vertical-velocity indicator (VVI) and was formerly known as a rate-of-climb indicator. It is a rate-of-pressure change instrument that gives the pilot an indication of any deviation from a constant pressure level.

Inside the instrument case is a capsule very much like the one in an airspeed indicator. Both the inside of this capsule and the inside of the instrument case are vented to the static system, but the case is vented through a calibrated orifice that causes the pressure inside the case to change more slowly than the pressure inside the capsule. As the aircraft ascends, the static pressure becomes lower and the pressure inside the case compresses the capsule, moving the pointer upward, showing a climb and indicating the number of feet per minute the aircraft is ascending. When the aircraft levels off, the pressure no longer changes, the pressure inside the case becomes the same as that inside the capsule, and the pointer returns to its horizontal, or zero, position. When the aircraft descends, the static pressure increases and the capsule expands, moving the pointer downward, indicating a descent.

The pointer indication in a VSI lags a few seconds behind the actual change in pressure, but it is more sensitive than an altimeter and is useful in alerting the pilot of an upward or downward trend, thereby helping maintain a constant altitude.

Some of the more sophisticated vertical-speed indicators, called instantaneous-vertical-speed indicators (IVSI), have two accelerometer-actuated air pumps that sense an upward or downward pitch of the aircraft and instantaneously create a pressure differential. By the time the pressure caused by the pitch acceleration dissipates, the altitude pressure change is effective.

calibrated orifice. A hole of specific diameter used to delay the pressure change in the case of a vertical speed indicator.

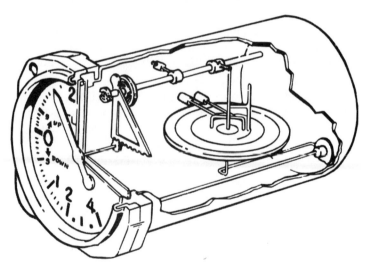

Figure 81. Vertical-speed indicator indicates the rate of climb or descent in thousands of feet per minute.

Chapter 29 **Gyroscopic Instruments**

A gyroscope, or gyro, is a small wheel with its weight concentrated around its periphery. When spun at a high speed, it becomes rigid and resists any attempt to tilt it or turn it in any direction other than around its spin axis.

Flight without reference to a visible horizon can be safely accomplished by using instruments based on the two fundamental characteristics of a gyro: rigidity in space and precession.

Attitude and heading instruments operate on the principle of rigidity. The gyro remains rigid in its case and the aircraft rotates about it. Rate indicators, such as turn indicators and turn coordinators, operate on precession. The gyro precesses, or rolls over, proportionate to the rate the aircraft rotates about one or more of its axes.

rigidity in space. The characteristic of a gyroscope that prevents its axis of rotation tilting as the Earth rotates.

precession. The characteristic of a gyroscope that causes an applied force to be felt, not at the point the force is applied, but at a point 90° in the direction of rotation from that point.

Attitude Indicator

The primary attitude instrument was originally called an artificial horizon, then later a gyro horizon, and now it is more properly called an attitude indicator, or AI. *See* Figure 82. Its operating mechanism is a small brass wheel with a vertical spin axis, spun at a high speed by either a stream of air impinging on buckets cut into its periphery or by an electric motor. The gyro is mounted in a double gimbal which allows the aircraft to pitch and roll about the gyro as it remains fixed in space.

A horizon disk is attached to the gimbals in such a way that it remains in the same plane as the gyro and the aircraft pitches and rolls about it. On early instruments a bar represented the horizon, but the more modern instruments have a disc with a line representing the horizon, and both pitch marks and bank-angle lines. The top half of the horizon disc is blue, representing the sky, and the bottom half is brown, representing the ground. A slotted bank index at the top of the instrument shows the angle of bank marked on the banking scale for 10°, 20°, 30°, and 60°.

A small symbolic airplane is mounted in the instrument case in such a way that it appears to be flying relative to the horizon. A knob at the bottom center of the instrument case raises or lowers the airplane to compensate for pitch trim changes as the airspeed changes. The dot in the center of the

double gimbal. A type of support, similar to a universal joint, that allows a gyroscope to remain in an upright condition as the aircraft rolls or pitches.

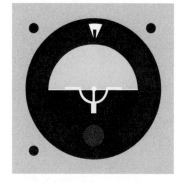

Figure 82. The dial of this attitude indicator has reference lines to show pitch and roll.

symbolic airplane's wings represent a pitch change of approximately 2°.

For an AI to function as it should, the gyro must remain vertically upright while the aircraft rolls and pitches around it. The bearings in these instruments have a minimum of friction, but even this small amount places a restraint on the gyro that produces a precessive force that causes the gyro to tilt. To minimize this tilting, an erection mechanism inside the instrument case applies a force to return the gyro to its vertical position any time the gyro tilts.

When the aircraft engine is first started and pneumatic or electric power is supplied to the instruments, the gyro is not erect, and a self-erecting mechanism inside the instrument actuated by the force of gravity applies a precessive force that causes the gyro to rise to its vertical position. This erection can take as long as five minutes, but is normally complete within two to three minutes.

Modern AIs are free from most errors, but depending upon the speed with which the erection system functions, there may be a slight nose-up indication during a rapid acceleration and a nose-down indication during a rapid deceleration. There is also a possibility of a small bank angle and pitch error after a 180° turn. These inherent errors are small and correct themselves within a minute or so after flight returns to straight and level.

Heading Indicator

A magnetic compass is a dependable instrument and is used as an emergency backup instrument in even the most exotic cockpits. But it has so many inherent errors that it has been supplemented with gyroscopic heading indicators since the very first "blind flights" in the late 1920s.

Gyro heading indicators, with the exception of slaved gyro indicators, are not north-seeking and must be set to the appropriate heading by referring to a magnetic compass. Rigidity causes them to maintain this heading indication without the oscillation and other errors inherent with a magnetic compass.

The gyro in a heading indicator like the one in Figure 83 is mounted in a double gimbal, with its spin axis horizontal, and it senses rotation about the vertical axis of the aircraft. The gyro drives a vertical dial that looks much like that of a vertical-card magnetic compass. The heading of the aircraft is shown against the nose of the symbolic airplane on the instru-

Figure 83. The heading indicator is not north-seeking, but must be set to agree with the magnetic compass.

ment glass which serves as the lubber line. A knob in the front of the instrument may be pushed in and turned to rotate the gyro and dial. The knob is spring loaded so it will disengage from the gimbals as soon as it is released. This instrument should be checked about every 15 minutes to see if it agrees with the magnetic compass and reset as needed.

Rate Instruments

Precession causes the gyro in a rate instrument to roll over an amount that is proportional to the rate the aircraft is rotating about the axis the instrument is measuring.

Turn and Slip Indicator

The first gyroscopic aircraft instrument was the turn indicator (which was the needle of the needle and ball) or turn and bank indicator, which is more accurately called a turn-and-slip indicator. The ball portion of this instrument is now called a slip-skid indicator.

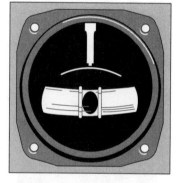

Figure 84. The turn and slip indicator

The clinometer in the instrument is a black glass ball sealed inside a curved glass tube that is partially filled with a liquid, much like compass fluid. This ball measures the relative strength of the force of gravity and the force of inertia caused by a turn. When the aircraft is flying straight and level, there is no inertia acting on the ball, so it remains in the center of the tube between two wires. In a turn made with too steep a bank angle, the force of gravity is greater than the inertia, and the ball rolls down to the inside of the turn. If the turn is made with too shallow a bank angle, the inertia is greater than gravity, and the ball rolls upward to the outside of the turn. The ball does not indicate the amount of bank, neither is it limited to an indication of slip.

The turn indicator uses a small gyroscopic wheel mounted in a single gimbal with its spin axis parallel to the lateral axis of the aircraft and the axis of the gimbal parallel with the longitudinal axis. *See* Figure 85 on the next page. When the aircraft yaws, or rotates about its vertical axis, it produces a force in the horizontal plane which, because of precession causes the gyro and its gimbal to rotate about the gimbal axis. It is restrained in this rotation by a calibration spring so that it rolls over exactly enough to cause the pointer to deflect one needle width when the airplane is making a standard rate turn—a turn of 3° per second, or 360° in two minutes.

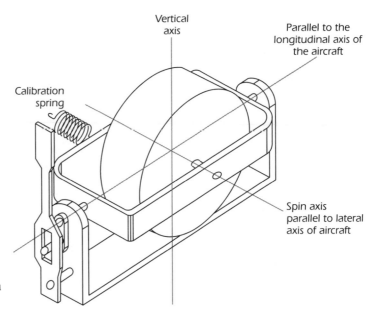

Figure 85. The rate gyro in a turn and slip indicator

Figure 86. A turn coordinator senses rotation about both the roll and yaw axes.

Turn Coordinator

The major limitation of the older turn and slip indicator is that it senses rotation only about the vertical axis of the aircraft. It tells nothing of the rotation about the longitudinal axis, which, in normal flight, occurs before the aircraft begins to turn.

A turn coordinator like the one in Figure 86 operates on precession, the same as the turn indicator, but its gimbal frame is angled upward about 30° from the longitudinal axis of the aircraft. This allows it to sense both roll and yaw. Rather than using a needle as an indicator, the gimbal moves a dial on which is the rear view of a symbolic airplane. The bezel of the instrument is marked to show wings-level flight and bank angles for a standard-rate turn.

The clinometer, similar to the one in a turn and slip indicator, is called a coordination ball, which shows the pilot the relationship between the bank angle and the rate of yaw. The turn is coordinated when the ball is in the center, between the marks. The aircraft is skidding when the ball rolls toward the outside of the turn and is slipping when it moves toward the center of the turn.

A turn coordinator does not sense pitch, and some instrument dials are marked "NO PITCH INFORMATION."

Gyroscopic Instrument Power Sources

Aircraft and instrument manufacturers have designed redundancy into the flight instruments so that any single failure will not deprive the pilot of his or her ability to safely conclude the flight.

Gyroscopic instruments are the most crucial for instrument flight, and to prevent a total loss, some are operated by electricity and others by air, or by a separate electrical power supply.

Electrical Systems

Many general aviation aircraft that use pneumatic attitude indicators use electric rate indicators and vice versa. Some instruments identify their power source on their dial, but it is extremely important to consult the POH to determine the power source of all instruments to know what action to take in the event of an instrument failure.

DC electrical instruments are available in 14- or 28-volt models, depending upon the electrical system in the aircraft. AC is used to operate some attitude gyros and automatic pilots; aircraft with only DC electrical systems have a solid-state DC to AC static inverter that changes 14 or 28 volts DC into three-phase 115-volt, 400-Hz AC.

Pneumatic Systems

Pneumatic gyros are driven by a jet of air impinging on buckets cut into the periphery of the wheel. On many aircraft this stream of air is obtained by evacuating the instrument case and allowing filtered air to flow into the case through a nozzle to spin the wheel.

Venturi Tube Systems

Airplanes that do not have an engine-driven vacuum pump to evacuate the instrument cases can use venturi tubes mounted on the outside of the aircraft like the system in Figure 87 on the next page. Air flowing through these tubes speeds up in the narrowest part, and according to Bernoulli's principle, the pressure drops. From this location a tube is connected to the instrument case. The two attitude instruments operate on approximately 4 in. Hg. suction and the turn and slip indicator needs only 2 in. Hg. so a pressure-reducing needle valve is used to decrease the suction. Filtered air flows into the instruments through filters built into the instrument cases.

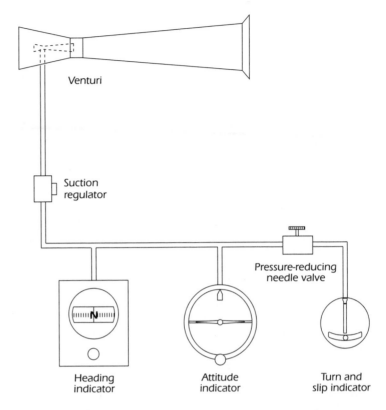

Figure 87. A venturi tube provides the low pressure inside the instrument case to drive the gyros.

This system has the obvious drawback in that ice can clog the venturi tube and stop the instruments when they are most needed.

Engine-Driven Vacuum Pump Systems

Wet-type air pumps have been used for many years to evacuate the instrument cases, and the discharge air is used to inflate rubber deicer boots on the wing and empennage leading edges. The vanes in these pumps are lubricated by a small amount of engine oil metered into the pump. This oil is then discharged with the air. To keep the oil from deteriorating the rubber boots, it must be removed with an oil separator like the one in Figure 88. Most modern systems use dry-type air pumps with carbon vanes which do not require any lubrication so there is no need for an oil separator.

The vacuum pump moves a greater volume of air than is needed for the instruments, so a suction relief valve is installed in the inlet side of the pump. This spring-loaded valve allows just enough air to enter the system to maintain the required low pressure inside the instruments as is shown on the suction gage in the instrument panel. Filtered air enters the instrument cases from a central air filter, the element of which is replaced on periodic maintenance inspections.

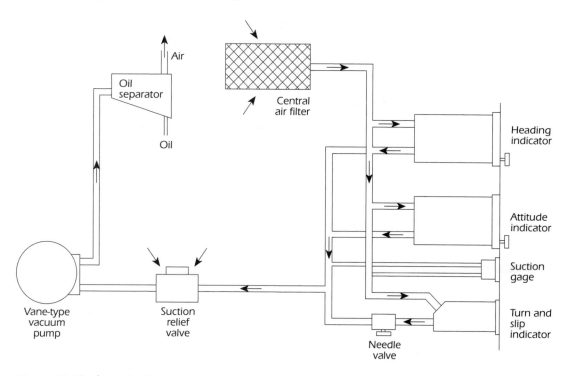

Figure 88. Single-engine instrument vacuum system using a wet-type vacuum pump.

Dry Air Pump Pressure System

As long as aircraft fly at relatively low altitudes, enough air is drawn into the instrument cases to spin the gyros at a sufficiently high speed. However, as flight altitudes increase the air becomes less dense and more air must be forced through the instruments.

Figure 89 is a diagram of the instrument pneumatic system of a twin-engine general aviation airplane. Two dry air pumps are used with filters in their inlet to filter out any contaminants that could damage the fragile carbon vanes in the pumps. Pressurized air flows through a pressure regulator, where excess pressure is bled off to maintain the pressure in the system at the desired level. The regulated air then flows through inline filters to remove any contamination picked up from the pump, and from there into a manifold check valve. If either engine should become inoperative, or if either pump should fail, the check valve will isolate the inoperative system and the instruments will be driven by air from the operating system. After the air passes through the instruments and drives the gyros, it is exhausted from the case. The gyro pressure gage measures the pressure drop across the instruments.

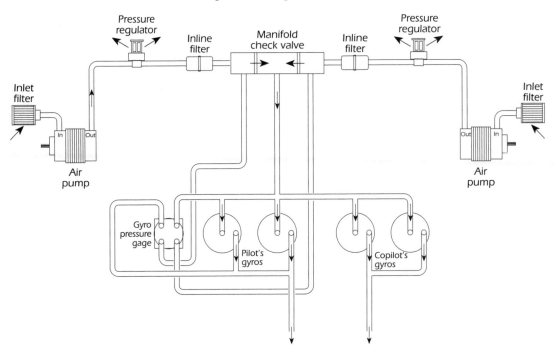

Figure 89. Twin-engine gyro instrument pressure system using a carbon-vane dry-type air pump.

Automatic Flight Control Systems

Automatic flight systems are important, not only because they free the human pilot of the need to continuously fly the aircraft, but they fly the aircraft with a greater degree of precision and are able to navigate the aircraft by coupling onto the various electronic navigation aids.

Modern automatic flight control systems use attitude gyros, rate gyros, altimeter aneroids, and signals from the various electronic navigation aids to program the desired flight profile that the aircraft can follow with extreme precision. These pickups and servos are the input and output devices for flight computers.

An automatic flight control system consists of four subsystems: command, error-sensing, correction, and follow-up.

The pilot programs the desired flight parameters into the command subsystem. The error-sensing subsystem detects when the aircraft is not in the condition called for by the command and a signal is sent to the correction subsystem which moves a control to achieve the appropriate changes. The follow-up subsystem senses the changes in the parameter and removes the error signal as soon as the correction is completed.

automatic pilot (autopilot).
An automatic flight device that controls an aircraft about one or more of its three axes.

Command Subsystem

The command subsystem is the portion of the automatic flight control system that allows the pilot to program the aircraft to do what is needed. A typical controller is seen in Figure 90.

- Depressing the **AP button** engages the autopilot and an indicator light shows that it is engaged.

- Depressing the **HDG button** ties the system to the HSI and the aircraft will fly the heading that is selected on it.

- Depressing the **NAV button** commands the aircraft to fly along the VOR radial or RNAV course selected on the appropriate navigation receiver.

- Depressing the **APPR button** causes the system to capture the chosen ILS localizer and follow it to the runway. If a back course approach is to be made depressing the **REV button** causes back-course information to be presented. When the **GS button** is depressed, the light will indicate that it is armed, and when the aircraft intercepts the glide slope, it will lock on it and descend along its electronic path.

- Depressing the **ALT button** commands the aircraft to fly to a selected barometric altitude and hold it.
- The **YAW button** engages the rudder trim which automatically trims the rudder for changes in airspeed.
- Rotating the **TURN knob** commands the aircraft to initiate a banked turn to the left or right as commanded.
- The **PITCH control** can be moved to the UP or DN position to command a change in pitch attitude. When it is released, it returns to its spring-loaded center position.
- The **ELEV indicator** shows whether or not the elevator is in its neutral position and gives an indication of any pitch trim changes that are needed.
- The **ROLL TRIM** allows the pilot to trim the aircraft about its roll axis when no other command is active.

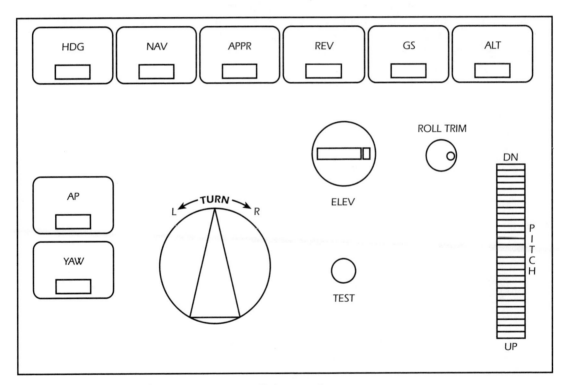

Figure 90. The controller for a typical automatic flight control system

Error-Sensing Subsystem

Error-sensing is normally done with gyros. The gyro in an attitude indicator senses any deviation from level flight, either in pitch or roll. The gyro in a heading indicator senses any deviation from the heading that is selected by the pilot. The amount of error signal is related to the amount the aircraft has deviated from its chosen attitude.

Because of the ease with which modern electronic systems can interface with automatic flight control systems, the output from the VOR and ILS as well as other navigation systems can be used to produce error signals. The pilot can tune to the appropriate localizer frequency on the VHF nav receiver and command the aircraft to follow an ILS approach. Any time it deviates from the glide slope or the localizer, an error signal is established that causes the aircraft to return to the desired flight path.

Altimeters can be included in the error-sensing subsystem. If the pilot has commanded the aircraft to fly to a given altitude, an error signal is established when the aircraft is not at that altitude, and the controls are adjusted to cause it to attain that altitude and level off. The altitude-hold command causes an error signal any time the aircraft departs from the commanded altitude.

Correction Subsystem

The error-sensing subsystem acts as the brains of the system to detect when a correction is needed. Its signal is sent to the controller and then to the servos which act as the muscles of the system.

Some automatic flight control systems have hydraulic servos, others use electric motors with drum-type capstans mounted on their shafts as servos. In some installations the primary control cable is wrapped around the capstan and in

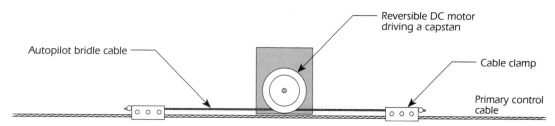

Figure 91. The capstan, driven by a reversible DC motor, pulls on the bridle cable which is clamped to the primary control cable.

other installations a smaller bridle cable is wrapped around the capstan and this cable is secured to the primary control cable with clamps shown in Figure 91.

Electric servos have the unusual requirement that they must start, stop, and reverse their direction rapidly when the controller directs, and they must have sufficient torque to move the controls. Some larger aircraft use three-phase AC motors to drive the capstan, and smaller aircraft use DC motors.

Follow-Up Subsystem

The follow-up subsystem stops the control movement when the surface has deflected the proper amount for the signal sent by the error sensor.

When a signal from the error-sensing system causes a control to deflect, the position pickup follows the movement of the surface and cancels out the signal from the error sensor when the surface attains the correct deflection.

For example, if the left wing drops, the gyro senses an error and sends a signal to the aileron servo that moves the left aileron down. When the aileron moves an amount proportional to the amount the wing has dropped, the follow-up system generates a signal equal in amplitude, but opposite in polarity, to the error signal and cancels it.

The left wing is still down and the aileron is deflected, and since the signals have canceled, the autopilot does not call for any more aileron deflection. As the aerodynamic forces bring the wing back to its level-flight attitude, an error signal opposite to the one that started the action is produced. This signal is gradually canceled, and by the time the wing comes level, the aileron is in the streamlined position and there is no overshooting or oscillation.

Flight Director Indicator

When installed, the flight director typically replaces the standard attitude indicator.

One of the advances in flight instrumentation is the flight director like the one shown in Figure 92. This instrument functions much like an attitude indicator with the addition of the "bow tie" shaped steering bars. The triangular delta symbol represents the airplane, and the steering bars are controlled by the autopilot command and error-sensing systems. Rather than the signals being sent to the appropriate servos to actually control the aircraft, the signals are sent to the steering bars which tell the pilot what to do. The flight director in Figure 92 is telling the pilot to pitch the nose up and turn to the right. The flight director shows the pilot the changes to make in pitch and roll in the same way the horizontal situation indicator (HSI) shows the pilot the proper changes to make in directional flight.

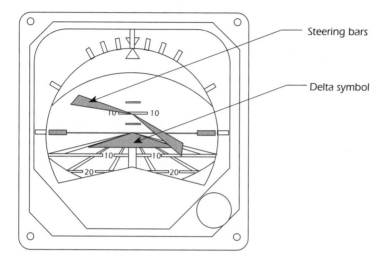

Steering bars

Delta symbol

Figure 92. Flight director

Horizontal Situation Indicator

The HSI in Figure 93 on the next page shows the pilot the relationship of the aircraft to the VOR radial or ADF bearing, the magnetic direction, the desired course and heading, and also the relationship of the aircraft to the glide slope.

When installed, the HSI typically replaces the standard heading indicator.

The pilot wants to approach the VOR station by flying inbound on the 120° radial. This gives a course of 300° to the station. This is set into the HSI with the course select knob. The airplane is flying a compass heading of 330° as shown opposite the lubber line, and is slightly to the left of the desired course as is shown by the lateral deviation bar which is to the right of the airplane symbol. If the pilot continues on this heading, the 330° radial will be intercepted, but the pilot has turned the heading select knob until the selected heading marker, or "bug," is over 315°. This commands the autopilot to change the heading of the airplane 15° to the left. In this case the pilot believes that the 15° difference between the heading and the course will correct for wind drift and allow the airplane to track inbound on the 120° radial.

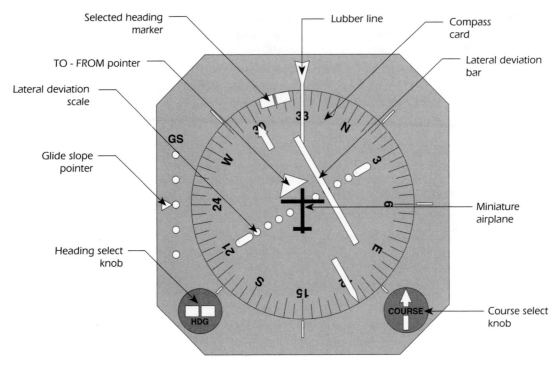

Figure 93. Horizontal Situation Indicator (HSI)

Chapter 30 Powerplant Instruments

It is important that the pilot know the condition of the engine and its systems at all times. It is for this reason that all aircraft have the familiar powerplant instruments. These instruments may be considered in three logical groups: those that measure pressure, temperature, and mechanical movement.

Pressure Measuring Instruments

Manifold Pressure Gage

The power produced by a piston engine is determined by two variables: the amount of pressure forcing the piston down on each power stroke and the number of power strokes each minute.

The pressure inside the cylinder is difficult to measure, but the absolute pressure of the air inside the induction system just ahead of the intake valve has a definite relationship to the pressure inside the cylinder.

When the engine is not running, the pointer indicates the existing barometric pressure which is the same as that read on the barometric scale of the altimeter when the altimeter pointers are adjusted to the existing airport elevation.

When the engine is started and is idling, the manifold pressure drops to around 15 inches of mercury. A naturally aspirated (nonsupercharged) engine can never develop a manifold pressure greater than that of the atmosphere, but supercharged engines can. *See* Figure 94.

Engine Oil Pressure Gage

One of the most important pressures in an aircraft engine is the gage pressure of the lubricating oil. This is the pressure of the oil as it circulates through passages in the engine and lubricates the bearings.

It is important that the oil pressure gage shows an indication of pressure within 30 seconds of the engine starting (some engines allow one minute in cold weather). If there is no indication of pressure within this time, shut the engine down and determine the cause.

The line between the pressure gage and the engine is filled with a lightweight oil such as kerosine. This lightweight oil

absolute pressure. Pressure referenced from zero pressure or a vacuum. Absolute pressure is normally measured in inches of mercury (in. Hg.).

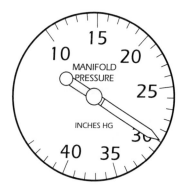

Figure 94. The manifold pressure gage for a turbocharged horizontally-opposed general aviation engine

gage pressure. Pressure referenced from the existing atmospheric pressure.

speeds up the indication of oil pressure in cold weather because it does not become as viscous as engine oil. The fitting
in the engine to which this line connects has a very small orifice that smooths out the pulsations in the oil pressure and
prevents a major loss of oil if the line to the instrument should
break.

Oil Temperature Measured by Pressure

The oil temperature of most small general aviation piston
engines is measured by a pressure gage.

A temperature-sensing bulb is installed in the oil screen
inside the engine just before the oil flows to the bearings. This
bulb is made of thin stainless steel and is connected to the oil
temperature gage with a small-diameter copper tube. The bulb,
tube, and instrument mechanism are partially filled with a
volatile liquid and are sealed as an integral unit. The pressure
of the vapor above the liquid is proportional to the temperature
sensed by the bulb, and this is read on the dial of the temperature gage in degrees Fahrenheit or Celsius.

Fuel Flow Measured by Pressure

The fuel flowmeter used with a fuel injected horizontally-
opposed piston engine is actually a pressure gage that measures the pressure drop across the injector nozzles.

The line to the flowmeter indicator attaches to the flow
divider and measures the gage pressure of the fuel delivered to
the nozzles. The nozzles for turbocharged engines have turbocharger discharge pressure, called upper deck pressure,
directed into shrouds around the nozzles. The pressure measured by the flowmeter is a differential pressure—the difference between the fuel pressure at the flow divider and the
upper deck air pressure.

One of the major problems with measuring fuel flow as a
function of the pressure drop is that a clogged injector nozzle
which decreases the amount of fuel delivered to the engine
causes an increased pressure drop and indicates an increased
flow.

differential pressure. A single
pressure which is the difference
between two opposing pressures.

Engine Pressure Ratio

The thrust produced by a jet engine is determined by the
change in momentum of the air passing through the engine
and thrust produced by an axial flow engine is measured by an
engine pressure ratio (EPR) indicator. This is the ratio of the

total pressure. The pressure a
moving mass of fluid would have if it
were stopped. Total pressure is the
sum of the static pressure and the
pressure caused by the ram effect.

total pressure at the compressor inlet and the total pressure at the last stage of the turbine.

Temperature Measuring Instruments

Engine Oil Temperature

Oil temperature is measured as the oil enters the engine. It can be measured with a pressure gage as described on Page 146, or it can be measured electrically.

An electrical oil temperature gage measures the resistance of the temperature probe. This probe is a coil of fine wire sealed inside a stainless steel tube that is mounted inside the oil screen. The resistance of the wire changes with the temperature of the oil surrounding it. The indicator is a special resistance-measuring instrument with a dial calibrated in degrees Fahrenheit or Celsius. The instrument is powered from the aircraft electrical system and when the power is off, the pointer moves off scale on the low temperature side.

Carburetor Air Temperature

A float carburetor is a highly effective refrigerator that lowers the temperature of the air passing through it. Even when the surrounding temperature is well above freezing, it is possible for the evaporation of the gasoline and the expansion of the air to lower the temperature enough to cause moisture in the air to condense out and freeze, blocking the air passage into the engine.

Hot air from around some portion of the exhaust system may be directed into the carburetor to prevent the formation of ice, but too much heat will cause the engine to detonate and too little will not prevent ice formation. The ideal place to measure this temperature would be in the throat of the venturi, but any restriction there would disrupt the flow of air. A usable compromise is to measure the air temperature as it enters the carburetor. This temperature is higher than that of the fuel-air mixture, but by a series of flight tests the aircraft manufacturer has determined the allowable range of carburetor inlet air temperatures that will prevent the formation of carburetor ice and yet not cause detonation.

A carburetor air temperature gage is the same type of electrical instrument as an oil temperature gage.

A carburetor air temperature gage measures the temperature of the air entering the carburetor. By adjusting the carburetor heat valve, the temperature of the air entering the carburetor may be kept warm enough to prevent ice and cool enough to prevent detonation.

Cylinder Head Temperature Indicator

A cylinder head temperature indicator shows the temperature of one cylinder head that has been chosen by the aircraft manufacturer as being the cylinder that is most likely to run the hottest in normal operation.

A CHT indicator is a self-powered electrical instrument that measures temperature by measuring the current that is generated in a thermocouple which is a special loop of wire made of two different metals. One junction (the hot junction) of the two wires is embedded in a spark plug gasket or in a spring-loaded bayonet that presses against the cylinder head. The other junction (the cold junction) is inside the indicator. The amount of current flowing in these wires is proportional to the temperature difference between the two junctions. The indicator is a sensitive milliammeter that measures this current and displays it on the dial in degrees Celsius or Fahrenheit. When the engine is cold the pointer in the CHT indicator shows the temperature inside the cockpit.

Exhaust Gas Temperature Indicator

The adjustment of the fuel-air mixture ratio produced by the carburetor or fuel injection system can be done precisely and uniformly by using an exhaust gas temperature (EGT) indicator. An EGT system uses a thermocouple similar to, but of different metals than that used with a CHT. The indicator is a milliammeter similar to a CHT and the hot junction is a probe that sticks into the exhaust stack near the cylinder head.

When the engine is set up for cruise flight with the desired RPM and manifold pressure, the mixture can be leaned for the most economical cruise. As the mixture control is moved toward lean, the temperature of the exhaust gases rises, as is shown on the EGT indicator. When the fuel-air mixture is the most efficient and is releasing the maximum amount of energy, the EGT peaks and further leaning causes it to drop. The peak is used as a reference and the engine manufacturer recommends that the mixture be leaned to peak EGT and then enriched until the EGT drops a specific number of degrees.

A single probe EGT is limited because uneven fuel-air mixture distribution causes different cylinders to have peak EGT at different times. It is not necessarily correct to assume that the cylinder at which the probe is mounted is the leanest cylinder. To overcome this limitation, modern EGT systems have probes at every cylinder and the temperature of all cylinders is displayed on the indicator in the form of a bar graph. It serves as

thermocouple. An electrical generating device consisting of wires of two dissimilar metals connected to form two junctions. An electrical current is generated in the wires that is proportional to the temperature difference between the two junctions.

a useful troubleshooting instrument because a glance at it shows which cylinder is operating the leanest.

The EGT system for a turbine engine is an averaging system in which there are a number of probes in the tail pipe of the engine connected in such a way that they measure the average temperature of the exhaust gases leaving the engine.

Mechanical Movement Measuring Instruments

Tachometer

All aircraft engines must have a means of displaying its rotational speed as this relates to the power the engine is developing.

Small single-engine airplanes use simple mechanical tachometers similar to the mechanical speedometer used on automobiles. The indicator is connected to the engine with a flexible cable inside a metal housing. The cable drives a magnet inside the instrument which in turn causes a pointer to move over the dial to show the speed of the engine in units of RPM times 100. Because of the length of cable required, most multiengine airplanes use electric tachometers.

The power produced by an engine with a fixed-pitch propeller is indicated by the tachometer, but on an engine equipped with a constant-speed propeller the indication of the manifold pressure gage must be correlated with the RPM to determine the power. The RPM of the engine is controlled by the propeller pitch control, and the pressure inside the cylinders which is indicated by the manifold pressure gage, is controlled by the throttle.

Torque Meter

An extremely important instrument in a turboprop airplane is a torque meter. This instrument measures the reaction between the propeller shaft and the turbine shaft. The indicator is calibrated in foot-pounds of torque and the horsepower the engine is developing may be found by the relationship between the RPM and torque.

torque. A force that produces, or tries to produce, rotation.

Chapter 31 **Instrument Marking**

Some powerplant instruments have colored marks to show the pilot at a glance whether or not a particular system or component is operating in a safe and desirable range. Figure 95 lists the colors and types of marks used, and the meaning of each. Figure 96 lists the range markings required for powerplant instruments.

Color and type of mark	Meaning
Green arc	Normal operating range
Yellow arc	Caution range
White arc	Special operations range
Red arc	Prohibited range
Red radial line	Do not exceed indication
Blue radial line	Special operating condition
Red triangle, dot or diamond	Maximum limit for high transients such as starting

Figure 95. The color, type and meaning of range marks used on powerplant instruments

Carburetor air temperature
Green arc...................................Normal operating range
Yellow arc ....Range where carburetor ice is most likely to form
Red radial line ....Maximum allowable inlet air temperature

Cylinder head temperature
Green arc...................................Normal operating range
Yellow arc ....Operation approved for limited time
Red radial line ....Never-exceed temperature

Manifold pressure gage
Green arc...................................Normal operating range
Yellow arc ....Precautionary range
Red radial line ....Maximum permissible manifold absolute pressure

Fuel pressure gage
Green arc...................................Normal operating range
Yellow arc ....Precautionary range
Red radial line ....Maximum and/or minimum permissible fuel pressure

Oil pressure gage
Green arc...................................Normal operating range
Yellow arc ....Precautionary range
Red radial line ....Maximum and/or minimum permissible oil pressure

Oil temperature gage
Green arc...................................Normal operating range
Yellow arc ....Precautionary range
Red radial line ....Maximum and/or minimum permissible oil temperature

Tachometer (Reciprocating engine)
Green arc...................................Normal operating range
Yellow arc ....Precautionary range
Red arc ....Restricted operating range
Red radial line ....Maximum permissible rotational speed

Tachometer (Turbine engine)
Green arc...................................Normal operating range
Yellow arc ....Precautionary range
Red radial line ....Maximum permissible rotational speed

Tachometer (Helicopter)
Engine tachometer
Green arc ....Normal operating range
Yellow arc................................Precautionary range
Red radial line ....Maximum permissible rotational speed
Rotor tachometer
Green arc ....Normal operating range
Red radial line ....Maximum and minimum rotor speed for power-off operational conditions

Torque indicator
Green arc...................................Normal operating range
Yellow arc ....Precautionary range
Red radial line ....Maximum permissible torque pressure

Exhaust gas temperature indicator (Turbine engine)
Green arc...................................Normal operating range
Yellow arc ....Precautionary range
Red radial line ....Maximum permissible gas temperature

Figure 96. Required range markings for powerplant instruments

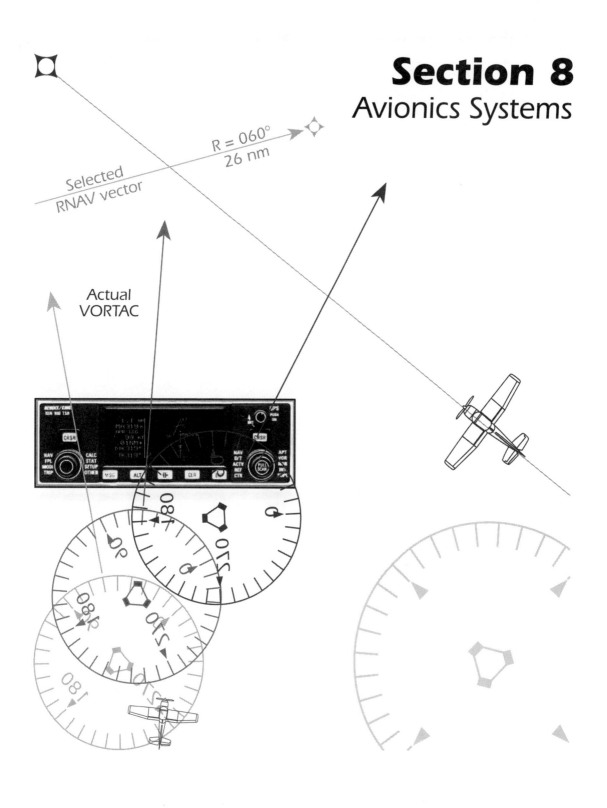

R = 060°
26 nm

Selected
RNAV vector

Actual
VORTAC

Chapter 32 **Communications**

Introduction

The utility of an aircraft has been multiplied many times over by efficient electronic communications and navigation systems. This section contains an overview of some of these important systems.

It is difficult to visualize flying without continual contact with the ground. But this type of communication has not always been available to general aviation. Before World War II all radio equipment used vacuum tubes, was heavy, and required high-voltage power supplies. The receivers and transmitters operated in the low- and medium-frequency ranges which required long wire antennas. In these ranges, static made communications difficult and in many instances impossible.

As a result of developments made during WWII, very-high frequency (VHF) communications became available. VHF receivers and transmitters were crystal controlled and were limited to very few channels. This equipment used short antennas and low power, but the range was limited. The range limitation has been overcome by the proliferation of ground stations and repeaters.

Basic Radio Theory

Radio is a method of transmitting intelligence from one location to another by means of electromagnetic radiation.

The block diagram in Figure 97 illustrates the principle of a basic aircraft amplitude-modulation (AM) radio transmitter. This transmitter contains an oscillator that produces alternating current with a very accurately controlled frequency in the VHF range between 30 and 300 megahertz (30,000,000 and 300,000,000 cycles per second). The intelligence to be trans-

Frequency Bands

Low frequency (LF)
30–300 kHz

Medium frequency (MF)
300 kHz–3 MHz

High frequency (HF)
3–30 MHz

Very high frequency (VHF)
30–300 MHz

Ultrahigh frequency (UHF)
300 MHz–3 GHz

Superhigh frequency (SHF)
3–30 GHz

amplitude modulation (AM).
A system of changing the voltage of a radio-frequency (RF) carrier to allow it to carry information.

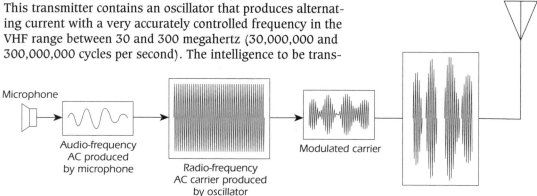

Figure 97. Block diagram of a simple radio transmitter

mitted is changed into an audio frequency (AF) electrical signal by the microphone, and it modulates, or changes, the carrier so that its voltage varies in exactly the same way as the voltage from the microphone. Notice that both sides of the modulated carrier are the same as the AF signal. The voltage of the modulated carrier is amplified so that it has enough power to radiate into space when it goes to the antenna.

The signal radiated into space from the transmitter antenna is picked up by the receiver antenna, as shown in Figure 98. The signal picked up by the antenna is a very weak imitation of the amplified modulated RF signal that was sent to the transmitter antenna. The weak signal is amplified, and then demodulated to remove the RF carrier but leave both halves of the AF signal. Because the resultant voltage of the AF is zero, one half must be removed. This is done in the detector, or rectifier. The resulting voltage has the same waveform as that produced by the microphone attached to the transmitter. This signal has too low a voltage to be useful, so it is amplified and then used to drive a speaker. The audio output of the speaker is the same as the input to the microphone.

detector. The circuit in a radio receiver that converts the received radio-frequency signal to an audio-frequency signal that can be heard.

The frequency of the oscillator is accurately maintained by sophisticated digital circuitry, and only this one frequency radiates from the transmitter antenna. The receiver antenna, on the other hand, picks up not only the signal from the desired transmitter, but signals from every other transmitter in the area as well as electromagnetic radiation (noise) from all sorts of electrical devices. Circuitry inside the receiver selects the frequency to which it is tuned and rejects all others.

VHF communications for air traffic control operate in the range between 118.0 and 136.975 MHz and most transceivers cover this range in 760 channels with 25 kHz spacing between each channel.

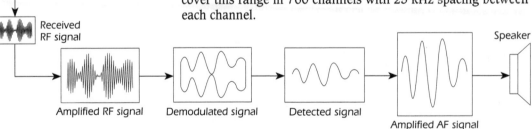

Figure 98. Block diagram of a simple radio receiver

When a frequency is selected on the transceiver it tunes both transmitter and receiver to the same frequency. Most transceivers show two frequencies, a USE frequency and a STANDBY frequency with a switch that shifts the circuitry between the two frequencies. To select a frequency, enter it into the STANDBY mode and then switch it into the USE mode. For example, the two selected frequencies allow you to talk with ground control on one frequency and then contact the tower on their frequency by touching a single switch.

Some avionics use frequency modulation (FM) equipment. This operates on the same principle as AM except the modulation changes the *frequency* of the carrier whereas AM changes its *voltage*.

Some communications (comm) transceivers are mounted inside the same housing as a navigation (nav) receiver and use the same power supply and certain other components. Panel-mounted avionics equipment is housed in rectangular cases that are a little over six inches wide so they can be stacked in the instrument panel. The trays in which the equipment mounts are permanently installed in the aircraft and connected to the antenna, to other pieces of avionics equipment, and to the aircraft electrical system. Inside the tray are quick-disconnect connectors so that as the equipment slides into the racks, plugs on the back of the housing mate with the connectors.

The communications equipment for corporate and airline aircraft is mounted in racks in the electronics bay and only the controls and indicators are accessible to the pilot.

The antenna for VHF communications equipment is a blade-type antenna mounted on the top and/or bottom center line of the fuselage and is connected to the transceiver by a special coaxial cable.

transceiver. A piece of radio communications equipment in which all of the circuits for the transmitter and receiver are contained in the same housing.

coaxial cable. A type of two-conductor electrical cable in which the center conductor is held rigidly in the center of a braided shield which serves as the outer conductor. Coaxial cable, commonly called coax, is used to connect radio receivers and transmitters to their antenna.

Figure 99. A typical panel-mounted communications transceiver

Chapter 33 **Navigation**

Early Electronic Navigation

Electronic navigation has undergone many changes. The earliest was the radio direction finder (RDF) in which a fixed-loop antenna was installed inside the airplane. The pilot tuned the radio receiver to the appropriate radio beacon or commercial broadcast station and turned the airplane until the volume of the signal was the weakest. By altering the airplane heading to maintain this null, the airplane flew toward or away from the station. Noting whether or not the signal volume increased or faded was the only way to know which direction. This system used amplitude modulation in the low and medium frequencies where static often made the signal unusable.

null. The position of an ADF loop antenna when the signal being received is cancelled in the two sides of the loop and the signal strength is weakest.

Automatic Direction Finder (ADF)

After the RDF the next advancement was the automatic direction finder (ADF) which operates in the low- or medium-frequency (90 to 1,800 kHz) range, and is still in use today. A small directional loop antenna is rotated by an electric motor. To use ADF, tune the receiver to the appropriate radio beacon or broadcast station and the motor turns the loop until the signal produces a null. The same signal is picked up on another antenna (a nondirectional sense antenna) and is mixed with the signal from the loop to cause the pointer on the instrument to always point toward the station. The relationship between the position of the loop and the nose of the aircraft is shown by the pointer on the ADF indicator that resembles a compass dial.

Figure 100. N, or North, represents the nose of the airplane and the head of the ADF needle points to the station being received.

Four-Course Low-Frequency Radio Range

The first airways across the U.S. were defined by a series of low-frequency four-course A–N ranges. The antennas for these range stations sent out four different signal patterns, two opposite patterns transmitted the Morse code letter A (• –) and the other two patterns transmitted the Morse code letter N (– •). In the narrow area where these signals overlapped the pilot heard a steady tone, and as the airplane drifted to one side the N became predominant and on the other side the A was more distinct. Directly over the antenna the signals cancelled each other and a cone of silence existed.

These range signals were in the low-frequency band and were subject to static rendering them useless when most needed. Also, some weather conditions caused the legs of the range to move about which gave erroneous indications. The airways laid out along these ranges have all been replaced by VOR airways.

Very-High-Frequency Omnidirectional Range (VOR)

World War II brought about the very-high-frequency omni-directional range (VOR) that overcame most of the problems of the four-course range. A VOR station can be approached from any direction, the signals are in the VHF spectrum which is less affected by static, and the indication is visual rather than aural.

To use VOR, select the station to which you wish to fly, then verify that it is the correct station by its Morse code identifier. Rotate the omnibearing selector (OBS) until the needle on the course deviation indicator (CDI) comes to the center and the TO-FROM indicator shows TO, then turn the airplane to the heading indicated on the CDI. If the needle drifts off center, alter the heading toward the needle and hold it until the needle returns to center. *See* Figure 101 on the next page.

One of the weaknesses of VOR is that it defines the line to or from the station, but it does not show the location of the aircraft along this line. This is solved by DME.

Distance Measuring Equipment (DME)

The military services use a special navigation system called TACAN (Tactical Air Navigation). TACAN provides both direction and distance from a ground station that is normally colocated with a VOR station; the combined facility is called a VORTAC station. Civilian aircraft are allowed to use the distance measuring feature from TACAN and the direction feature from the VOR. The DME frequency is paired with the VOR frequency so only the VOR frequency need be set into the NAV receiver.

DME is an active system in which the airplane sends out a special random coded series of pulses that is picked up by the VORTAC or VOR/DME station, delayed for a specific number of microseconds, and then retransmitted to the airplane. The airplane receiver recognizes the random code that was transmitted and the computer inside the receiver measures the time

VOR system

Receiver
Antenna
Omni bearing selector (OBS)
Course deviation indicator (CDI)
To-From indicator

TACAN:

For direction and distance—
military
For distance—civilian

VORTAC:

VOR, for direction—civilian

required for the signal to reach the ground station, the time delay, and the time required to return to the airplane. This time is converted into nautical miles to the station. Some DME receivers have the ability to compute the ground speed and estimated time en route to the selected waypoint.

DME has two slight problems. One is that the horizontal distance to the station is shorter than the slant line, or direct, distance the signal must travel. However, this error is small and is of little consequence to most general aviation aircraft that fly at relatively low altitudes. The other problem is that DME is an interactive system between the airplane and the

radial. A line of radio bearing radiating outward from a VOR navigation facility.

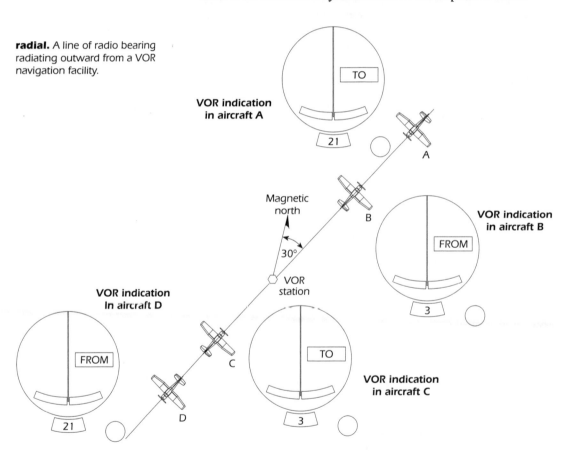

Figure 101. Airplane A is inbound on the 030° radial.
Airplane B is outbound on the 030° radial.
Airplane C is inbound on the 210° radial.
Airplane D is outbound on the 210° radial.

ground station, and the ground station can only accommodate 110 users at any one time. In practice, this limit is seldom reached.

Area Navigation (RNAV)

One of the main limitations of the VOR/DME is the number of stations available to the pilot. Area navigation, or RNAV, has solved this problem by allowing you to create a waypoint by virtually moving a VORTAC station to any location to which you want to fly. This is done by defining the location of the waypoint in terms of a radial from the chosen VORTAC and the DME distance along this radial. When this data is entered into the RNAV computer, the waypoint is created that allows you to fly directly to it in exactly the same way you would fly to a VORTAC. The course to the waypoint is given on the indicator along with the distance to the waypoint, the ground speed and the time to the waypoint. If the aircraft is so equipped, the indicator will also display the estimated time of arrival at the waypoint, the amount of fuel that will be used, and the amount of fuel remaining.

waypoint. A pseudo location to which a VORTAC station has been electronically moved by an RNAV system.

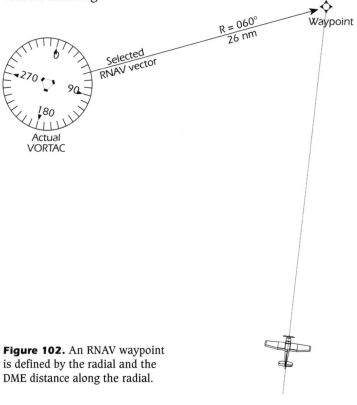

Figure 102. An RNAV waypoint is defined by the radial and the DME distance along the radial.

Instrument Landing System (ILS)

ADF, VOR, and RNAV allow you to fly from point A to point B, but the landing is the all important part of any flight and none of these systems direct you all the way to a safe landing. The ILS guides you to a safe touchdown at your destination.

An ILS consists of a localizer, glide slope, marker beacons, and approach lights.

**Instrument Landing
System (ILS)**
Localizer
Glide slope
Marker beacons
Approach lights

Localizer

The localizer is a VHF facility that provides course guidance down the extended center line of the instrument runway from approximately 18 miles out to the point of touchdown. Tune the NAV receiver to the localizer frequency which is listed on the approach plate. This will be between 108.10 and 111.95 MHz, and all localizer frequencies have odd numbers as the first digit after the decimal point. Identify the localizer signal by the Morse code for the normal three-letter identifier preceded by the letter I (• •). For example the VOR for Gregg County Airport, Texas is GGG (– – • – – • – – •) and the localizer for the Gregg County ILS is IGGG (• • – – • – – • – – •)

The same type of indicator used for VOR is used for the localizer, but it has different circuitry and works in a different way.

The localizer antenna transmits two different signals that overlap forming a narrow beam oriented along the centerline of the runway. The vertical needle indicates the signal that is predominant by moving to the side of the indicator dial that shows the direction you should change heading to get back on the localizer beam. For example, if the airplane drifts to the left of the localizer beam, the needle will deflect to the right and you should alter heading slightly to the right to bring the needle back to center. The needle is insensitive to the heading of the airplane; it indicates only the side of the localizer beam on which you are located.

There is a circle in the center of the dial called the doughnut with a series of four dots on either side. When using this instrument in the VOR mode, each dot indicates a deviation from the course of two degrees, but when operating in the localizer mode, they indicate only approximately one-half degree (0.5°).

Any time the localizer signal becomes unusable, a red flag will appear in the LOC window.

Glide Slope

The glide slope is the portion of an ILS that projects a vertical beam directing you to the runway surface some 1,000 feet from the approach end of the runway. The glide slope operates in the UHF frequency band and is paired with the localizer so when the NAV receiver is tuned to a particular localizer frequency, the appropriate glide slope is automatically tuned.

The glide slope transmits a beam approximately three degrees upward from its antenna and the signal from it activates the horizontal needle on the ILS indicator (Figure 103). When the airplane is above the glide slope, the needle will move down and the rate of descent must increase; when the needle moves up above the doughnut the airplane is below the glide slope and the rate of descent must decrease.

When a red flag shows in the GS window, the signal from the glide slope transmitter is unusable.

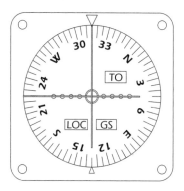

Figure 103. The ILS indicator is the same one used for VOR.

Marker Beacons

The localizer shows the direction along the center line of the instrument runway but does not give any indication of the distance along the localizer course. A complete ILS includes three lights: one blue, one amber, and one white.

The outer marker (OM) is a 75 MHz signal transmitted from a highly directional antenna located between four and seven miles from the instrument runway threshold. The signal is directed straight up, and when the airplane is directly over the OM a series of low pitch (400 hertz) dashes (– – – –) is heard through the radio and the blue light flashes the same pattern of dashes.

The middle marker (MM) is located approximately 3,500 feet from the approach end of the runway and it identifies the missed approach point. It is also a 75 MHz signal and is transmitted vertically. When directly above the antenna, a series of medium pitch (1,300 hertz) dots and dashes, dits and dahs (• – • – • –) is heard and the amber light flashes in the same pattern.

The white light is activated by certain other marks along an instrument approach or an airway. It is also a 75 MHz signal and is modulated with a series of high pitch (3,000 hertz) dots (• • • •) and the white light flashes in the same pattern when the airplane is directly above the transmitter antenna.

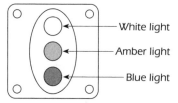

Figure 104. The marker beacon lights are used to indicate your position along the localizer beam.

LORAN

Long range navigation, or LORAN-C was originally developed for the U.S. Coast Guard (USCG) to provide radionavigation service for U.S. coastal waters. It was later expanded in cooperation with the FAA to include complete coverage of the continental U.S. as well as most of Alaska. It provides navigation, location, and timing services for both civil and military aircraft and is approved as an en route supplemental air navigation system for both IFR and VFR operations.

LORAN provides information on position, velocity, time, and/or data and operates in the low-frequency band at 100 kHz.

The USCG operates 27 stations, comprising eight chains, in the U.S. National Airspace System (NAS). A chain is a linked group of transmitters, one master station, and between two and five secondaries.

A LORAN receiver gets its signal from a master station and at least three secondaries that are typically located hundreds of miles apart. The master station in each chain transmits a series of grouped pulses. The time interval between these groups, measured in microseconds, is called the "group repetition interval" (GRI) and is the identifier for the particular chain. For example, transmitters in the northwest U.S. chain operate with a GRI of 99,400 microseconds which is shortened to 9940 for convenience.

If the time difference, measured in microseconds, between the reception of the signal from the master and that from one of its paired secondaries were plotted, it would form a hyperbolic line of position as shown in Figure 105. The intersection of the lines of position from the master and two secondaries defines the location of the aircraft. The receiver converts this intersection information into latitude and longitude.

When the present location and the desired destination are both entered, the receiver will display the distance and bearing to the destination, the ground speed, and the estimated time en route to the destination. A course deviation indicator will show the deviation from the course between the two locations. *See* Figure 106. Certain LORAN-C receivers are approved by the FAA for IFR enroute navigation and for some nonprecision approaches.

An updatable database in the LORAN receiver includes the locations of airports, VORs, NDBs, and intersections. The airport information includes such data as its name, city, identifier, radio frequencies, latitude and longitude coordinates, eleva-

nonprecision approach.
An instrument approach to an airport that does not incorporate the use of a glide slope.

tion, difference between local and UTC time, its relationship to Class B, C, or D airspace type of instrument approaches, and information on runways which includes lighting, length, and type of surface. There are provisions for entering the location of user-selected waypoints in the database by either latitude and longitude or radial and distance from an existing waypoint.

UTC time. Universal Time Coordinated—Universal time corrected for seasonal variations in the Earth's rotation. It is the same as Greenwich Mean Time (GMT) which is the time at the Royal Observatory in Greenwich, England. It is also known as Zulu time.

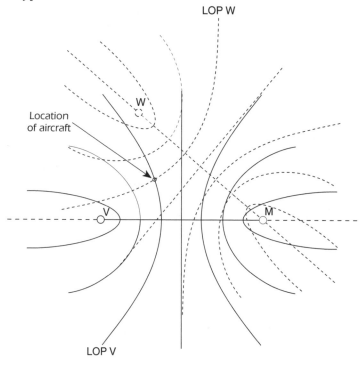

Figure 105. A LORAN fix is determined by the intersection of two lines of position from the master and one secondary that have the same time difference.

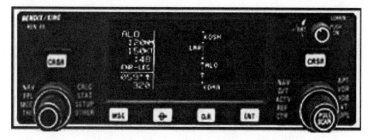

Figure 106. A modern panel-mounted Loran receiver

global positioning system (GPS). Navigation system that uses satellite rather than ground-based transmitters for location information.

Global Positioning System (GPS)

GPS is a navigation system developed by the Department of Defense (DOD). Because of its versatility and high degree of accuracy, GPS will eventually replace ADF, VOR, DME, and ILS.

The space segment of GPS consists of 24 operational satellites in six circular orbits 10,900 nautical miles above the Earth. There are actually 27 satellites in orbit to ensure that at least 24 will be operational at all times. The satellites are spaced in orbit in such a way that at any time a minimum of 4 satellites are in view to users anywhere in the world. These satellites are tracked by the DOD and their exact positions are relayed back up to them. This information is included as a portion of the position and time data that is continuously broadcast by the satellite in a series of coded signals. The GPS receiver measures the time between transmission of the signal and its reception. By knowing the speed of the signal (186,000 miles per second), the time it takes to reach the receiver, and the location of the satellite, the computer inside the receiver determines the exact distance to the satellite. The receiver takes this measurement from three satellites, computes the location of the receiver and displays it on a screen in terms of latitude and longitude in degrees, minutes and hundredths of a minute, and the altitude in feet MSL.

A database card which is available on a regularly updated basis is inserted into the receiver and provides at least this information:

Airports. Identifier, city and state, facility name, latitude and longitude, elevation, fuel service, and controlled approaches.

VORs. Identifier, city and state, facility name, latitude and longitude, frequency, colocated DME or TACAN, magnetic variation and weather broadcast information.

NDBs. Identifier, city and state, facility name, latitude and longitude, frequency, and weather broadcast information.

Intersections. Identifier, latitude and longitude, and nearest VOR.

Communications frequencies. Approach, arrival, control area, departure, ATIS clearance delivery, tower, ground, UNICOM, and pretaxi.

Runways. Designation, length, surface, lighting, ILS localizer frequency and identifier, and pilot-controlled lighting frequency and instructions.

FSS. Identifier, reference VOR and frequency.

Airspace. Class A, B, and C; MOAs, and restricted and prohibited airspace.

Provisions are made to create your own waypoint by entering its latitude and longitude, or by depressing the LOAD PRESENT POSITION button.

To navigate from one location to another, enter your present location and the destination location. The display will show the magnetic bearing to the destination and the distance in nautical miles, and the altitude in feet MSL. The computer in the receiver computes the ground speed in knots and displays it and the estimated time en route in hours and minutes.

Many GPS receiver displays incorporate a CDI that shows the track error in degrees right or left of the desired track. Others have a moving map display that shows the location of the airplane relative to the desired track. In the enroute mode it shows various types of airspace, and in the approach mode it shows a diagram of the airport.

Proximity alarms that warn of the approach of a waypoint or the vicinity of restricted or prohibited airspace, or the minimum safe altitude may be set by the pilot.

One extremely useful function is the emergency facility search capability. When the emergency search feature is selected, the moving map display shows the bearing and distance to the nearest suitable airport.

GPS is the easiest to use and most accurate navigation system now available, and both the FAA and DOD are working to make it the universally used type of electronic navigation for both enroute and approach flight.

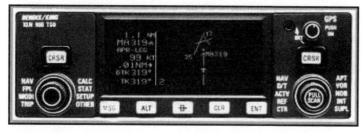

Figure 107. A GPS receiver with a cathode ray tube type moving map display

Emergency frequencies:
VHF—121.5 MHz
UHF—243.0 MHz

Emergency Locator Transmitter (ELT)

General aviation airplanes carry one piece of electronic equipment that we hope we never need, but when needed, are thankful that it is installed and working. This is the emergency locator transmitter, or ELT.

The ELT is a self-contained, battery-powered transmitter mounted in the tail of the aircraft in a location that normally survives a crash. This little transmitter is actuated automatically any time it receives a jolt along its fore and aft axis. It then transmits a series of downsweeping tones on 121.5, 243.0 and 406 MHz.

The first two frequencies are transmitted by an analog device and the 406 MHz signal is transmitted by a digital transmitter. The signal from the digital transmitter is stronger than that of the analog, and it transmits the owner's contact information and aircraft data along with the signal.

Analog 121.5/243.0 MHz ELTs should only be tested during the first 5 minutes after any hour. If operational tests must be made outside of this period, they should be coordinated with the nearest FAA Control Tower or FSS. Tests should be no longer than three audible sweeps. If the antenna is removable, a dummy load should be substituted during test procedures.

Digital 406 MHz ELTs should only be tested in accordance with the unit's manufacturer instructions. Airborne tests are not authorized. If an ELT has been activated, maintenance might be required before the unit is returned to the "ARMED" position. You should contact the nearest air traffic facility and notify it of the inadvertent activation.

A wise part of a preflight and a pre-shutdown check is to tune the COMM receiver to 121.5 MHz and listen for the ELT signal. Naturally, there should be none.

Because the ELT is battery powered, the batteries should be fresh or fully charged. The required replacement date must be marked on the outside of the transmitter case, and this should be checked on each annual inspection. If the expiration date has been reached, an AMT must replace them.

Section 9
Aircraft Environmental Control Systems

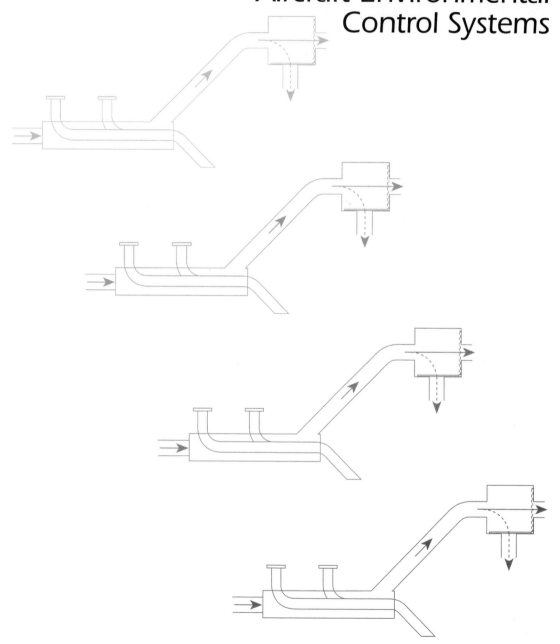

Chapter 34 Heating Systems

Introduction

Modern airplanes fly at altitudes that place the occupants in a hostile environment. The air is so thin that there is not enough oxygen to sustain life, and the temperature is so low that the cabin must be heated. When the aircraft is on the ground in the summer the cabin temperature becomes far too high for comfort and a cooling system is needed. This section covers the heating and cooling systems, the supplemental oxygen systems, and the ultimate environmental system, the pressurized cabin.

Cabin Heat

The cabins of small general aviation airplanes are heated by directing air around some portion of the engine exhaust system and then bringing it into the cabin through a cabin heat valve. When the cabin heat valve is off, the heated air is dumped overboard. *See* Figure 108.

This type of heater system is simple and fairly effective, but on airplanes using this type of heater, the exhaust system must be inspected with special care as a slight crack can allow deadly carbon monoxide (CO) to enter the cabin.

Carbon monoxide is a colorless, odorless gas that is a normal by-product of incomplete combustion of almost all hydrocarbon fuels and is present in all smoke. It is lethal even in small concentrations, so its presence must be detected early.

CO detectors are used in the cabin and cockpit areas. The most widely used CO detectors are small cards with a transparent pocket containing silica gel crystals treated with a chemical that causes them to change color when exposed to CO. The

Carbon monoxide (CO) is odorless, colorless, and **deadly**. It is present in engine exhaust gas **so all exhaust system components must be carefully inspected for leaks**.

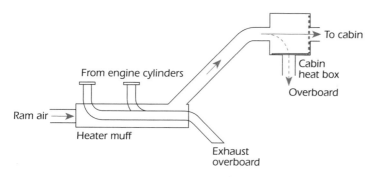

Figure 108. A shroud around part of the exhaust system serves as a source of heat for smaller aircraft cabins.

crystals are normally yellow or tan, but darken when exposed to CO. The more drastic the change, the higher the content of CO in the air. They turn black when exposed to a level of CO that could cause illness. These small detectors have an adhesive backing that allows them to be attached to the instrument panel, in easy view of the flight crew to warn of the presence of CO. They must be periodically replaced with fresh indicators.

Larger aircraft may be equipped with a combustion heater that uses gasoline from the aircraft fuel tanks and burns it in a special sealed combustion chamber. Combustion air flows through the heater and is discharged overboard. Ventilating air flows over and around the combustion chamber and absorbs heat which is taken into the cabin. Combustion heaters are efficient and safe.

Turbine-powered aircraft use hot compressor bleed air from the engine to heat the cabin.

Chapter 35   **Cooling Systems**

Heaters are necessary to make an aircraft cabin habitable while flying, but when the aircraft is on the ground in the summertime it becomes unbearably hot. Therefore the air conditioning systems that have become so ubiquitous in automobiles have been adapted for use in aircraft.

Refrigerant

These are vapor cycle cooling systems that use a freon refrigerant known as R-12, or the more environmentally friendly R-134a. This refrigerant is liquid when it is held under pressure, but when the pressure is released, it evaporates (changes from a liquid to a gas) and in doing so absorbs a great deal of heat from the air, cooling it.

The refrigerant is sealed inside the closed system as shown in Figure 109 on the next page. When the air conditioning control is turned to COLD, the clutch on the compressor allows the engine to drive it, compressing the refrigerant and raising both its pressure and temperature. The hot gas flows through a condenser coil which is installed in a location where air from outside the aircraft can blow across it and cool it by absorbing some of its heat.

When the refrigerant is cooled, it condenses and becomes a liquid. This liquid flows into a receiver-dryer which contains a filter and some crystals that absorb any moisture that might possibly be in the refrigerant. From the receiver-dryer the hot liquid refrigerant flows into a thermostatic expansion valve that meters and sprays the refrigerant in tiny droplets into the evaporator coils inside the airplane cabin. The refrigerant evaporates, or changes into a gas, and as it does, it loses much of its heat energy and becomes cold.

A fan blows cabin air over the evaporator coils where it is cooled and distributed throughout the cabin. The cooled refrigerant vapor then goes to the compressor where energy is added to raise its pressure and temperature and it cycles through the system again.

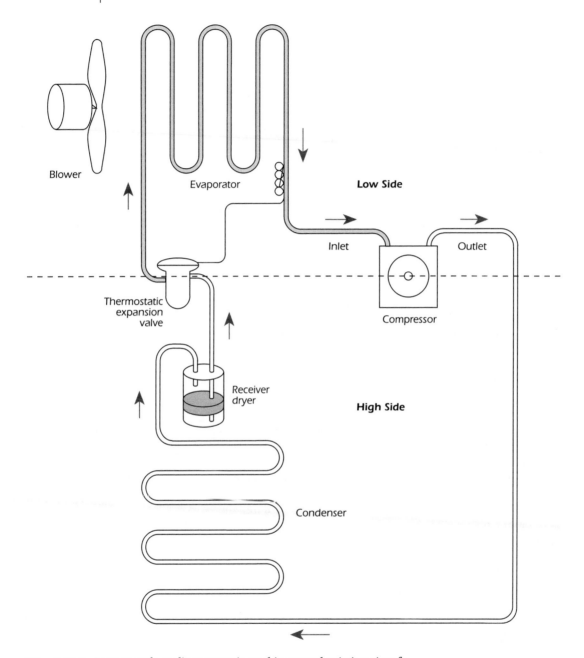

Figure 109. A vapor-cycle cooling system is used in general aviation aircraft.

Chapter 36 **Oxygen Systems**

Physical Effects

The human body is much like an aircraft engine. It takes in fuel (food, a hydrocarbon) and combines it with oxygen from the air so it will release its energy allowing us to function. After the oxygen has done its work, it combines with the carbon and is expelled in the form of carbon dioxide (CO_2). Figure 110 shows the effect of being deprived of oxygen.

Use Supplemental Oxygen

The simplest way to function effectively at altitude is to carry supplemental oxygen and breathe it.

When oxygen is needed only occasionally, gaseous oxygen may be carried in small portable self-contained high-pressure metal bottles fitted with a regulator and masks. Aircraft that routinely fly at high altitudes have built-in oxygen systems with regulators and outlets into which the masks may be plugged.

Most oxygen systems for general aviation use are of the continuous-flow type in which oxygen flows into a plastic bag attached to the mask as long as the regulator is turned on. When you inhale, you get oxygen-rich air from the bag, and when you exhale, the used air fills the bag. The first air out of your lungs still contains usable oxygen, but the air near the end of the exhale contains less oxygen and it is forced overboard by the flow of fresh oxygen entering the bag.

The flight crew on corporate jets and airliners are fed oxygen through demand regulators that meter oxygen to the mask when the wearer inhales, but cuts it off during exhale. The regulator dilutes the oxygen with cabin air to maintain the proper mix of oxygen and air as the air density changes with altitude.

At very high altitudes where the air pressure is too low to force oxygen and air into the lungs, the regulator forces the oxygen into the mask under pressure. Therefore a different breathing technique is required, one that allows the air to enter the lungs without conscious effort but the exhale must be against this pressure.

Altitude (feet)	Effect
5,000	Deterioration of vision
10,000	Judgment and abilities impaired
14,000	Blurred thinking
16,000	Disorientation and belligerence
18,000	Possible unconciousness
Above 18,000	Unconciousness and possible death

Figure 110. Effects of lack of oxygen on the human body

For optimum protection, pilots are encouraged to use supplemental oxygen above 10,000 feet during the day, and above 5,000 feet at night. 14 CFR §91.211 requires that at the minimum, flight crew be provided with and use supplemental oxygen after 30 minutes of exposure to cabin pressure altitudes between 12,500 and 14,000 feet and immediately on exposure to cabin pressure altitudes above 14,000 feet. Every occupant of the aircraft must be provided with supplemental oxygen at cabin pressure altitudes above 15,000 feet.

Chapter 37 **Pressurization Systems**

Cabin Environment

The ultimate in environmental control systems is the pressurization system that controls the environment to make the air pressure, temperature, and air movement in the aircraft cabin comfortable for the occupants.

The air we breathe is a mixture of gases that contains approximately 21% oxygen and 78% nitrogen with traces of several other gases. This percentage remains constant as the pressure and temperature change, but as the altitude increases, the pressure drops too low to force enough air into the lungs to supply the needed oxygen so supplemental oxygen must be used. An alternative to using supplemental oxygen is pressurization in which the pressure inside the cabin is increased enough to allow sufficient air, and thus oxygen, into the lungs to sustain life and physical action.

Pressure Differential

The cabin of a pressurized airplane is made strong enough to withstand the pressure differential between the low outside pressure at altitude and an inside pressure that is high enough to support life. The cabin is sealed and compressor bleed air from the turbine engine or, on piston engine airplanes, air from the engine turbocharger is introduced into the cabin.

The pressurization controller can be set to maintain a specific cabin altitude up to the differential pressure for which the cabin is approved and above this the controller will maintain this differential. The cabin pressure is controlled by an outflow valve that opens to allow air to escape from the cabin or closes to allow the pressure to build up.

Heat for a pressurized cabin of a turbine-powered aircraft comes from the hot compressor bleed air, and an air-cycle cooling system can be used that cools the bleed air by allowing it to expand through an expansion turbine to drop its temperature.

Things to Watch For

The environmental systems determine your comfort and efficiency while operating an airplane, so there are several things you should watch for on a preflight inspection.

If the aircraft gets its cabin heat from the engine exhaust system, check as much of the heater shrouds around the muffler as you can see. If there are any apparent cracks, looseness or any indication of leaks, call this to the attention of your AMT.

Be sure there is a carbon monoxide indicator in plain sight of the pilot. If it shows any indication of CO, be sure to find the source. Remember that CO is odorless, but it is also deadly.

The air cooling system should put cool air into the cabin. If it does not:

- Be sure the A/C circuit breaker is in so the engine can drive the compressor.

- Check to be sure that the evaporator coils (the place where the cool air comes out) are not clogged with lint, or are otherwise obstructed.

- Check the condenser, the radiator-like component where outside air takes the heat out of the refrigerant. It must be clear so air is free to blow across it.

If all of this looks good, have your AMT check to ensure that the compressor is being driven by the engine, and the system has a full charge of refrigerant.

Anytime a flight is being planned to an altitude requiring oxygen, be sure that the oxygen bottles are full, and that the masks and tubing are on board for all occupants. Furthermore, ensure that they are in good condition.

For pressurized aircraft, be sure that all door seals are in good condition and that all checks required by the Pilot's Operating Handbook have been observed.

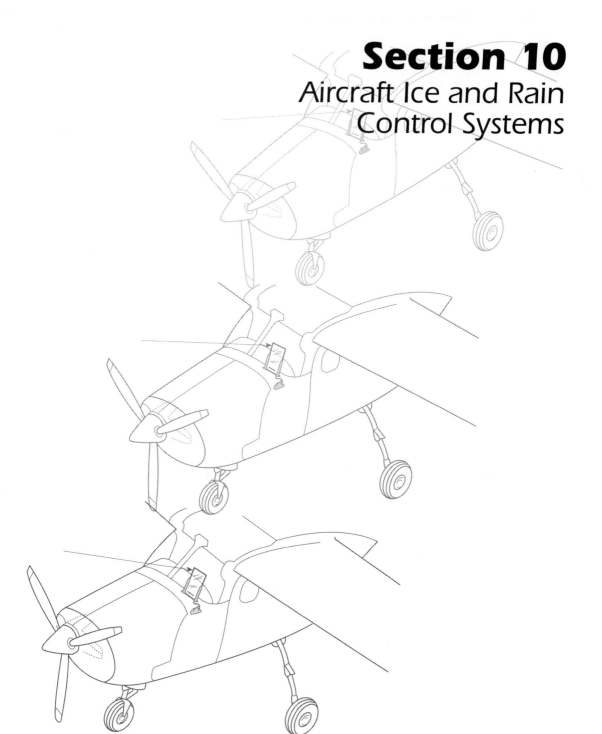

Section 10
Aircraft Ice and Rain Control Systems

Chapter 38 **Ice Control Systems**

Ice affects both engines and airframes and causes a large number of aircraft accidents. Reciprocating-engine-powered aircraft are susceptible to carburetor ice which shuts off the airflow to the engine. Structural ice forms on the airfoil surfaces adding weight, as well as disturbing the smooth flow of air needed to produce lift.

Dangers of Inflight Icing

Some aircraft are certificated for flight into known icing conditions, but the ice control systems on these aircraft in reality only give them time to fly out of the icing conditions rather than deliberately remain in them. No aircraft can withstand unrestricted exposure to icing.

There are three types of structural ice that affect an aircraft in flight: rime ice, glaze ice, and frost.

Rime Ice

Rime ice is a rough, opaque ice that forms when small droplets of water freeze as soon as they strike the aircraft. It builds up slowly and its rough surface causes a great deal of drag and deforms the airfoil, increasing the stall speed. Rime ice is relatively easy to break loose with deicer boots.

Types of structural ice:
- clear, or glaze ice
- rime ice
- frost

Glaze Ice

Glaze ice is the most dangerous type. It forms when flying through supercooled water or freezing rain. Glaze ice adds a large amount of weight and is difficult for the boots to break loose.

Three factors must be present for rime or glaze ice to form on an aircraft in flight. There must be visible moisture in the air which can be in the form of rain, drizzle, or clouds. The surface of the aircraft must be below the freezing temperature of water, and the drops of water must be large enough to form ice.

supercooled water. Water in its liquid state at a temperature below its normal freezing temperature. When supercooled water is disturbed, it immediately freezes.

Frost

Frost forms on an aircraft when the surface temperature is below freezing and water sublimates from the air, or changes directly from water vapor into ice crystals without passing through the liquid state. Frost does not add appreciable weight, but the tiny ice crystals create a rough surface that increases the thickness of the boundary layer and adds so much drag that flight may be impossible. All traces of frost must be removed before flight. This can be done by sweeping it off with a broom or by spraying the aircraft with a mixture of ethylene glycol and isopropyl alcohol.

Types of Ice Control Systems

There are two types of ice control systems used on general aviation aircraft: anti-icing systems, which prevent the formation of ice, and deicing systems, which remove ice after it has formed.

Anti-Icing Systems

anti-icing system. A system that prevents the formation of ice on an aircraft structure.

There are a number of critical areas upon an aircraft on which ice should not be allowed to form. These include carburetors, pitot tubes, windshields, turbine engine air inlets, and any components that are located ahead of these inlets. Anti-icing systems prevent ice from forming on these components.

Pitot heads installed on aircraft that are likely to encounter icing have an electrical heater built into them to prevent ice from clogging their air inlet. This heater produces enough heat to damage the head if there is no cooling air flowing over it, so it should not be turned on while the aircraft is on the ground except for brief preflight checking.

Except for a brief preflight check, pitot heat should not be used on the ground.

You can be sure the heater is operating properly in flight by watching the ammeter when the pitot heat is turned on. The heater draws enough current that the ammeter will show its operation.

Some flush static ports have heaters built into them, but on most aircraft there are two separate ports located at widely separated locations. It is unlikely that both ports will ice over at the same time. In the unlikely event that they should both become plugged, the system is equipped with an alternate static air source valve that allows you to select alternate air. This valve picks up static air from inside the aircraft where ice cannot form.

Aircraft that routinely fly into icing conditions have some method of preventing ice from forming on the windshield and obstructing the pilot's visibility. Three types of ice control are used: double-panel windshields with warm air blown through the space between the panels, anti-icing fluid sprayed on the outside of the windshield, and electrically heated windshields.

Some general aviation aircraft have a heated anti-icing panel that can be installed on the outside of the windshield. A panel of this type is seen in Figure 111. This panel is made of two sheets of plate glass separated by a layer of vinyl compound. A fine resistance wire embedded in the vinyl is heated with DC supplied through a connector enclosed in a streamlined housing near the panel. The panel is removable and is installed only on flights when icing conditions are likely. Prior to entering possible icing conditions, the system is turned on, and once in operation, temperature sensors cycle the power to maintain a temperature of approximately 100°F.

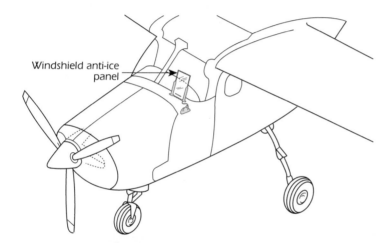

Windshield anti-ice panel

Figure 111. A removable heated panel may be installed in some general aviation aircraft to provide an ice-free area in the windshield directly in front of the pilot.

Snow, Ice, and Frost Removal

Aircraft that operate in the winter months are often faced with the problem of taking off into conditions of snow and ice. Test data has shown that ice, snow, or frost formations with a thickness and surface roughness no greater than that of medium or coarse sandpaper, on the leading edge and upper surface of a wing, can reduce wing lift as much as 30 percent and increase drag by as much as 40 percent. For this reason all snow, ice, and frost must be removed.

Aircraft that have been sitting in the open and are covered with snow may be prepared for flight by sweeping the snow off with a brush or broom, making very sure that no frost is left to roughen the surface enough to destroy lift. An engine heater

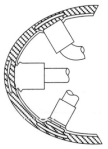

A When system is not operating, suction holds all three tubes deflated and tight against leading edge.

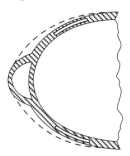

B When system is first turned on, center tube inflates and cracks the ice. Center tube remains inflated for specific number of seconds, then deflates.

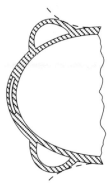

C Outer two tubes inflate and raise cracked ice from surface so wind can blow it away.

Figure 112. The operating cycle of a typical three-spanwise-tube deicer boot.

that blows warm air through a large hose may be used for melting ice, but unless this is done properly it can create additional problems. Be sure that no water from melted ice is allowed to run down inside the aircraft because it can refreeze and lock up the flight controls.

It is usually wise to remove the streamline wheel fairings (wheel pants) if the airplane is being operated from slush-covered runways or unpaved surfaces because water or slush can freeze inside these fairings while in flight and completely lock the wheels so they cannot turn.

Pneumatic Deicing System

Pneumatic deicing systems have boots made of soft pliable rubber or rubberized fabric containing inflatable tubes attached to the leading edges of the wings and empennage. The surface ply of the boots is made electrically conductive so it will dissipate the static electrical charges that build up as air flows over them. If this charge does not flow off the boot, the voltage could build up high enough to discharge through the boot to the skin, and in doing so burn a hole in the boot.

The typical three-spanwise-tube boot in Figure 112 shows the operation of this system. When the system is not in operation, suction from the engine-driven vacuum pump holds the tubes deflated and tight against the leading edge, as seen in Figure 112A.

When icing is encountered in flight, the pilot allows ice to form over the boots. Then the system is turned on. Air from the discharge side of the vacuum pump inflates the center tube in the boot as in Figure 112B to crack the ice. The timer holds the center tube inflated for a specific number of seconds, then deflates it and inflates the two outer tubes. These tubes lift the cracked ice so air can get under it and blow it from the surface. This is shown in Figure 112C.

The first deicer boots were attached to the surface with screws, but in all modern installations the boots are bonded to the surfaces with an adhesive.

Any grease or oil must be removed from the boots with a rag damp with naphtha or varsol, and then the entire area washed with a mild soap and water solution. Small holes in a boot may be patched with cold patches similar to those used for bicycle tubes, but not the same material. Only patching material provided by the boot manufacturer may be used, and the manufacturer's procedures must be followed in detail.

The boots may be periodically resurfaced with a black, conductive neoprene cement to seal any tiny pinholes and ensure that the boots remain electrically conductive.

Single-Engine Airplane Deicing System

Small aircraft that are equipped for flight into known icing conditions have a wing and empennage deicing system similar to that in Figure 113 on the next page. The air pump that is used for the instruments supplies the necessary 18- to 20-psi positive pressure to operate the boots and the suction used to hold them tight against the leading edges when the system is not operating.

If the air pump is of the "wet" type that uses engine oil as a lubricant, an oil separator is installed in its discharge side to remove the lubricating oil. Dry-type air pumps have carbon vanes and require no lubrication. Therefore, when a dry pump is used there is no need for an oil separator.

When the deicing system is not operating, the shuttle valve is held over to allow suction from the air pump to hold the boots deflated and tight against the leading edges of the surfaces.

When ice has formed on the wings, the pilot can depress the momentary-on DEICE switch. This opens the control valve and allows air pressure to reach the shuttle valve. The shuttle moves over so air pressure can reach the timer. The timer begins a sequence of operation that inflates the empennage boots for about six seconds, then the inboard wing boots for six seconds, and finally the outboard wing boots for six seconds. When there is sufficient pressure at the boots for proper inflation, the deice pressure light on the instrument panel illuminates. When the cycle is completed, the control valve opens the passage to the overboard dump, and the shuttle moves over so the suction can again hold the boots tightly against the skin.

Turbine-engine aircraft have a ready source of warm compressor bleed air for anti-icing, and they normally use thermal ice control. Some of the smaller turbine engines do not have an adequate quantity of bleed air for thermal ice control but do have enough for inflating pneumatic deicing boots. Systems that use compressor bleed air for this purpose have a pressure regulator that lowers the pressure to the correct value, and a venturi downstream of the regulator that produces a suction when the boots are not being inflated. This suction holds the tubes deflated and tight against the leading edges.

deicer. A system or component used to remove ice from a surface after it has formed; not to be confused with anti-icers that prevent the formation of ice.

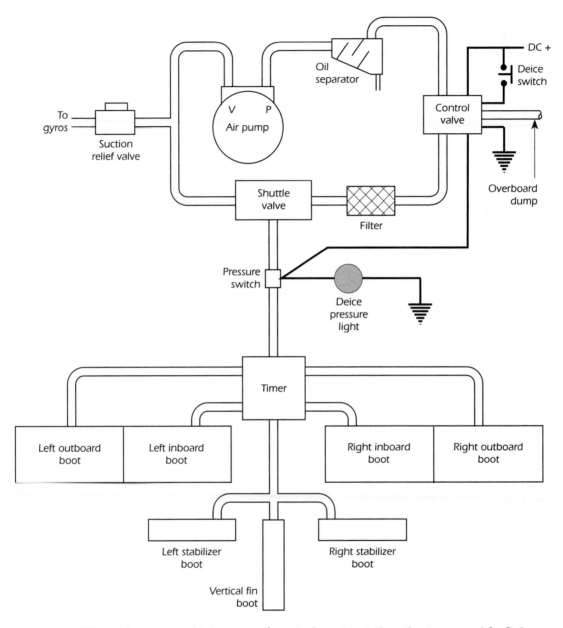

Figure 113. Wing and empennage deicing system for a single-engine airplane that is approved for flight into known icing conditions.

Powerplant Ice Protection

Powerplant ice affects both reciprocating and turbine engines. Most reciprocating engines are prone to carburetor or induction system icing, and turbine engines are mostly bothered by ingestion of ice that has broken off of some portion of the aircraft ahead of the intake.

Reciprocating Engines

Carburetor ice is the most prevalent type of powerplant ice and can affect the safety of flight even when there is no visible moisture in the air and no danger of other types of ice forming. A float-type carburetor acts as a very effective mechanical refrigerator. Liquid fuel is sprayed into the induction air in the form of tiny droplets which evaporate, or change from a liquid into a vapor. Heat is required to make this change, and it comes from the air flowing through the carburetor. When heat energy is removed from the air, its temperature drops enough to cause moisture to condense out and freeze in the throat of the carburetor. This ice chokes off the air flowing into the cylinders and causes the engine to lose power. Severe carburetor icing can cause engine failure. There is about a 70°F drop in temperature when the fuel evaporates, and it is possible for carburetor ice to form when the outside air temperature is as high as 100°F if the humidity is high.

Carburetor ice is normally prevented by heating the air before it is taken into the carburetor. Aircraft certificated under 14 CFR Part 23 that have a sea-level engine with a venturi carburetor must have the ability to increase the temperature of the induction air by 90°F. Aircraft having an altitude engine must be able to provide a temperature rise of 120°F. This heating is normally done by routing the air around the outside of some part of the exhaust system before taking it into the carburetor. The heated air bypasses the inlet air filter; therefore, carburetor heat should not be used for ground operation.

Fuel-injected engines are not bothered by carburetor ice, but ice can form on the intake air filter and choke off the air flowing into the engine. These aircraft normally have an alternate air valve that allows air from inside the engine cowling to be taken into the fuel injection unit if the screen should ice over.

Some larger engines spray isopropyl alcohol into the throat of the carburetor. This coats the venturi and throttle valves so any ice that might be picked up will not stick to the carburetor.

carburetor ice. Ice that forms inside the throat of a carburetor installed on an aircraft reciprocating engine. When air flows through the carburetor venturi, it speeds up, and both its pressure and temperature drop.

Carburetor heat should not be used on the ground because the heated air is not filtered and dust or sand can damage the engine.

Most carburetor ice forms at the point the liquid fuel droplets evaporate, and this is in the carburetor body where the airflow would be disturbed by a temperature probe. Flight tests have shown that there is a definite relationship between the temperature of the air entering the carburetor and the temperature of the air at the point of fuel evaporation. A temperature probe can be installed at the carburetor air inlet, and as long as the air temperature it senses remains above a specific value, there is little chance of carburetor ice forming. The pilot can control the temperature of this air by using the carburetor heat control.

carburetor air heater. A sheet metal jacket surrounding part of the engine exhaust system through which air from inside the engine nacelle or compartment flows and picks up heat. When the air temperature is low or the humidity is high, heated air can be directed through the carburetor heat valve into the carburetor. Air that flows through the carburetor air heater is not filtered.

Turbine Engines

Turbine engines are susceptible to damage from chunks of ice that get into the compressor. For this reason anti-icing systems are used to prevent the formation of ice ahead of the compressor inlet. Many aircraft have air passages in the compressor inlet case, inlet guide vanes, nose dome, and nose cowling. Hot compressor bleed air flows through these passages to prevent the formation of ice.

Ice can form when the engine is operated at high speed on the ground when the temperature is as high as 45° if the air is moist. The high velocity of the inlet air creates a pressure drop that lowers the temperature of the air enough for ice to form.

In flight, the anti-icing system should be turned on before entering areas of visible moisture (rain or clouds) when the inlet temperature is between about 40°F and 5°F. Below 5°F, there is so little moisture in the air that ice is not likely to form.

Sometimes when turbine-powered aircraft sit on the ground, water collects in the compressor and freezes. If this should happen, a flow of warm air should be directed through the engine until all of the ice is melted and the rotating parts turn freely.

Propellers

Ice on a propeller changes its airfoil shape and creates an unbalanced condition. Both of these conditions produce vibration and can cause damage to the engine as well as to the airframe.

The earliest propeller ice control, and a system that is still in use, is chemical anti-icing. A mixture of isopropyl alcohol and ethylene glycol is carried in a tank in the aircraft and when icing conditions are anticipated, some of it is pumped into a slinger ring around the hub of the propeller and then out along the leading edges of the blades. Some propellers have molded rubber feed shoes bonded to the blade roots to help concentrate the flow of fluid along the portions of the blade that are most susceptible to ice formation. Keeping the blade surfaces perfectly smooth and waxed will assist in preventing ice from sticking when it forms. *See* Figure 114 on the next page.

Propellers are deiced with an electrothermal system that has rubber boots bonded to the leading edge of the blades. These boots have electrical heating elements embedded in them that are supplied with current from a propeller deicing timer.

Figure 115 on Page 191 is the electrical schematic diagram of a typical system used on a twin turboprop airplane. Current flows from the bus through the 20-amp Auto Prop Deice circuit breaker/switch into the deicer timer unit. When the manual-override relays are not energized, this current flows through brushes riding on slip rings mounted on the propeller spinner bulkhead into the heating elements bonded to the propeller blades. The slip rings are connected to the heater elements through flexible conductors that allow the blades to change their pitch angle.

The timer sends current through the right propeller for about 90 seconds, then switches over and sends current through the left propeller for 90 seconds.

Some propeller deicing systems have two separate heating elements on each blade. Current flows through the right propeller outboard element for about 30 seconds, then through the right propeller inboard element for the same length of time. After the right propeller is deiced, the timer shifts over and sends current through the left propeller outboard elements and then through the left propeller inboard elements.

Current cycles of the two propellers are controlled by the timer as long as the propeller Auto Prop Deice switch is ON. When the Manual Prop Deice switch is held in its momentary ON position, the two manual-override relays are energized and current flows directly from the bus to the blades without going through the timer.

You can easily tell whether or not the deicing system is operating correctly in the AUTOMATIC mode by watching the propeller ammeter. It will show a flow of current each time one of the heater elements draws current.

Continued on Page 192

propeller anti-icer. A system that spreads a mixture of alcohol and glycerin along the propeller blades when the aircraft is flying in icing conditions. The alcohol and glycerin prevent water reaching the metal of the propeller blade and freezing on it.

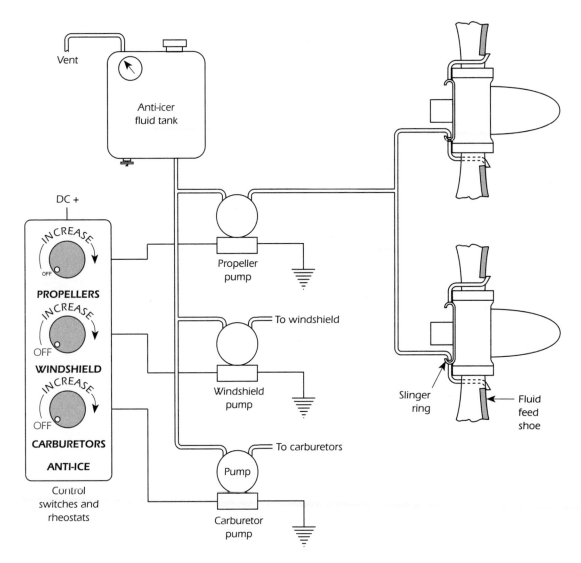

Figure 114. A typical chemical anti-icing system for a propeller

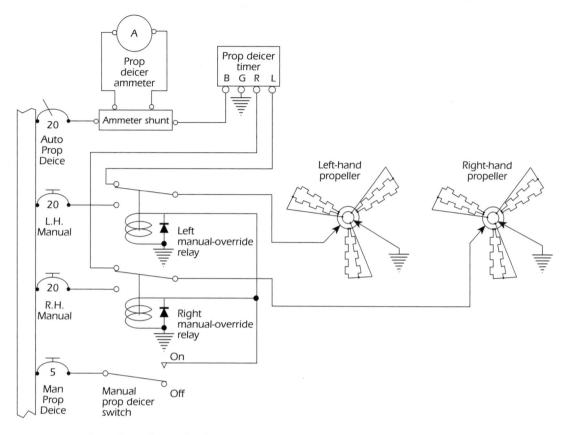

Figure 115. Electrothermal propeller deicing system

Rain Removal Systems

Rain removal systems are used in most of the larger aircraft to keep the windshield free of water so the pilot can see for the approach and to safely maneuver the aircraft on the ground.

Small general aviation aircraft have acrylic windshields that are easy to scratch, so windshield wipers are not used. Rain is prevented from obstructing visibility on these aircraft by keeping the windshield waxed with a good grade of paste wax. Water does not spread out on the waxed surface, but it balls up and is blown away by the propeller blast.

Rain is removed from the heated, tempered-glass windshields of large jet aircraft by mechanical windshield wipers, by chemical rain repellant that prevents the water from adhering to the glass, or by a blast of high-velocity hot turbine-engine compressor bleed air.

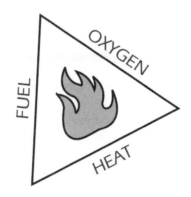

Section 11
Aircraft Fire
Extinguishing Systems

Chapter 39 **Ingredients for Detection and Protection**

Aircraft carry large volumes of highly flammable fuel in a lightweight, vibration-prone structure. This structure also carries one or more engines that continually produce huge quantities of extremely hot exhaust gases. Add to this a complex electrical system with motors and relays that produce sparks, and radio and radar transmitters that emit electromagnetic radiation. All of this combines to produce an ideal environment for fires.

Yet with all of its possibilities, there are relatively few fires in the air, and this is because of the effectiveness of the fire detection and protection systems that are available in modern aircraft.

Aircraft fire detection systems consist of fire detectors, overheat detectors, rate-of-temperature-rise detectors, smoke detectors, and carbon monoxide detectors.

How a Fire Happens

Fire is the result of a chemical reaction between some type of fuel and oxygen. When this reaction occurs, energy is released in the form of heat and light. For a fire to occur, there must be fuel, oxygen, and a temperature that is high enough to start the reaction. Fires may be extinguished by removing the fuel or oxygen or by reducing the temperature to a level below that needed for the reaction.

For a fire to exist there must be fuel, oxygen, and enough heat to start the chemical action. If any of the three are removed, the fire will go out.

In order to best understand fires and the way to combat them, the National Fire Protection Association has categorized them and identified the types of extinguishing agents that are best used on each of them. The four categories are: Class A, B, C, and D.

Class A fires have solid combustible materials such as wood, paper, and cloth as its fuels. These fires normally occur in aircraft cabins and cockpits, and any extinguishing agent used for Class A fires must be safe for the occupants.

Class B fires have combustible liquids such as gasoline, jet-engine fuel, lubricating oil, and hydraulic fluid as their fuel. Class B fires normally occur in engine compartments.

Class C fires involve energized electrical equipment. These fires can occur in almost any part of an aircraft and demand special care because of the danger of electrical shock.

Class D fires are those in which some metal such as magnesium burns. These fires normally occur in the brakes and wheels, and burn with a ferocious intensity. Water should never be used on a burning metal as it only intensifies the fire.

Fire-Extinguishing Agents

Water

Class A fires can be extinguished with an agent that lowers the temperature of the fuel. A commonly used agent for aircraft cabin fires is water. Small hand-held fire extinguishers contain water that is adequately protected with an antifreeze agent. When the handle of these extinguishers is twisted, the seal in a carbon dioxide (CO_2) cartridge is broken, and the CO_2 pressurizes the water and discharges it in the form of a spray. When the water changes from a liquid to a vapor, it absorbs heat from the air above the fire and drops its temperature sufficiently to cool the fuel enough to cause the fire to go out.

Water must never be used on Class B, C, or D fires.

Water must never be used on Class B, C, or D fires. Most flammable liquids float on water, and the use of water on Class B fires will only spread the fire. Water conducts electricity, and its use on a Class C fire constitutes a definite danger of electrocution. Water sprayed on the burning metal in a Class D fire will actually intensify the fire rather than extinguish it.

Carbon Dioxide

Carbon dioxide (CO_2) is heavier than air, and when it is sprayed on a fire it remains on the surface and excludes oxygen from the combustion process, so the fire goes out. CO_2 has been a favored extinguishing agent for many years. It is relatively inexpensive, nontoxic, safe to handle, and has a long storage life.

Hand-held CO_2 extinguishers can be used to extinguish fires in energized electrical equipment, but they should not be used unless the nozzles are made of a nonconductive material. Fortunately most nozzles are made of pressed nonconductive fiber.

CO_2 is normally a gas, and it is stored in steel bottles under pressure. When it is released, it expands and cools enough to change into a finely divided snow of dry ice. CO_2 may also be produced directly on a fire by covering the fire with a dry powder such as sodium bicarbonate, potassium bicarbonate, or ammonium phosphate. Dry powder is useful for Class D fires such as those in an aircraft brake.

Halogenated Hydrocarbons

This classification of fire-extinguishing agents includes the most widely used agents today, as well as some of the agents that were used in the past but are no longer considered suitable.

These agents are hydrocarbon compounds in which one or more of the hydrogen atoms have been replaced with an atom of one of the halogen elements such as fluorine, chlorine, or bromine.

In the process of combustion, the molecules of the fuel combine with those of oxygen in an orderly fashion, but if one of the halogen compounds is mixed with the oxygen this combination is interrupted and may be stopped entirely—the fire will go out.

The two most widely used halogenated hydrocarbons are Halon 1301 and Halon 1211. Both of these compounds, often called by the trade name of Freon, have a very low toxicity, with 1301 being the least toxic of all commonly used agents. Both are very effective as fire-extinguishing agents. They are noncorrosive, evaporate rapidly, leave no residue, and require no cleanup or neutralization.

Hand-Held Fire Extinguishers

14 CFR Part 135 Operating Requirements: Commuter and On-Demand Operations and Rules Governing Persons On Board Such Aircraft. This regulation requires that passenger-carrying aircraft operated under this part have at least one hand-held fire extinguisher located on the flight deck and at least one in the passenger compartment. For years, the most popular extinguishers have been CO_2 type, but modern developments have made Halon 1301 and Halon 1211 the extinguishers of choice. These extinguishing agents are the least toxic of all and are effective on almost all types of fires likely to be encountered in an aircraft cabin. These extinguishers are available in small, medium, and large sizes. The small extinguishers are adequate for fires of up to one square foot in area, medium extinguishers are adequate for fires up to two square feet in area, and the large sizes are adequate for fires up to five square feet.

Halon 1211 extinguishers use compressed nitrogen for a propellant, but Halon 1301 has enough pressure that it does not require a separate propelling agent. All Halon extinguishers have built-in pressure gages to indicate the pressure of the extinguishing agent.

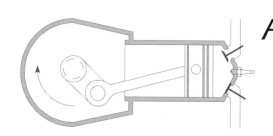

Section 12
Aircraft Piston Engines

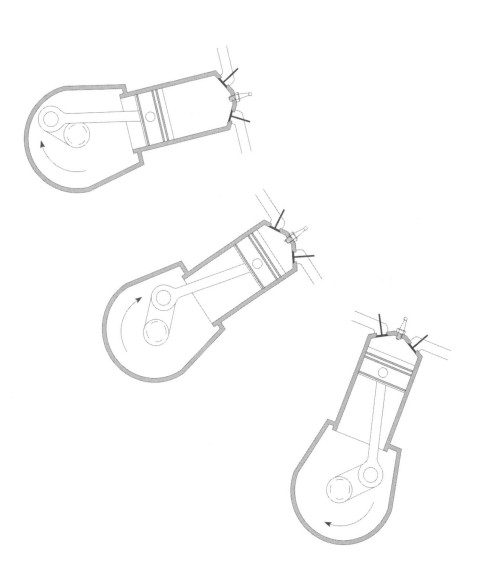

Chapter 40 **Theory of Operation**

Aircraft reciprocating, or piston, engines operate on the same basic principle as automobile engines, and for that matter as the engine in the Wright Flyer of a century ago. These engines all operate on the four-stroke, five-event Otto cycle.

Aircraft engines differ from automobile engines in that they are lighter weight and turn slower. They operate with a rather constant speed and load for long periods of time rather than the continual changing conditions encountered by automobile engines in traffic.

Most modern aircraft piston engines are horizontally-opposed, air cooled, and may turn the propeller directly from the crankshaft or its speed may be reduced by gears.

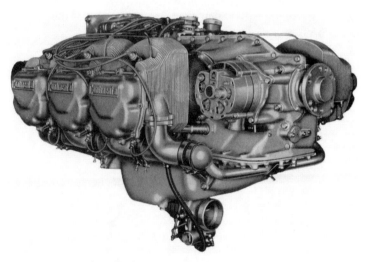

Figure 116. A six-cylinder, air-cooled, horizontally-opposed aircraft engine that drives the propeller through a reduction gear.

reciprocating engine. A form of heat engine that uses chemical energy from burning fuel to heat the air inside the cylinders that drives pistons. The reciprocating motion of the pistons is converted into rotary motion of the crank-shaft to turn the propeller or drive a helicopter transmission.

Aircraft piston engine configurations:

Inline: The cylinders are all in a line

Upright: Cylinders are above the crankcase

Inverted: Cylinders are below the crankcase (4- and 6-cylinder models most popular)

V: Two banks of inline cylinders in the form of a V

Upright or inverted (8- and 12-cylinder models most popular)

Horizontally opposed—Two banks of cylinders with one bank on each side of the crankcase. (This is the most popular modern configuration with most engines having 4 or 9 cylinders.)

Radial—Cylinders radiating out from a small central crankcase. (Most popular engines through WWII had 5, 7 or 9 cylinders in one row, 14 or 18 cylinders in two rows, or 28 cylinders in four rows.)

Internal Combustion

All internal combustion heat engines produce power by burning fuel inside the engine to convert the chemical energy in the fuel into heat which expands the air inside the engine. This expansion performs useful work.

There are three essentials for a heat engine to operate:

- There must be fuel
- There must be enough air to mix with the fuel to make a combustible mixture
- There must be heat to ignite the fuel.

combustible mixture. An air-fuel mixture of between 8 pounds of air to 1 pound of gasoline to 18 pounds of air to 1 pound of gasoline.

The Otto Cycle

The Otto cycle of energy transformation is used by almost all certificated aircraft piston engines. Every other inward stroke of the piston is a power stroke. Many ultralight aircraft use two-stroke engines in which every inward stroke of the piston is a power stroke.

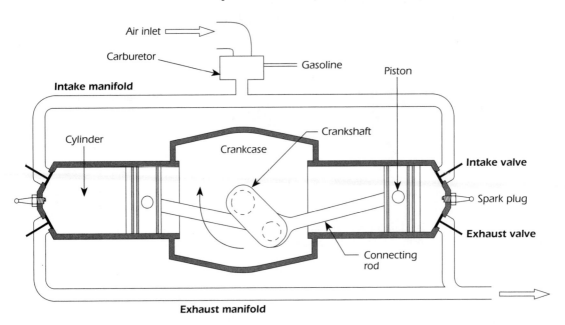

Figure 117. Piston engine nomenclature

Two-stroke engines are simpler and have more power strokes per minute than four-stroke engines but are less efficient and are therefore not commonly used. However, two-stroke turbocharged compression-ignition (diesel) engines hold promise for general aviation aircraft in the future.

The four strokes and five events are:

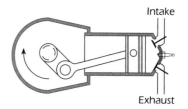
Figure 118. Intake stroke

Intake

On the intake stroke the piston moves inward with the intake valve open. The low pressure created as the volume of the cylinder increases pulls air and fuel vapors into the cylinder through the carburetor.

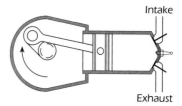
Figure 119. Compression stroke

Compression

As the piston passes the inward end of its stroke (bottom center) and moves outward, both valves are closed and the vapors inside the cylinder are compressed to approximately one-sixth of their original volume. The pressure and temperature of the fuel-air mixture inside the cylinder are increased.

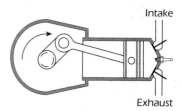
Figure 120. Ignition

Ignition

When the crankshaft has turned until it is about 30° of rotation before the outward end of its stroke (top center), the compressed air and fuel vapor inside the cylinder is ignited by sparks from the two spark plugs and begins to burn. Heat from the burning vapor expands the air inside the cylinder, increasing its pressure.

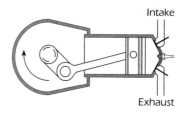
Figure 121. Power stroke

Power

By the time the piston reaches the outer end of its stroke and starts back inward, the pressure has risen to the highest value and pushes the piston in. The force of this push produces the torque that turns the propeller and creates thrust that moves the airplane through the air.

Exhaust

After the piston passes bottom center it starts back outward. The exhaust valve is open, and the piston forces the burned gases out of the cylinder, preparing it for the next cycle of operation.

The firing sequence of the cylinders is timed to give the propeller a smooth rotation, and failure of any cylinder to

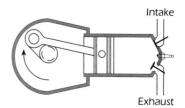
Figure 122. Exhaust stroke

produce its even push on the crankshaft at its proper time causes the engine to vibrate and lose power.

The amount of power an aircraft engine produces is determined by four things:

- Area of the piston heads acted on by the expanding gases. This is determined by the bore (diameter) of the cylinder and the number of cylinders.
- Distance the piston moves on each power stroke. This is called the stroke.
- Pressure inside the cylinder at the beginning of the power stroke.
- Number of power strokes per minute.

The first two factors, the bore and the stroke, are determined by the size and configuration of the engine. The last two are controlled by the pilot.

Pressure is determined by the amount of fuel burned in the cylinders which is controlled by the throttle. The number of power strokes per minute is determined by the crankshaft speed (RPM), and is controlled by the pitch of the propeller.

The end product of an aircraft powerplant is thrust, the forward force produced by a propeller as it accelerates a large mass of air rearward. Aircraft piston engines are inefficient as they convert less than one third of the energy in the fuel into useful work and only about 80% of this work is converted into thrust by the propeller.

Chapter 41   **Piston Engine Construction**

Crankcase

The crankcase is a two-piece aluminum alloy casting with webs that support the bosses for the crankshaft and the camshaft bearings. Pads to which the cylinders mount are machined on both halves and the parting surfaces between the halves are machined smooth so they form an oil-tight seal without the use of gaskets. The front end has a bearing cavity for a thrust bearing or provisions for a propeller reduction gear system. The rear of the crankcase has provisions for the gears that drive the camshaft, magnetos, alternator, and the various pumps. The engine is held in the airframe by engine mounts attached to the crankcase.

crankcase. The housing of a reciprocating engine which encloses the crankshaft, camshaft, and many of the accessory drive gears. The cylinders mount on the crankcase, and the engine is attached to the airframe by the crankcase.

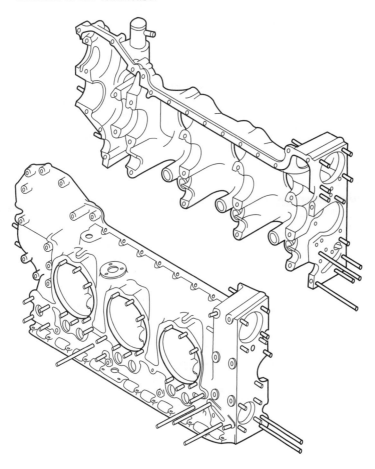

Figure 123. Typical aircraft piston engine crankcase

The bottom of the crankcase has provisions for mounting an oil sump that holds the lubricating oil supply. Passages are cast into the crankcase to carry oil from the oil pump to the crankshaft and camshaft bearings and to the gears at the front and rear of the engine.

Some engines have the carburetor mounted on the bottom of the oil sump and the fuel-air mixture is carried in intake pipes surrounded by the oil. This heats the fuel-air mixture and keeps the carburetor warm to help prevent carburetor ice.

Crankshaft

The propeller of an airplane or the rotor system transmission of a helicopter is driven by the crankshaft.

The crankshaft is the strongest and heaviest component in an aircraft piston engine. It rides inside the crankcase in plain bearings with replaceable inserts. It receives the push from the pistons through the connecting rods to transform their in and out motion into rotation that drives the propeller.

torsional vibration. A twisting vibration in a crankshaft caused by the power impulses transmitted from the pistons into the crankshaft.

The power produced by a piston engine is supplied in a series of pushes, or pulses. When the frequency of these pulses is the same as the resonant frequency of the crankshaft, enough torsional vibration can result that the crankshaft can be broken. To prevent this, the crankshaft for some larger engines have counterweights mounted on blades that are forged parts of the crankshaft. The counterweights are free to rock back and forth to change the resonant frequency of the crankshaft and prevent damage from torsional vibration.

front and rear ends of an engine. The front end of an engine is the end that has the propeller even though it may be mounted as a pusher. The technical name for the rear end of the engine is the antipropeller end.

The front end of the crankshaft for a direct drive engine has either a flange, a taper, or a spline. For geared engines, the drive gear is attached to the front end.

The crankshaft is hollow with passages for oil to flow from one of the main bearing bosses through passages to the throws where the connecting rods mount. Each throw has a sludge plug pressed into it to trap any sludge in the oil and

Figure 124. Crankshaft of a four-cylinder horizontally-opposed engine

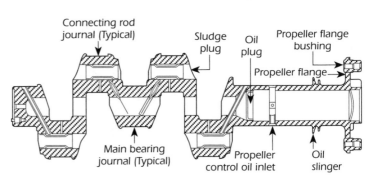

Connecting rod journal (Typical) — Sludge plug — Oil plug — Propeller flange bushing — Propeller flange — Main bearing journal (Typical) — Propeller control oil inlet — Oil slinger

hold it until the engine is overhauled. Oil from the propeller governor flows through the hollow crankshaft and into the propeller to change the propeller pitch.

Connecting Rods

The pistons are connected to the crankshaft throws by forged steel connecting rods. The small end has a bronze bushing pressed into it that rides on the smooth steel wrist pin in the piston. The big end has a two-piece plain bearing insert similar to those used for the main bearings in the crankcase.

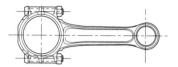

Figure 125. Typical forged steel connecting rod for a horizontally-opposed engine

plain bearings. Bearings made of a material such as lead or babbit that has a low coefficient of friction.

Cylinders

The cylinders have an alloy steel barrel with fins for air cooling machined on their outer surface, and a heavy flange near their open end where they are bolted to the crankcase (Figure 126 on the next page). The upper end of the barrel is threaded and a cast aluminum alloy head is screwed and shrunk onto it.

The cylinder head has cooling fins cast onto its outer surface, with holes for the valve seats and valve guides. It also has passages that allow fuel air mixture to flow into the combustion chamber and exhaust gases to leave. There are two holes in the cylinder head for the spark plugs. These holes are fitted with stainless steel Heli-Coil inserts to prevent the soft cast aluminum alloy being damaged by repeated changing of the spark plugs.

The top end of the cylinder head has the valve operating mechanism enclosed in an oil-tight housing. The intake and exhaust pipes bolt to the cylinder head to allow passage of the fuel-air mixture into the intake valve chamber and the exhaust gases to leave through the exhaust valve.

Valve guides are pressed into the cylinder head to provide a smooth bearing surface for the valve stems to ride back and forth. Hardened valve seats are shrunk into the head to provide a wear resistant surface on which the valve faces provide their airtight seal.

The cylinders for fuel-injected engines have holes for the injector nozzles in the wall of the intake valve cavity. Fuel is sprayed into this cavity where it evaporates. When the intake valve is pushed off its seat, the air from the intake pipe forces these fuel vapors into the combustion chamber of the cylinder.

cylinder. The component in a reciprocating engine that houses the piston and valves; they form the combustion chambers of the engine.

Heli-Coil insert. A patented stainless steel coil of wire having a diamond-shaped cross section. It is screwed into the spark plug hole in a cast aluminum alloy cylinder head to form wear-resistant threads.

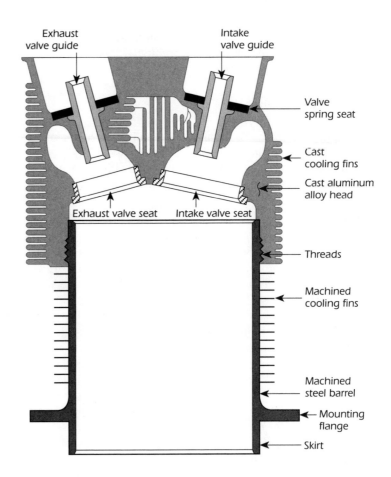

Figure 126. Typical cylinder for an air-cooled horizontally-opposed engine

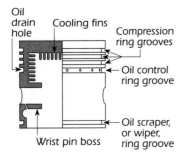

Figure 127. Typical aircraft engine piston

Pistons

Cast or forged aluminum alloy pistons ride inside the cylinders to compress the fuel-air mixture and to transmit the force from the expanding heated air to the crankshaft. A polished high-strength steel wrist pin rides in holes in the sides of the piston. This anchors the connecting rod that transmits the forces from the piston to the crankshaft, while allowing the connecting rod to rock back and forth as the crankshaft rotates.

Three or more springy cast-iron piston rings are fitted into grooves around the periphery of the piston above the wrist pin. They press tightly against the cylinder walls to form a gas-tight seal. The top one or two rings are called compression rings; they seal the piston to the cylinder walls. There is also an oil control ring that controls the amount of oil allowed to remain between the piston and the cylinder wall. Some pistons have an oil scraper ring that scrapes the oil up into the space between the piston and the cylinder wall.

Camshaft

The camshaft is a hollow steel shaft with lobes and bearing journals machined on it. The lobes and journals are ground and polished then case hardened to increase their resistance to wear. The camshaft is gear driven from the crankshaft at one half crankshaft speed.

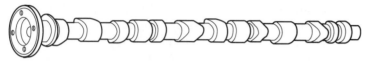

Figure 128. A camshaft for a typical six-cylinder horizontally-opposed engine

The camshaft is geared to the crankshaft and timed in such a way that the valves open and close at the proper time relative to the position of the piston in the cylinders.

Valves

Each cylinder has an intake and an exhaust valve. To increase the area for the gases to enter and leave the cylinder, some engines have two intake and two exhaust valves in each cylinder.

The valves operate in the most hostile environment and are made of the highest grade of alloy steel. The exhaust valves are subject to especially high heat and to prevent the valve overheating some have hollow stems partially filled with metallic sodium. Sodium is a solid at normal room temperature, but at the high operating temperature of the valve it becomes a liquid and absorbs heat from the valve head, then it sloshes up into the stem and carries this heat to the valve guide where it is transferred into the cylinder head and carried off by the air passing through the fins.

The valves are actuated by a camshaft driven from a gear on the crankshaft. The shape and position of the cam lobes times the opening and closing of the exhaust and intake valves. *See* Figure 129 on the next page.

Hydraulic valve lifters ride on the cam lobes and, at the high point of the lobe, press against a push rod that pushes up on the rocker arm and forces the valve off its seat against the force of the valve springs. When the camshaft rotates so the valve lifter is no longer on the high point of the lobe, the springs close the valve.

The hydraulic unit in the valve lifter takes up any wear or slack in the system by continually being filled with oil from the engine lubricating system.

The valve seats on which the valves seal are high-strength replaceable inserts shrunk into the cast aluminum head. They withstand the pounding of the valve and the extreme heat from the exhaust gases as they leave the combustion chamber. The valve guides are also replaceable components that provide a good bearing surface in which the valve stems ride.

The valve mechanism is lubricated by engine oil that flows from passages in the crankcase up through the hollow push rods into the valve chambers cast into the cylinder head and then drains back either through an external return tube or through the housing that encases the push rod.

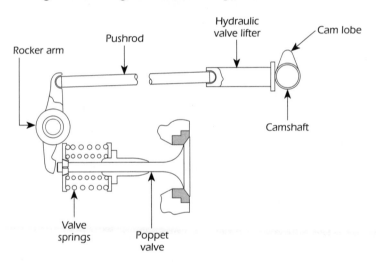

Figure 129. Valve operating mechanism

Gears

Gears that drive the camshaft and accessories such as the magnetos and pumps are housed in an oil-tight compartment, usually at the rear of the engine. The propeller reduction gears, if they are used, are driven from the crankshaft at the front of the engine.

Propellers lose their efficiency when their tips approach the speed of sound, but the power produced by a piston engine is determined by its speed. To allow the propeller to operate at an efficient speed when the engine is operating at a high speed, a reduction gear system is used between the crankshaft and the propeller shaft.

Most modern horizontally-opposed engines use a simple spur gear arrangement, but the larger radial engines use planetary gears.

spur gear. A gear wheel with teeth radiating outward from its periphery.

planetary gears. A system of gears that reduces the speed of the propeller shaft without changing its direction of rotation as is done with a simple spur gear system.

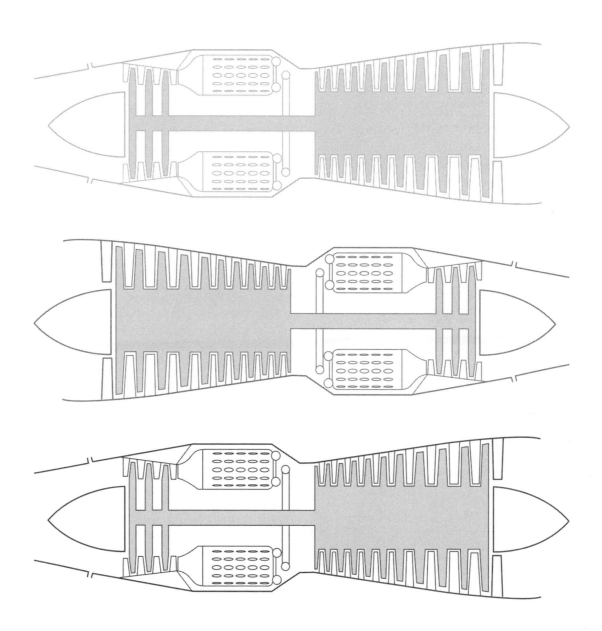

Chapter 42 Types of Turbine Engines

Introduction

The greatest evolution that has taken place in transportation since World War II has been the advent of the turbine engine. The heavy, vibrating, piston engine with its short time between overhauls (TBO) and a low specific weight is in the process of being replaced with a much lighter, more dependable engine with a far longer TBO.

The main limitation of the turbine engine has been high operating temperatures that have required the development of new materials and it is the expensive research involved that keeps the cost of these engines so high. But their light weight and efficiency have made them indispensable for the military, airlines, and business operations.

The flexibility of the turbine engine makes it especially suitable for an aircraft powerplant. It may be used as a straight turbojet, turbofan, or turboprop for airplanes or turboshaft for helicopters.

specific weight. The ratio of the weight of an aircraft engine to the brake horsepower it produces.

Turbojet Engines

The first successful aircraft turbine engine was a turbojet. A turbojet engine takes in a huge volume of air through its inlet air duct. This air is compressed and a large amount of fuel is burned in it. The heated air accelerates and passes through the turbine where it gives up most of its energy by driving the compressor. The remaining energy leaves the engine through the exhaust nozzle as a high velocity jet of hot gas. The thrust the engine produces is proportional to the change in momentum of the air as it passes through the engine.

Turbojet engines are noisy and fuel inefficient and have been replaced to a great extent by turbofan engines.

momentum. The product of a mass times its velocity.

Turbofan Engines

A turbojet engine creates thrust by accelerating a small mass of air through a large change in velocity. A propeller produces thrust by accelerating a much larger mass of air through a smaller change in velocity. Turbojet engines are most efficient at high speeds and propellers are most efficient at low speeds.

A turbofan engine may be thought of as a compromise between a turbojet engine and a propeller. The turbine drives a set of lengthened compressor blades that accelerates a large mass of air around the outside of the engine. Between 30% and 75% of the total thrust produced by a turbofan engine is produced by the fan. Turbofan engines are the most efficient type of engine for operating at speeds of around Mach 0.8 (80% of the speed of sound) and are the type of engine used in almost all jet transport airplanes.

Turboprop Engines

turboprop engine. A form of gas turbine engine that uses one or more stages of turbines to drive a set of reduction gears, which in turn drives a propeller. Most of the heat energy in the exhaust gases is converted into torque, rather than into a stream of high-velocity exhaust gases, as is done in a turbojet engine.

free turbine. A turbine or stage of turbines in a gas turbine engine that is independent of the turbine used to drive the compressor in the gas-generator section of the engine.

Jet aircraft are most efficient at high speed and high altitude, but propeller-driven airplanes are more efficient at low altitude and low speed. Turbine engines produce their power with a far lighter weight than piston engines, so it is a logical step to use a turbine to drive a propeller through a series of reduction gears.

Turboprop engines have an extra stage or stages of turbines to drive the propeller. Free-turbine engines have a separate turbine to drive the propeller and single-shaft engines have the extra stages of turbines on the same shaft as the compressor. So much energy is extracted by these turbines that the gases leaving the engine do not produce an appreciable amount of jet thrust.

Most short haul commuter airliners are turboprop powered because of the tremendous weight savings and their long time between overhauls.

Turboshaft Engines

A lightweight turbine engine operating at a constant speed is an ideal powerplant for a helicopter, and the engine of choice for a helicopter is a turboshaft engine.

Turboshaft engines have extra stages of turbines to extract the maximum amount of energy from the fuel being burned so little is left in the gases as they leave the engine. Most turboshaft engines are free turbine engines.

Chapter 43 **Theory of Operation**

A turbine engine is a heat engine that converts the chemical energy in the fuel into heat and then this heat into mechanical energy. It uses the Brayton cycle of operation which is a constant-pressure cycle, rather than the constant-volume cycle of the Otto-cycle engine.

The turbojet as illustrated in Figure 130 is the most basic form of aircraft turbine engine and was the type first developed. By understanding it, you will be able to understand the other configurations of the turbine engine.

A turbine engine has the same events: intake, compression, ignition, expansion, and exhaust as a piston engine, the difference being that they are all continuous actions that occur in different locations within the engine. In a piston engine they occur in the same location but at different times.

Air is taken into the engine through an inlet air duct and compressed, then it flows into a diffuser which decreases the velocity of the air and increases its pressure. This air now flows into the combustor, a special thin-wall steel housing where the fuel is sprayed under pressure and ignited by a continuously burning fire. The burning fuel heats and expands the air which leaves the combustor at about the same pressure but at a very high speed. It then passes through one or more stages of turbines that act in much the same way as a windmill. The turbines extract a great amount of energy from the hot, high-velocity gases to drive the compressor. The energy remaining in the gas after it drives the compressor produces thrust as it leaves the engine through a specially shaped tail pipe as a high-velocity jet of hot air.

Brayton cycle. The constant-pressure cycle of energy release used in a gas turbine engine. Fuel is added to the air passing through the engine and burned. Heat from the burning fuel expands the air, and since the air is not confined, it accelerates as it moves through the engine.

power. The amount of work in foot-pounds divided by the time in seconds or minutes used to do the work. One horsepower is equal to 33,000 foot-pounds of work done in one minute or 550 foot-pounds of work done in one second.

work. A physical measurement of force used to produce movement. It is the product of the force applied to an object multiplied by the distance the force causes the object to move.

torque. A force that produces, or tries to produce, rotation.

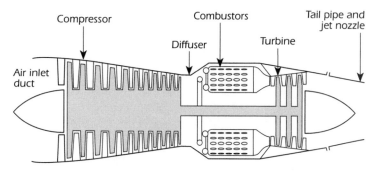

Figure 130. Basic components of a turbojet engine

thrust. The forward aerodynamic force produced by a propeller, fan, or turbojet engine as it forces a mass of air to the rear, behind the airplane.

Turbojet and turbofan engines are not rated by power because power involves movement. A turbojet engine operating on a test stand is not producing power, but it is producing thrust. The amount of thrust is proportional to the acceleration of the mass of air flowing through the engine.

Chapter 44 **Turbine Engine Construction**

Inlet Air Ducts

On most turbojet and turbofan, and some turboprop engines, the inlet air duct is shaped in such a way that the air is slowed down slightly and its pressure increased before it enters the compressor. Some turboprop engines have the air inlet at the rear and the air is taken into a plenum chamber which acts as a diffuser before it enters the compressor.

Compressors

There are two types of compressors used on turbine engines: centrifugal and axial flow.

Centrifugal Compressor

A centrifugal compressor has a disk-like impeller with vanes on one or both of its faces. Air is taken into the eye, or center, of the impeller and is slung outward by centrifugal force which increases the velocity of the air. This high-speed air then passes through a diffuser which slows it down and increases its pressure before it flows through a manifold and into the combustor. To increase the volume of the air moved by a centrifugal compressor, some have vanes on both sides of the impeller disk. These are called double-entry centrifugal compressors.

plenum chamber. An enclosed chamber in which air can be held at a pressure slightly higher than that of the surrounding air. A plenum chamber allows the air pressure to stabilize before it enters the compressor of a gas turbine engine.

diffuser. A duct installed in the compressor outlet of a turbine engine to reduce the velocity of the air leaving the compressor and increase its pressure before it enters the combustor.

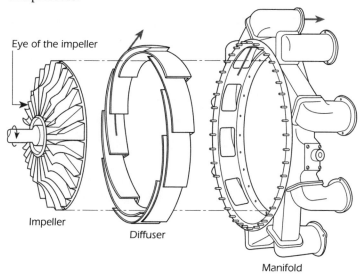

Eye of the impeller

Impeller

Diffuser

Manifold

Figure 131. A typical single-entry centrifugal compressor

Centrifugal compressors were used on some of the early turbine engines because they are rugged and light weight, but they have two disadvantages that prevent their use on large turbojet and turbofan engines. While they have a large pressure rise for each stage, they are limited to only two stages, and they have a large diameter for the amount of air they move.

Centrifugal compressors are used on many modern turbo-prop engines and some smaller turbofan engines. These engines may have two stages of small-diameter centrifugal compressors or a high-pressure centrifugal compressor in the output of a low-pressure axial-flow compressor.

Axial-Flow Compressors

axial-flow compressor. A type of compressor used in gas turbine engines in which the air passes through the compressor in essentially a straight line, parallel to the axis of the compressor.

Axial-flow compressors are used on all large turbojet and turbofan engines. They are heavier than a centrifugal compressor, and are much more complex and costly, but their efficiency is much higher. The pressure rise per stage is considerably lower than it is for a centrifugal compressor but there may be many stages.

Each rotor blade is like a small propeller that is turned by the turbine. As the air flows past the rotor blades it is accelerated. Following each stage of rotor blades is a set of stator vanes that act as diffusers to slow the air down by converting some of its velocity energy into pressure energy. By the time the air reaches the end of the compressor its velocity and direction of flow are essentially the same as when it entered the compressor, but its pressure is greatly increased.

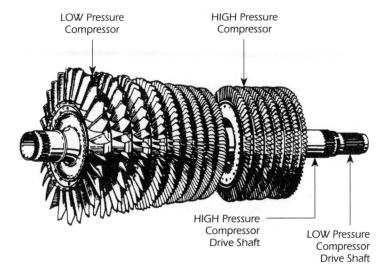

LOW Pressure Compressor

HIGH Pressure Compressor

HIGH Pressure Compressor Drive Shaft

LOW Pressure Compressor Drive Shaft

Figure 132. The rotor of a two-spool axial-flow compressor

Some large turbojet and turbofan engines have increased efficiency by using two axial-flow compressors, each driven by its own turbine at its best operating speed. Figure 132 shows the rotor of such a compressor.

Combustors

The combustors, or burners, are some of the most highly engineered components in a turbine engine. The heat energy released inside these thin steel components is many thousand times greater than that released in any commercial furnace.

Only about one fourth of the air that flows through a turbine engine is used in the burning process; the rest is used for cooling. The air from the compressor flows through holes in the combustor walls and forms a film of air that prevents the flames from reaching the metal in the walls.

combustor. The section of a gas turbine engine in which the fuel is injected, mixed with air and burned. The intense heat from the combustion expands the air flowing through the combustor and directs it out through the turbine.

Turbines

The turbine is a form of windmill that extracts energy from the hot exhaust gases leaving the combustors. About 75% of the power developed by the turbine is used inside the engine to drive the compressor. The rest is available to drive a fan or propeller or to create the jet of hot gases that propels a jet airplane.

The stages of turbines are made up of a disk with a series of removable blades around its periphery. The turbine disk is attached to a shaft on which the compressor is mounted. Just ahead of the turbine disk is a set of turbine inlet guide vanes that straighten the hot gases as they leave the combustors and direct them into the turbine blades at the correct angle.

When more power is needed than can be supplied by a single stage of turbines, more stages are used. Some of the largest engines have as many as seven stages of turbines.

Exhaust Nozzle

The exhaust nozzle of a turbojet engine is a specially shaped duct attached to the rear of the engine that converts some of the velocity energy in the gases as they leave the engine into pressure.

Thrust Reverser

The exhaust nozzle on some turbojet and turbofan engines have thrust reversers in them. Soon after landing, the reversers are deployed to deflect some of the exhaust gases forward to slow the airplane before the brakes become fully effective. Thrust reversers produce a rearward thrust of between 40% and 50% of the engine's forward thrust.

Afterburner

The majority of the air that flows through a turbine engine is not involved in the combustion process and still contains its normal amount of oxygen. Military fighters and supersonic transport airplanes spray a large amount of fuel into this fast-moving stream of hot exhaust gas and ignite it. The resulting expansion of the gas increases the thrust by as much as 50%. Afterburners are used only when the large increase in thrust warrants the tremendous amount of fuel used to get this increase.

Chapter 45 **Turbine Engine Systems**

Ignition System

The fuel-air mixture inside a turbine engine burns continually and needs an ignition system only for starting and as a backup system in the event of a flameout at high altitude.

Two igniters which are similar to a special type of spark plug are installed in combustion chambers on opposite sides of the engine. High voltage, high energy pulses of electricity are generated in the ignition exciter units and sent to the igniters. Here an extremely high intensity spark jumps across electrodes and ignites the fuel-air mixture inside the combustor. When the fuel is ignited the ignition spark is discontinued.

Fuel Metering System

The tremendous amount of air flowing through a turbine engine demands a complex fuel metering system that can provide the correct amount of fuel to produce the power or thrust called for by the pilot without allowing the engine to flame out because of either an excess or deficiency of fuel.

The fuel control unit senses a number of parameters and integrates them to meter the fuel to the combustors for any desired power or thrust while ensuring the turbine inlet temperature does not exceed its allowable limits. The basic parameters sensed are:

Power lever angle—This is the input by the pilot specifying the amount of power or thrust desired.

Compressor inlet pressure—This relates to the density of the air entering the engine.

Compressor RPM—This is a measure of the steady-state operating conditions and limits the rate of acceleration or deceleration.

Combustor pressure—This relates to the weight of the air flowing through the engine.

Many modern turbine engines are equipped with Full-Authority Digital Electronic Control (FADEC) which is a highly precise digital electronic fuel control that functions during all engine operations. It includes the electronic engine control and functions with the flight management computer to meter the fuel to the nozzle in such a way that prevents overshooting of power changes and overtemperature conditions.

Lubrication System

Aircraft turbine engines do not have all the components needing lubrication that a piston engine has, so their lubrication system is far simpler. A special synthetic lubricating oil is used in turbine engines, and this is carried in a relatively small tank which may be part of the engine or mounted on the outside of the engine.

Oil flows from the tank to a pressure pump where its pressure is increased and it is filtered. Then it flows to nozzles that spray the oil into the bearings that support the compressor and turbine. Oil drains down from the bearings and is moved back to the oil tank by scavenger pumps.

Some engines have an oil cooler in the line between the pressure pump and the bearings while others have the cooler in the return lines between the scavenger pumps and the oil tank.

Cooling System

In a turbine engine, fuel is burned continually, releasing so much heat that it could destroy the engine if it were not removed.

Of the huge volume of air flowing through the engine, only about one fourth is used in the combustion process; the remainder is used for cooling. The cooling air flows through louvered slots or holes in the combustion chamber liners and forms a high-velocity film on either side of the metal of which the liners are made. This air carries the heat away before it can be absorbed into the metal.

The amount of power or thrust a turbine engine can produce is determined by the air temperature as it passes through the turbine inlet guide vanes and the first stage turbine blades. The higher this temperature, the greater the power. These guide vanes and turbine blades are made of materials that can sustain these high temperatures, but they also have air passages in them that allow cooling air to flow into them and exit through holes that form a film of cooling air over their surfaces to insulate them from the extreme heat.

It is only necessary to cool the inlet guide vanes and the first stage of turbine blades because the gases lose enough of their energy passing through the first stage that their temperature drops enough that it will not damage the following stages.

Starting System

A turbine engine is started by rotating the compressor with the starter until it is turning fast enough to move air through the engine and purge it of any fuel vapors that may have collected. The ignition is then energized, and when the engine has reached a specified RPM, fuel is sprayed into the combustors and the engine starts. As soon as it reaches a self-sustaining idle speed, the starter and the ignition system are deactivated. This start sequence is programmed so the pilot has only to initiate the action and the rest follows automatically.

The large turbofan engines on a jet transport airplane are started with an air turbine starter. A large volume of compressed air from the onboard auxiliary power unit (APU) or from a ground power unit (GPU) spins a high-speed turbine inside the starter. This turbine turns the starter drive shaft through a series of reduction gears to increase its torque. When the engine starts and reaches a self-sustaining speed, the output shaft turns faster than the turbine that was driving it, and centrifugal force disconnects the output shaft and holds it disconnected from the starter. An electrical solenoid valve then shuts off the air flow to the starter.

reduction gears. A gear arrangement in which the output shaft turns more slowly than the input shaft, used to increase the torque produced by the rotor of a turbine engine.

Small turbine engines are usually started with an electrical starter-generator. This is a special generator that has an extra set of windings in it, so it can act as a high-torque motor. When the start switch is placed in the START position, the automatic start sequence is put into action and current flows into the starter-generator which rotates the compressor. When the engine starts and reaches its self-sustaining speed, current is cut off to the starter windings, the ignition exciter is de-energized, and the generator output is connected to the aircraft electrical system.

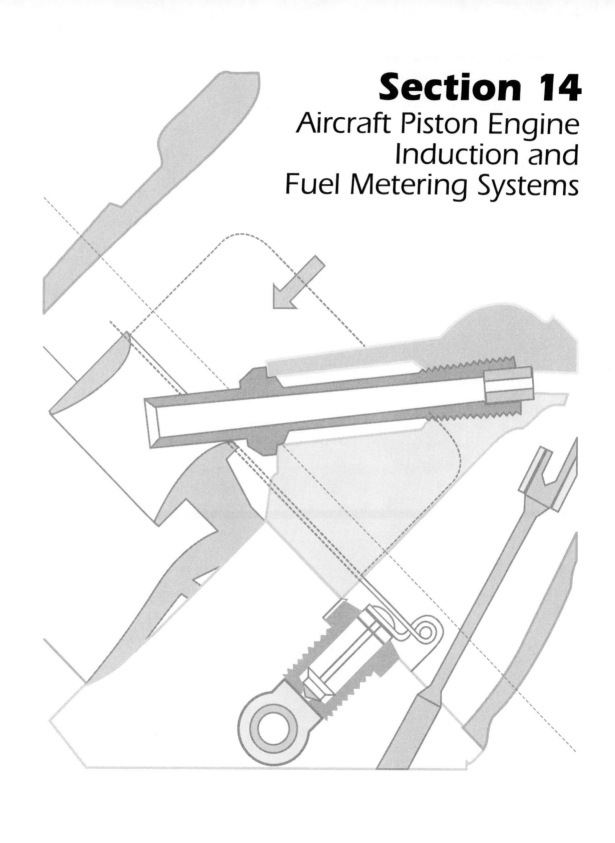

Section 14
Aircraft Piston Engine Induction and Fuel Metering Systems

Chapter 46 **Induction Systems**

An aircraft piston engine is an air-breathing engine, and in order to convert the chemical energy in the fuel into heat and then into mechanical energy, enough air must be taken into the cylinder to form a combustible mixture. A typical cruise mixture ratio requires about 15 pounds of air for every pound of fuel. This means that an engine burning 12 gallons of gasoline per hour at sea level must take in approximately 240 cubic feet of air per minute.

240 cubic feet of air is slightly more air than is in a six-foot cube.

Induction air is drawn into the engine by the low pressure caused by the pistons moving inward in each of the cylinders. It must pass through an air filter, then through the carburetor and through the intake pipe and into the cylinder through the intake valve. At full takeoff power the intake valve is open for only about 15 milliseconds (0.015 second) during each intake stroke.

To further complicate the picture, as the airplane goes up in altitude, the air becomes thinner (less dense) and more cubic feet of air must be taken into the engine each minute to get the proper weight of air to burn the fuel.

Unsupercharged Engines

The induction system of a naturally aspirated, or unsupercharged, engine consists of an air scoop, induction air filter, alternate air valve with a source of heat, fuel metering device and induction pipes to carry the fuel-air mixture into the cylinders.

naturally aspirated engine. A reciprocating engine that uses atmospheric pressure to force the charge of fuel-air mixture into the cylinders.

The air scoop converts some of the ram air pressure from the forward motion of the airplane into a pressure that forces the fuel-air mixture into the cylinders. A well-designed air scoop can increase the power of an engine by as much as 5%.

It is extremely important that the air entering the engine be filtered to remove dust and dirt particles that can drastically shorten the life of the engine. This is done with a replaceable filter in the inlet to the fuel metering system. This filter must be cleaned or replaced at all routine engine inspections and more often when operating under excessively dusty conditions.

Heated air taken into the carburetor is less dense than cold air and it is the volume, not the weight, of air flowing through the carburetor that determines the amount of fuel discharged. There are fewer pounds of air for the fuel and the mixture will become overly rich, the engine will lose power. A check to determine that the carburetor heat is operating properly is to momentarily apply carb heat during engine runup and note the drop in RPM.

Fuel injected engines do not have a problem with carburetor ice, but there is the possibility when flying through icing conditions that the induction air filter may ice over and shut off the air flowing into the engine. Fuel injected engines have an alternate air control that allows the pilot to switch the inlet air from the filter to warm air taken from a location inside the cowling.

Altitude Engines

For an airplane engine to produce its rated power at a high altitude the air must be compressed before it is taken into the cylinders.

supercharger. An air pump used to increase the pressure of the air taken into the cylinders of a reciprocating engine.

Some engines have a gear-driven supercharger. This is a centrifugal blower geared to turn faster than the crankshaft that takes the air after it passes through the fuel-metering system and compresses it before sending it to the cylinders.

Gear-driven superchargers take power from the crankshaft to drive the impeller but there is another type of supercharger that is more efficient—the turbocharger. Some engines have both a turbocharger and a supercharger.

Turbochargers

Turbocharger is a shortened name for exhaust-driven turbosupercharger.

About half of the energy in the fuel used in an aircraft engine is wasted as it leaves the engine in the hot exhaust gases. Some of this energy is salvaged by the turbocharger which uses the hot gases to spin a turbine which drives a centrifugal compressor in the induction system. The compressed air in the induction system increases manifold pressure so the engine can maintain sea-level power up to its critical altitude.

critical altitude. The maximum altitude at which a turbocharged aircraft engine can produce its rated takeoff power.

The turbine restricts the exhaust, causing the engine to lose some power, but the power gained by compressing the intake air more than overcomes this loss.

Turbocharger Controls

The pressure produced by a turbocharger is controlled by its speed; this is done by varying the amount of exhaust gas that flows through the turbine. Figure 133 shows a typical turbocharger control system.

Hot gases leave the cylinders through the exhaust valves and flow through the turbine, then overboard through the engine exhaust tail pipe. A "Y" in the exhaust pipe allows some of the hot gases to bypass the turbine and flow directly out of the tail pipe. The amount of gases that flow through this bypass is controlled by a hydraulically-operated waste gate valve. For starting and low-altitude operation the waste gate valve is fully open and very little gases flow through the turbine, but at altitude where the air density is low, the turbocharger controls sense the loss in manifold pressure and cause a flow of engine oil to begin closing the waste gate, forcing more of the exhaust to flow through the turbine. The compressor is on the same shaft as the spinning turbine and as the turbine speeds up the manifold pressure increases and forces more air into the cylinders. The turbocharger controls can maintain any power the pilot selects by controlling the position of the waste gate. When the engine reaches its critical altitude, the waste gate is fully closed and all of the gases flow through the turbine.

Some turbocharger controls are automatic, others manual, and some are fixed, limiting the amount of exhaust gas allowed to flow through the turbine.

manifold pressure. The absolute pressure inside the intake manifold that forces the fuel-air charge into the cylinders.

waste gate. A controllable butterfly valve in the exhaust pipe of a reciprocating engine equipped with an exhaust-driven turbocharger. When the waste gate is open, the exhaust gases leave the engine through the exhaust pipe; but when closed, the gases must pass through the turbine that drives the turbocharger compressor. By controlling the opening of the waste gate, the speed of the turbocharger can be controlled, and this speed determines the manifold pressure in the engine.

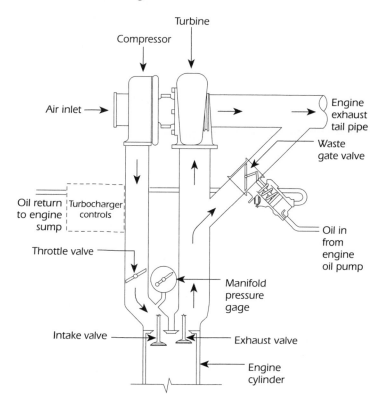

Figure 133. A typical turbocharger system

Chapter 47 **Fuel Metering Systems**

Liquid gasoline will not burn, but its vapors are highly flammable. For gasoline to release its energy inside the engine it must first be vaporized then mixed with the proper amount of air, compressed and ignited at the proper instant by a spark from a spark plug.

Either of two devices may be used on modern airplane engines to measure the air entering the engine and meter the correct amount of fuel into it. These are float carburetors and fuel injection systems.

Float Carburetors

Aircraft float-type carburetors are relatively simple but must perform their functions flawlessly. They must measure the air that flows into the engine and meter the correct amount of fuel for the air. Then they must spray this fuel into the air in the form of tiny droplets so it will rapidly evaporate and form a combustible vapor. This vapor must then be carried from the carburetor to the cylinder heads through thin-wall metal tubes. When the intake valve opens, this vapor and air is pulled into the cylinder, compressed, and ignited.

Float carburetors have two main limitations: they are susceptible to carburetor ice, and the difference in the length and configuration of the intake pipes between the carburetor and the cylinders prevents the mixture being uniform among all of the cylinders.

Main Metering System

A float carburetor gets its name from a metal or plastic float that actuates a needle valve that controls the level of fuel in the float bowl. When the fuel level drops, the needle valve moves off its seat and allows fuel to flow into the bowl. This maintains the fuel level at a specified distance from the discharge nozzle. *See* Figure 134.

venturi. *A specially shaped restriction in an air passage that is designed to speed up the flow of air. As the air speeds up its pressure drops.*

Air flows through the carburetor air filter upward into the engine through the venturis. As air flows through a venturi it speeds up, and as a result its pressure drops and at the narrowest part the pressure is the lowest. Note that there are two venturis in Figure 134: the discharge of the smaller, or boost, venturi is at the narrowest part of the main venturi, and the fuel discharge nozzle is at the narrowest part of the boost venturi.

Not shown in Figure 134, but located just above the main venturi, is a circular flat-plate valve that is actuated by the throttle control in the cockpit. When the throttle is forward (for full power) the butterfly valve is parallel with the air flow and the maximum amount of air flows into the engine. When the throttle is pulled back to idle, the valve is almost closed and only a minimum amount of air flows into the cylinders. The position of the throttle valve controls the amount of air that can enter the engine which determines the low pressure at the discharge nozzle, and thus the amount of fuel metered into the air.

After the fuel passes through the metering jet at the bottom of the discharge tube, a measured amount of air bleeds into the fuel to break it up into tiny droplets so it will evaporate just as soon as it gets into the air flowing into the engine.

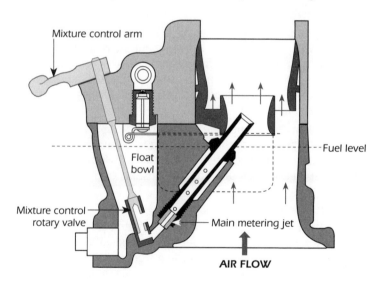

Figure 134. The metering system of a float carburetor

Idling System

The low pressure that pulls the fuel from the main metering jet requires a certain volume of air to flow through the venturis. When the engine is idling there is not enough airflow for the main metering system to operate.

All of the air that flows into the cylinders at idling must flow around the edges of the almost closed throttle valve. At this point the air velocity is high and the pressure is low. The idling system acts much like a small carburetor that takes its fuel from the float bowl and discharges it at the edge of the throttle valve.

The idling RPM and the idling mixture must be adjusted by an AMT so the engine will operate smoothly at the proper speed.

As soon as the throttle is partially opened, the pressure of the air flowing past the edge of the throttle valve rises and no more fuel is discharged from the idling system.

Acceleration System

There is normally a momentary lack of fuel flow between the time the idling system stops working and the time enough air flows through the venturis for the main metering system to discharge fuel. To prevent this interruption of fuel and the hesitation it causes, an acceleration system is incorporated in the carburetor.

Usually a pump, operated by the throttle, sprays an additional spurt of fuel into the air flowing into the engine when the throttle is opened suddenly. This fuel provides a momentarily rich mixture that prevents the hesitation.

Mixture Control

rich mixture. An air-fuel mixture that contains less than 15 parts of air to 1 part of fuel, by weight.

lean mixture. An air-fuel mixture that contains more than 15 parts of air to 1 part of fuel, by weight.

For aviation gasoline to release the maximum amount of its energy, it must be mixed with air on the basis of the *weight* of the air. But the amount of fuel drawn from the float bowl is determined by the *volume* of air flowing into the engine. As the airplane goes up in altitude, the air becomes less dense. The volume of air remains the same, but its weight decreases and therefore more fuel is metered into the air than at low altitude. The mixture becomes overly rich (too much fuel for the air) and the engine loses power.

Aircraft carburetors are equipped with a mixture control that allows the pilot to manually decrease the amount of fuel going to the cylinders without affecting the amount of air. The mixture may thus be leaned as the altitude increases to allow the engine to produce all the power it can with the reduced weight of air.

Power Enrichment System

Aircraft piston engines are designed in such a way that they can absorb or dissipate only a specific amount of heat, and when more than this amount is released by the fuel the engine may be damaged. The cooling and lubrication systems take care of most of this heat but there is another important way that some of this heat is removed.

When the throttle is fully open and the maximum amount of power is being produced (the maximum amount of heat is being released), a system inside the carburetor adds additional fuel to the air. When this extra fuel evaporates, it drops the temperature of the air and absorbs some of the heat that would otherwise damage the engine. This action is called power enrichment.

Carburetor Heat

One of the major problems with a float carburetor is its susceptibility to carburetor ice. When gasoline evaporates it removes heat from the air, and the gasoline that evaporates in the venturi of a carburetor can cause a temperature drop of about 70°F. When the humidity is high, the temperature drop in the air passing through the carburetor will cause moisture to condense from the air and freeze. This ice can restrict the flow of air through the carburetor enough to cause the engine to quit.

To prevent the formation of carburetor ice, heated air from around some exhaust system component, such as the muffler, is directed into the carburetor. Care must be taken when using carburetor heat because this air is not filtered and should not be used on the ground where sand can enter the engine. Also, when carburetor heat is used during full-power operation there is a possibility that the induction air will be so hot that detonation can occur.

Heated air taken into the carburetor is less dense than cold air and it is the volume, not the weight, of air flowing through the carburetor that determines the amount of fuel discharged. There are fewer pounds of air for the amount of fuel so the mixture will become overly rich; therefore the engine will lose power. A check to determine that the carburetor heat is operating properly is to momentarily apply it during engine runup and note the drop in RPM.

detonation. An explosion or uncontrolled burning of the fuel in the cylinder of an engine when the temperature or the pressure of the fuel reaches its critical value. Detonation can destroy an engine.

Fuel Injection Systems

The two limitations of the float carburetor, that is, susceptibility to carburetor ice, and uneven fuel-air mixture distribution between the cylinders, are problems that are both eliminated with fuel injection systems.

The intake pipes in a fuel injected engine carry only air, and the metered fuel is discharged from nozzles in the cylinder head right at the intake valve. This hot location ensures immediate evaporation so there is no danger of ice forming.

The fuel lines between the fuel manifold and the cylinders are all the same length; therefore every cylinder receives exactly the same fuel charge, and all have the same mixture ratio.

Aircraft engine fuel injection systems are different from the electronic fuel injection systems used in automobiles and the injection systems for diesel engines. Aircraft engines use low-pressure, constant-flow systems that instead of sending a timed high-pressure spurt of fuel into the cylinder, send a constant flow of atomized fuel into the intake valve cavity of the cylinder head, just outside of the intake valve. The heat at this point vaporizes the fuel and when the intake valve opens, the fuel vapors are drawn into the cylinder along with fresh air from the intake pipe. The fuel vapor and air mix, and then inside the cylinder are compressed and ignited.

There are two types of fuel injection systems used on modern general aviation airplanes: the Precision Airmotive RSA fuel injection system and the Teledyne-Continental (TCM) fuel injection system. They do the same thing, but in slightly different ways.

Precision Airmotive RSA Fuel Injection System

This system, formerly the Bendix system, meters the fuel on the basis of the volume and density of air entering the engine. The air flowing into the engine is controlled by the throttle air valve as it is in a float carburetor. On the way to the cylinders the volume of the air is sensed by a venturi tube and the density is sensed by impact tubes. These two pressures act on an air diaphragm in the servo regulator.

Fuel from the engine fuel pump passes through a strainer in the fuel control unit and then through a mixture control valve which allows the pilot to lean the mixture as the air becomes less dense at altitude. From the mixture control it flows through the main metering jet which limits the amount of fuel that can flow to the engine during times of full-throttle, full-rich operation. From the main metering jet the fuel flows to the throttle fuel valve. This metering valve is linked with the throttle air valve so they open and close together.

Fuel pressure between the mixture control and the main metering jet is called unmetered fuel pressure and it acts on one side of a fuel diaphragm in the fuel control. The metered fuel, after it leaves the throttle valve, flows into the servo regulator on the opposite side of the fuel diaphragm from the unmetered fuel pressure. It then flows through the servo valve to the flow divider and then to the nozzles in the cylinder heads.

The amount of fuel allowed to flow to the flow divider is determined by a balance between two air metering forces and two fuel metering forces. The venturi and impact tube pressures work together to open the servo valve an amount

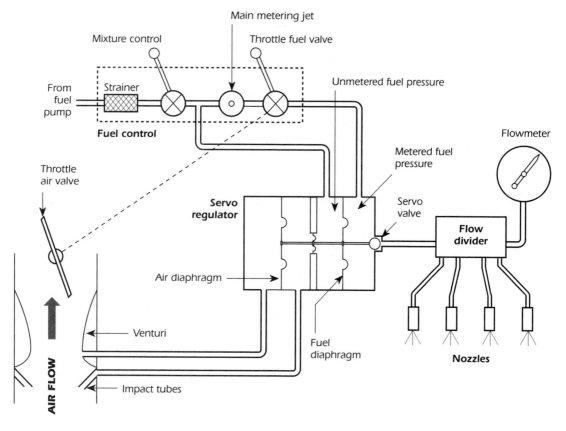

Figure 135. Simplified diagram of the RSA fuel injection system

proportional to the amount of air flowing into the engine. The unmetered fuel pressure acting on the fuel diaphragm creates a force on the servo valve that senses any fluctuations in the fuel pump pressure. The metered fuel pressure works with the air pressures to open the servo valve an amount determined by the throttle valve position and the amount of air entering the engine.

The flow divider is a spring-loaded valve that remains closed to shut off all fuel to the cylinders until the pressure from the servo regulator reaches a preset value, then it opens and sends fuel equally to all the cylinders. When the mixture control is put in the IDLE CUTOFF position, the pressure drops and the flow divider positively and instantly shuts off all fuel to the cylinders.

The fuel flowmeter used with aircraft fuel injected engines is actually a pressure gage that measures the pressure drop across the injector nozzles. This pressure is directly proportional to the amount of fuel flowing to all the nozzles. One problem with this type of system is that a clogged nozzle will restrict the amount of fuel that flows to the cylinders, but it will indicate on the flowmeter as an increased flow.

The injector nozzles are of the air bleed type. The fuel flows through a calibrated orifice in the nozzle and an air bleed hole allows air to mix with this fuel before it leaves the nozzle. This ensures that an emulsion of fuel and air is discharged rather than a stream of liquid fuel.

Teledyne-Continental Fuel Injection System

This TCM system does the same thing as the RSA system, but it determines the amount of fuel going to the cylinders by the RPM of the engine and the position of the mixture control and throttle.

The engine driven fuel pump is the heart of this system. Fuel enters the pump from an auxiliary fuel pump in the aircraft fuel system. It flows into the pump in such a way that any vapors trapped in the fuel are slung out by centrifugal action. The fuel then flows into a vane-type pump where its pressure is increased proportional to the engine speed. The fuel then flows to the fuel-air control unit.

The actual pressure produced by this pump is controlled by a relief valve and an adjustable orifice. These devices are in series with each other, but are in parallel with the pump. For idling, when the pump is putting out a small volume of fuel, the spring-loaded relief valve controls the pressure. It relieves back to the inlet side of the pump all pressure above the low-unmetered fuel pressure specified in the aircraft maintenance manual. When the engine is running at a high speed, this relief valve is completely off its seat and the high-unmetered fuel pressure is determined by the setting of the adjustable orifice. These two pressures are critical and must be adjusted by an AMT.

In the fuel-air control unit the fuel flows through a filter and then into the mixture control valve. This valve is actually a variable selector valve. For FULL RICH operation it sends all of the fuel to the main metering jet. In the IDLE CUTOFF position it sends all of the fuel back into the pump and the engine stops. The mixture control allows the pilot to vary the fuel flow for conditions between CUTOFF and FULL RICH to compensate for changes in air density with altitude. The fuel that flows back to the pump from the mixture control passes through a venturi in the top of the fuel inlet chamber creating a low pressure that pulls any vapors from this chamber. The fuel then flows back to one of the fuel tanks. It is important that fuel be used from this tank first so the return fuel will not cause it to overflow. The POH is very specific about this.

From the mixture control the fuel flows to the main metering jet which limits the amount of fuel that can flow to the cylinders during full throttle, full rich operation. The throttle fuel valve and throttle air valve are linked together so the amount of air and fuel can be regulated together.

The manifold valve in this system serves the same function as the flow divider in the RSA system and the flowmeter works in the same way as it does in the RSA system.

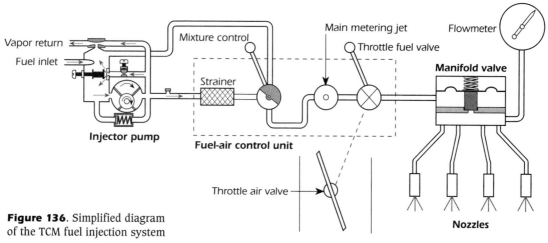

Figure 136. Simplified diagram of the TCM fuel injection system

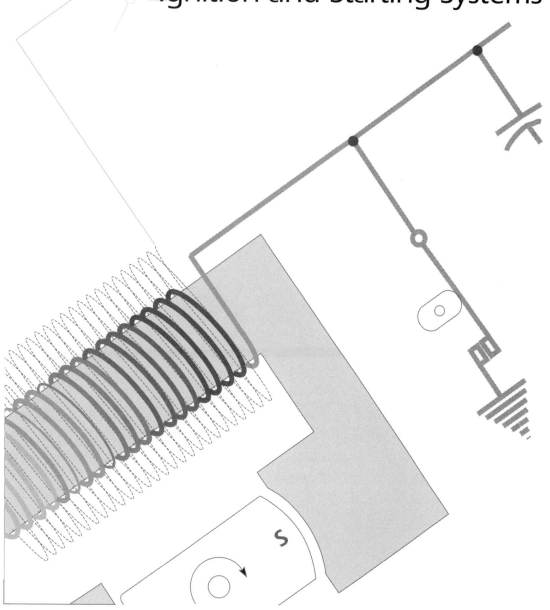

Section 15
Aircraft Piston Engine
Ignition and Starting Systems

Chapter 48 **Aircraft Magnetos**

Modern aircraft piston engines are spark-ignition engines that ignite the fuel-air mixture inside the cylinder with an electric spark. Almost all automobiles also use spark-ignition engines but they use electrical current from the battery to produce the spark. Aircraft engines use small, self-contained alternating current generators called magnetos to produce their sparks. The magnetos are completely independent of the aircraft electrical system and will continue to provide ignition even when the aircraft electrical system is turned off.

Before going too far in discussing the ignition system, it would be advantageous to review a few pertinent facts about electricity itself.

- When electrical current flows in a wire, a magnetic field surrounds the wire.

- When a wire passes through a magnetic field, current is caused to flow in the wire (electrons move through the wire).

- The electrical pressure that causes the flow of current is determined by the rate at which the wire moves through the magnetic field.

Operating Principles

There are three engine-driven rotating elements inside a magneto: the magnet, the cam, and the distributor finger. The magnet rotates inside a laminated soft iron frame and as it rotates, lines of magnetic flux pass through the iron and create a magnetic field that surrounds the coils of wire wound on part of the frame. As the magnet rotates, this field alternately builds up and collapses, producing alternating current in the coil of heavy wire in the primary circuit. When the breaker points are closed, the primary circuit is complete and current flows to ground. *See* Figure 137 on the next page.

When the cam opens the breaker points, the current can no longer flow to ground. Therefore the magnetic field collapses and the flux cuts across the many wire turns in the secondary winding of the coil. A very high voltage is produced in the secondary circuit and is carried to the finger of the distributor. From the distributor, it is directed to the correct spark plug through a shielded spark plug lead. The high voltage causes a spark to jump across the electrodes in the spark plug and ignite the fuel-air mixture.

magneto. *A small, self-contained electrical generator and a step-up transformer for ignition. A set of breaker points, timed to the crankshaft, interrupts the flow of current in the primary winding. This interruption induces a high voltage in the secondary winding at the proper time for a spark to occur at the spark plug inside the cylinder. If the aircraft electrical system fails completely, the engine will continue to run.*

primary winding. *The winding made of heavy wire in the step-up transformer inside a magneto. Current is induced into the primary winding by the rotating magnet.*

secondary winding. *The winding made of many turns of fine wire in the step-up transformer inside a magneto. When the breaker points interrupt the flow of current in the primary winding, its magnetic field collapses and induces a very high voltage in the secondary winding.*

The capacitor acts as an electronic shock absorber and helps the magnetic field collapse rapidly. It also prevents an arc from forming between the breaker points as they are opening.

The ignition switch is in the primary circuit and when the switch is OFF, it is closed; therefore the primary current goes directly to ground rather than through the breaker points and no spark is produced. This causes a safety hazard. If the wire between the magneto and the ignition switch (the P-lead) is broken or disconnected, the magneto cannot be grounded and is always "hot," so a cylinder could fire if the propeller were turned. When turning a propeller by hand, always consider the magnetos to be ON regardless of the position of the ignition switch.

Aircraft engines have dual ignition. This means that there are two independent ignition systems each having a magneto,

P-lead. The primary lead, or the wire that connects the primary circuit of a magneto to ground when the magneto is OFF.

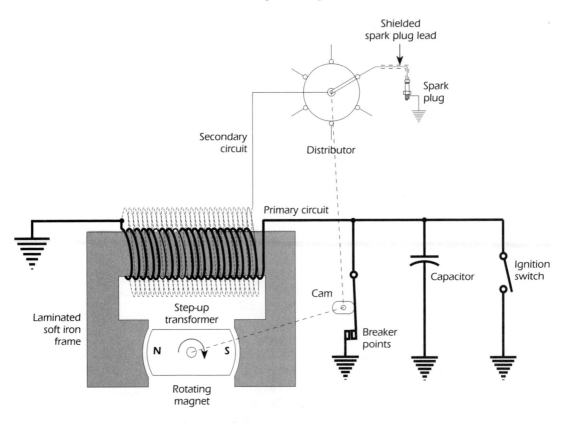

Figure 137. Operating principle of an aircraft magneto

a distributor and a spark plug in each cylinder. Some engines have a double magneto. This is a single magneto housing with one rotating magnet and cam but two of every other component.

Two spark plugs are used in each cylinder as a safety feature, but more important, they provide more efficient combustion. By igniting the fuel-air mixture at two locations, each flame has only half the distance to travel and the mixture inside the cylinder can be burned more rapidly than it could if ignited by only one spark plug.

> One purpose of the dual ignition system on an aircraft engine is to provide for improved engine performance.

Auxiliary Systems for Starting

One of the major shortcomings of a magneto is that the intensity of the spark produced is determined by the speed of the rotating magnet. When the engine is being started, the magnet rotates slowly and the spark is too weak to ignite the cold fuel-air mixture. There are two systems in use to provide a hot and late spark for starting: the impulse coupling and the induction vibrator system.

To review the five events in an aircraft engine operating cycle, remember that the spark normally occurs when the piston is approximately 30 degrees of crankshaft rotation before it reaches top center on the compression stroke. When the engine is turning very slowly for starting, a spark occurring at this point would cause the engine to kick back and it would not begin to run. To prevent this, the ignition for starting must be retarded so it does not occur until the piston has passed over its top center position and has started down on the power stroke.

> The five events in an aircraft engine operating cycle include intake, compression, ignition, power, and exhaust.

Impulse Coupling

An impulse coupling is a spring-loaded coupling between one of the magnetos and the engine that prevents the magnet from turning until the spring is wound up tight, allowing the piston to pass over top center. Then the spring is released and spins the magnet fast enough for it to produce a hot and late spark for starting. When the engine starts, centrifugal force holds the impulse coupling disconnected and the engine operates with its normally advanced spark timing.

Induction Vibrator Starting System

This system is best known by the name "Shower of Sparks." On engines equipped with this system, the left magneto has two sets of breaker points connected in parallel. The RUN points open at the correct time for the spark to occur with the normal advance. The other set, called the RETARD points, does not open until the piston has passed over top center and has started down.

The ignition switch used with this system has these positions: OFF, LEFT, RIGHT, BOTH, and a spring-loaded START position.

When the switch is in the START position, the right magneto is grounded (OFF), and a battery-operated vibrator produces pulsating direct current that is sent to the primary circuit of the left magneto and to ground through both sets of breaker points. It continues to go to ground through the RETARD points after the RUN points are open, but when the crankshaft has turned enough for the piston to be past top center, the RETARD points open and the pulsating current goes to ground through the primary winding in the magneto coil. This induces a high voltage in the secondary winding which causes a continuous spark between the electrodes of the spark plugs (thus the name Shower of Sparks) until the RUN points close.

When the ignition switch is returned to the BOTH position, the vibrator is deactivated and the engine runs with both magnetos operating.

Chapter 49 **Ignition Leads**

The high-voltage current in the secondary winding between the magneto distributor and spark plugs acts exactly as a radio signal and radiates out from any conductor through which it flows. This signal interferes with the communications and navigation equipment in the aircraft.

To prevent this interference, the ignition leads are encased in a braided metal shield that intercepts the radiated energy and directs it to ground. The shielding is covered with a plastic coating that protects it from abrasion or other damage. It is important that ignition leads be protected from excessive heat by ensuring that they do not touch a hot exhaust pipe, and they should not have any sharp bends that could break down the insulation.

The braided metal shielding around the ignition leads grounds the radiated energy and prevents ignition system interference with the aircraft avionics systems.

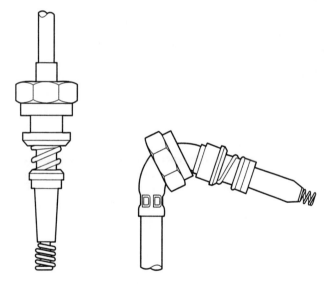
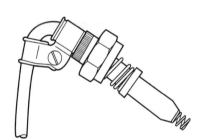

Figure 138. Spark plug terminals on ignition leads

Chapter 50 **Aircraft Spark Plugs**

Recess for
all-weather
seal

3/4–20
threads

Insulator

Resistor

Copper-filled
conductor

Fine-wire
center
electrode

Fine-wire ground electrode

Figure 139. A shielded aircraft spark plug

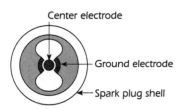

Center electrode

Ground electrode

Spark plug shell

Figure 140. The electrodes of a massive electrode aircraft spark plug

Aircraft spark plugs are simple, but extremely important components in an aircraft engine. They operate in a hostile environment and can tolerate very little damage from mishandling.

Types of Spark Plugs

Figure 139 shows a fine-wire electrode shielded spark plug that is typical of those used on high-performance aircraft piston engines. The case of this spark plug is made of steel and inside is a special ceramic insulator. Imbedded in this insulator is a copper-filled conductor with a fine wire tip made of iridium or platinum to withstand the extremely high temperatures inside the cylinders. One or more ground electrodes also made of iridium or platinum wire are swaged into the rim of the spark plug body.

The ignition lead is terminated with a plastic or ceramic cigarette that has a stainless-steel coil spring which contacts the conductor inside the insulator. *See* Figure 138 (on previous page). A rubber seal surrounds the ignition lead that fits into the recess in the top of the spark plug body to prevent moisture from getting into the spark plug terminal cavity. A nut on the lead screws onto the threads to form a rain proof and electrically-sound connection.

A resistor inside the spark plug between the lead and the center electrode stops the flow of current across the electrodes after the initial spark occurs. The shielding around the ignition lead acts as a capacitor and stores electrical energy that is radiated from the lead while current is flowing, and then returns it when the current from the magneto stops. The resistor stops the extra current and prolongs the life of the electrodes.

There are two basic types of electrodes in aircraft spark plugs: massive electrodes and fine-wire electrodes.

Spark plugs with massive electrodes, like those in Figure 140 are used in many aircraft engines that do not have a problem with lead fouling. These spark plugs are available with two, three, or four ground electrodes. These spark plugs are relatively inexpensive, but there is not enough open space for the lead-rich gases to be purged from around the center electrode and they become fouled with lead deposits.

Fine-wire electrode spark plugs like that in Figure 141 are used in engines in which lead fouling is a problem. The center electrode is a fine round wire made of platinum or iridium and the ground electrodes are square wires made of platinum or iridium. These small electrodes leave an open space that allows all of the lead-rich gases to be purged from the nose cavity of the spark plug. This prevents the spark plug from becoming fouled with lead deposits.

Fine-wire spark plugs cost several times more than those with massive electrodes but they will operate successfully in engines that cannot use the less expensive spark plug.

Spark Plug Servicing

The spark plugs are normally removed and cleaned on each annual or 100-hour inspection. Their appearance tells much about the condition of the cylinder from which they are taken.

The AMT removes the leads from each spark plug and carefully pulls the cigarette out so as not to crack it or the ceramic insulation inside the spark plug. Then he or she removes all the spark plugs and places them in a tray with numbered holes to identify the spark plug with the cylinder from which it came.

The insulator of a normally operating spark plug is covered with a brown deposit and there is normally some hard lead deposits in the cavity. The gap between the ground electrode and the center electrode will have increased until it is slightly wider than it should be.

If the electrodes show abnormal wear, there is a possibility that the cylinder from which the spark plug was taken has experienced detonation and the AMT should examine the cylinder carefully for other indication of damage.

If the nose cavity has an excessive amount of black fluffy carbon, the cylinder has probably been operating with too rich a mixture which indicates problems with the carburetor or fuel injection system.

Black and oily deposits indicate that the engine is pumping too much oil and the AMT will check for worn piston rings or worn valve guides.

When the firing-end cavity is filled with a hard, brittle deposit, the engine is not accommodating the amount of tetraethyl lead in the fuel causing these deposits to form. They can completely fill the cavity and provide a path for the high voltage to leak to ground without causing a spark.

Lead deposits are removed with a vibrator type cleaner that chips the contaminants out without damaging the nose core insulator. After the lead deposits are all out, the nose cavity is

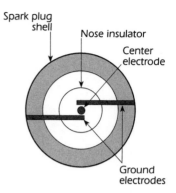

Figure 141. The electrodes of a fine-wire electrode aircraft spark plug

blasted with an abrasive to remove all the remaining deposits and clean the nose insulator. Then the gaps between the ground electrodes and the center electrode are adjusted by carefully moving the ground electrodes over until the distance between the electrodes is that specified by the engine manufacturer. The spark plugs are then tested to be sure they will spark when under pressure and a specified AC voltage is applied across the electrodes. If they pass this test they will spark properly in the engine.

When replacing the spark plugs in an engine, always replace them in the cylinder next in firing order from the cylinder from which they were removed, and replace the ones removed from the top of the cylinder to the bottom of the cylinder and vice versa.

As the sparks jump between the electrodes, metal is eroded from either the ground or center electrode depending upon the polarity of the sparks. This polarity reverses with each spark, and by replacing the spark plugs in the cylinder, next in firing order, the erosion of the electrodes is evened out.

The spark plugs in the bottom of the cylinders usually foul first and by replacing them from top to bottom and bottom to top, the amount of cleaning needed is evened out among all of the plugs.

New solid copper gaskets are put on the plug and a small amount of antiseize compound is applied to the threads. This prevents them from seizing in the cylinder head and being difficult to remove for the next inspection. The spark plugs are then screwed into the cylinder head and tightened with a torque wrench. The cigarettes are cleaned with a solvent such as acetone and put into the spark plug and the nut is tightened snugly.

It is extremely important that the proper spark plugs be used when any are replaced. The AMT has information that lists the spark plugs approved for the engine and these must be used.

Aircraft spark plugs are critical elements of engine performance. Only the specific spark plug approved for an engine should ever be used as a replacement.

Spark plugs are classified by:

Size: 14 or 18 mm

Electrodes: Fine wire or massive

Shielding: 5/8 – 24 thread or 3/4 – 20 thread

Resistor or no resistor

Reach: Length of the threads that screw into the cylinder head

Heat range: This is most important as it relates to the ability of the spark plug to resist fouling

Chapter 51 **Piston Engine
Starting Systems**

Large radial engines of World War II vintage used inertia starters in which the starter motor spun a heavy flywheel to a high speed. When the flywheel reached its peak speed, it was disengaged from the motor and engaged with the crankshaft. The energy stored in the flywheel turned the crankshaft fast enough for the engine to start. When more powerful electric motors were developed, direct-cranking starters became popular.

The starter used with a modern aircraft piston engine is a heavy duty electric motor with a special clutch drive that engages the crankshaft when the starter switch is placed in the START position. As soon as the engine starts and the crankshaft turns faster than the starter, the clutch disengages and current is shut off to the starter motor.

There are two popular types of starters used on modern general aviation aircraft: starters using a Bendix drive, and those using a helical spring drive.

Figure 142. The large gear at the propeller end of the engine is the starter gear that is turned by the starter mounted on the engine crankcase.

Starters With a Bendix Drive

Many Lycoming engines have a large starter gear around the propeller end of the crankshaft with the starter motor bolted to the crankcase. The starter for these engines uses a Bendix drive clutch.

When the starter switch is placed in the START position, the starter motor turns and the Bendix drive pinion (*see* Figure 143), moves forward on the helical splines, engages the large starter gear and turns the engine crankshaft. This stretches the Bendix drive spring. When the engine starts and drives the pinion faster than the starter motor, the drive spring and the helical splines pull the pinion out of engagement with the starter gear. Releasing the starter switch stops the starter motor.

Starters With a Helical Spring Drive

Many of the large Continental engines have a starter with a right-angle drive adapter which uses a helical spring drive as seen in Figure 144.

The starter shaft gear meshes with a gear on the accessory end of the crankshaft and turns with it at all times. This shaft has a knurled starter-clutch drum that rides inside, but does not touch a helical spring.

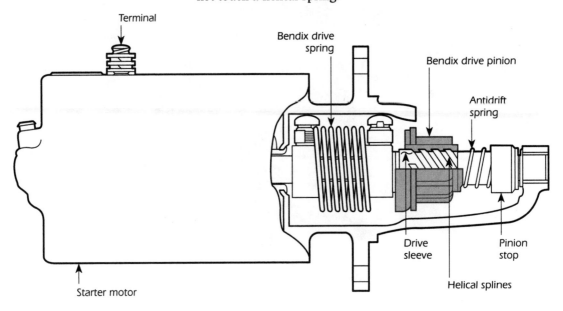

Figure 143. An aircraft engine starter using a Bendix drive

The starter motor has a worm gear on its shaft that engages the worm-gear wheel inside the starter adapter housing. When the starter switch is placed in the START position, the starter motor drives the worm-gear wheel and the helical spring. Friction between the outside of the spring and the inside of a sleeve in the adapter housing causes the spring to wind up, decreasing its inside diameter enough for it to grip the starter shaft drum. This locks the worm gear wheel to the starter shaft which turns the crankshaft. As soon as the engine starts, the starter shaft turns faster than the worm-gear wheel and the spring unwinds, increasing its diameter so that it no longer grips the clutch drum. Releasing the starter switch stops the starter motor.

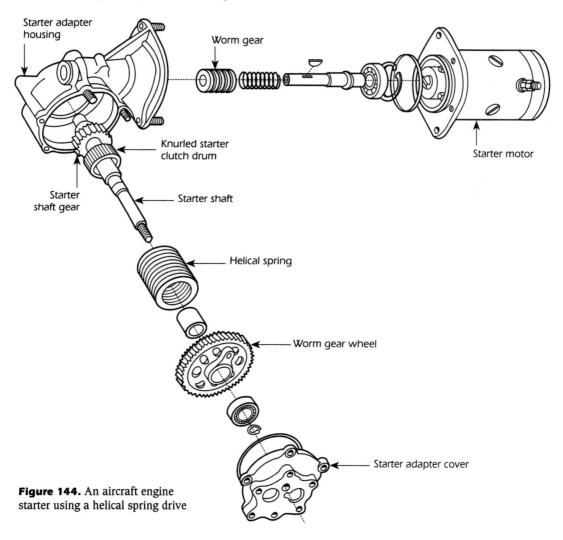

Starter adapter housing

Worm gear

Knurled starter clutch drum

Starter motor

Starter shaft gear

Starter shaft

Helical spring

Worm gear wheel

Starter adapter cover

Figure 144. An aircraft engine starter using a helical spring drive

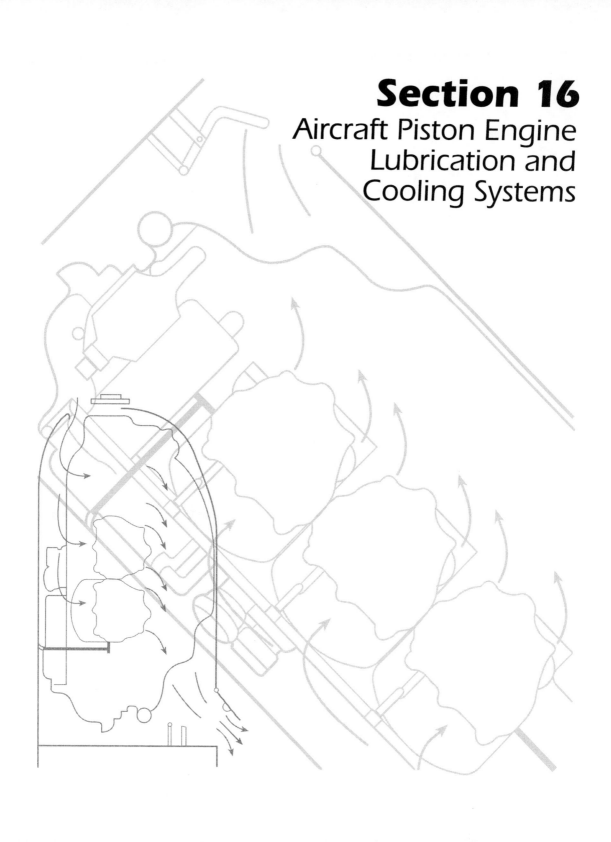

Section 16
Aircraft Piston Engine Lubrication and Cooling Systems

Chapter 52 **Aircraft Engine Lubricating Oil**

The lubrication system is one of the more important systems in an aircraft engine as the life and reliability of the engine depends upon it. There are two basic types of lubrication systems used in aircraft piston engines: dry sump and wet sump.

A dry sump engine carries its supply of oil in a reservoir, or oil tank, external to the engine. Oil is taken from the tank, pumped through the engine and returned to the tank through an oil cooler. A wet sump engine carries all the oil supply in the engine itself. It is held in a sump, or oil pan, which is a compartment at the bottom of the crankcase. Oil is taken from the sump and forced through the bearings by the oil pump and then it drains back into the sump.

Types of Oil

The oil used in an aircraft engine is a special blend of mineral oil and additives that improves its stability and adjusts its viscosity. Its weight, or ability to flow, is measured in terms of SAE numbers or commercial numbers with the lower number indicating the lighter viscosity.

Automobile engine oil should not be used in an aircraft engine because it is formulated for different operating conditions. It is normally recommended that new and freshly overhauled aircraft engines be operated for the first few hours with a MIL-L-6082 straight mineral oil that has no additives. This allows the engine parts to wear the initial roughness off their surfaces. After this initial break-in period, the oil and the filter are changed and the recommended grade of MIL-L-22851 ashless-dispersant (AD) oil is used.

AD oil has additives that hold all of the carbon and other contaminants suspended in the oil until they are trapped in the filter element. In just a few hours of operation AD oil will be quite black with these contaminants. This is good because it means that the oil is doing its job.

Detergent oils have been successfully used in automobile engines for years but are not suitable for aircraft engines. Detergent oils contain ash-forming additives that improve their antioxidation characteristics, but ash deposits can build up in the cylinders and absorb enough heat to cause preigni-

SAE (Society of Automotive Engineers). *A professional organization that formulates standards for the automotive and aviation industries.*

MIL standards. *A group of standard specifications used by the United States military services to describe the products they buy. MIL standards are known and used by most manufacturers to keep parts standardized and interchangeable.*

tion. The additives used in these oils have a strong detergent action that loosens sludge and carbon deposits which could then flow through the lubrication system and clog oil passages and filters.

Multiviscosity oil is used in most modern aircraft engines because of the wide range in operating temperatures encountered. When an oil is cold it is viscous, or acts like a heavy syrup, but when it gets hot it becomes thinner, more like water. For this reason, in the winter a low-viscosity oil such as SAE 20 would be recommended and in the summer time, a heavy oil like SAE 50 would be recommended. A multiviscosity oil, SAE 20W50 has special additives that stabilize the viscosity. When it is cold it acts like cold SAE 20 oil and when it is hot, it acts like hot SAE 50 oil.

You will see some aircraft engine oil referred to with a Grade number rather than an SAE number. This is a number for commercial aviation and is generally twice the SAE number. *See* Figure 145.

Turbine engines have different operating conditions from piston engines and use a synthetic base oil. Some synthetic oil has been used in piston engines, but it is not a good idea to use it unless it has been specifically approved for your engine.

SAE	Commercial Aviation	Military
SAE 5W		
SAE 10W	Grade 20	
SAE 20W		
SAE 20	Grade 40	
SAE 30	Grade 65	MIL 1065
SAE 15W50	SAE 15W50	
SAE 40	Grade 80	MIL 1080
SAE 20W50	SAE 20W50	
SAE 25W60	SAE 25W60	
SAE 50	Grade 100	MIL 1100
SAE 60	Grade 120	MIL 1120

Figure 145. Comparison of lubricating oil ratings

Chapter 53 **Lubrication System Servicing**

The POH specifies the grade and amount of oil that should be carried in the engine. It is not customary to keep the oil sump completely full for local or short duration flights because of the engine's tendency to blow some oil out through the crankcase breather. But do not start any flight with less than the minimum amount specified in the POH as the oil will not have an opportunity to lose the heat it absorbs, will get too hot and the oil pressure will drop.

An abnormally high engine oil temperature indication may be caused by the oil level being too low. There is not enough oil to adequately carry the heat away from the engine.

When adding oil, use only the grade specified for the existing ambient temperature. It is not important that the same brand of oil be used, but it is important that the oil has the same MIL spec. number as the oil in the engine.

Engine Oil Change

It is important to change the engine oil at the number of hours and/or the calendar time specified in the POH. When the airplane is not flown regularly or not flown for a long enough time to allow the engine oil to get completely hot, moisture can accumulate in the oil forming acids that are harmful to the engine. If the airplane is not to be flown for weeks or months, it is an unwise procedure to run it up on the ground for a few minutes. This would ensure that the oil would become contaminated and would lead to cylinder wall rust.

Short ground runs are not good for an engine. The oil does not get hot enough to adequately lubricate the moving parts and water can condense in the oil to form acids which cause steel parts to rust.

When the oil is drained and the filter replaced, it is a wise procedure for the AMT to cut the filter open, unfold the filter element and examine it for any indication of metal chips. New and freshly overhauled engines typically have some very fine hairlike threads of aluminum in the filter from engine parts that are wearing to fit, but any chunks of metal, and especially any particles that are attracted to a magnet, are warning signs of impending engine failure.

Many airplane owners and operators subscribe to a spectrometric oil analysis program. This is a program in which an AMT takes a sample of the engine oil at each oil change interval or some other specified time and sends it to a laboratory for analysis. The oil sample is burned in an electric arc and the resulting light is analyzed for the type and amount of various

A spectrometric analysis of a single sample of oil is meaningless. The value of this type of analysis is in tracking the increase in the amounts of various chemical elements in the oil.

chemical elements in the oil. The parts per million of certain elements are plotted over a period of samples and a trend of the growth of these elements in the oil is used to indicate any abnormal wear in the engine.

Chapter 54 **Cold Weather Operation**

Naturally, it is best to keep an airplane in a warm hangar during the winter months. Of course, this is not always possible, so precautions must be taken for engine care in the cold.

In very cold weather, use a pre-heater to warm the engine, taking care to blow the hot air over the oil sump. When starting the engine, check for an indication of oil pressure. If there is no indication of pressure within one minute (or other interval specified in the POH) shut the engine down and determine the cause. When preflighting the airplane, check the engine crankcase breather for ice accumulation. If it is blocked, the crankcase has no vent and excessive oil consumption will result.

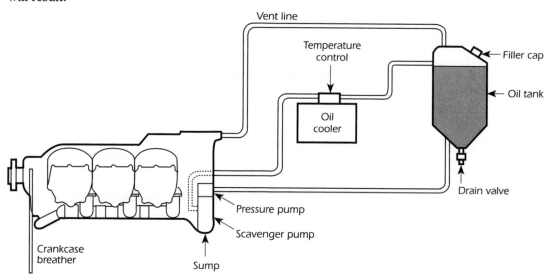

Figure 146. A typical dry-sump lubrication system.

Chapter 55 **Piston Engine Cooling Systems**

Aircraft piston engines are very inefficient as they convert about only one third of the energy in the fuel into useful work. Half of the energy is lost in the hot exhaust gases and part of the waste energy must be carried away by the cooling and the lubrication systems.

Most modern aircraft engines are air cooled, but there have been new developments in liquid cooling in which a high-velocity flow of a water and ethylene glycol mixture is used to cool the cylinder heads. A high-volume spray of engine oil is used to cool the cylinder walls and the underside of the piston heads.

Pressure Cooling for Air-Cooled Engines

Horizontally-opposed engines are the most widely used configuration of piston engines. They are enclosed in a cowling that provides pressure cooling which is seen in Figure 147.

The cowling is divided into two compartments, one above the engine and the other below. The upper compartment is formed by a vertical baffle at the rear of the engine and a horizontal baffle approximately along the centerline of the cylinders. Both the vertical and horizontal baffles are sealed against the cowling with a strip of rubber or rubberized fabric. Air enters the upper compartment through a large forward-facing air inlet at a pressure above ambient because of the ram effect from the forward speed of the aircraft and the acceleration of the air by the propeller. A low pressure below the engine caused by air flowing over a flared cooling-air exit or over a set of adjustable cowl flaps pulls the air downward into the lower compartment through the cooling fins on the cylinders. Close fitting intercylinder baffles and shrouds around the cylinders force all the air to flow through the fins so it can remove the maximum amount of heat.

cowl flaps. Movable flaps located at the exit of the cowling that houses an air-cooled aircraft engine. Opening or closing the cowl flaps controls the amount of air flowing through the cowling and this in turn controls the amount of heat removed from the engine cylinders.

The amount of air that flows through the intercylinder shrouds is determined by the pressure difference across the engine which is regulated by the amount the cowl flaps deflect the air. On the ground the cowl flaps should be fully open; but during climb and cruise, they are closed to regulate the temperature of the engine.

Air cooled engines that are designed to operate in an en-closed cowling must never be operated without the cowling in place. Without the cowling they cannot be adequately cooled.

Cooling air inlets are a favorite nesting place for birds, and if the aircraft has been left out in a tie-down area for a period of time, be sure to carefully inspect all openings in the cowling for possible bird nests.

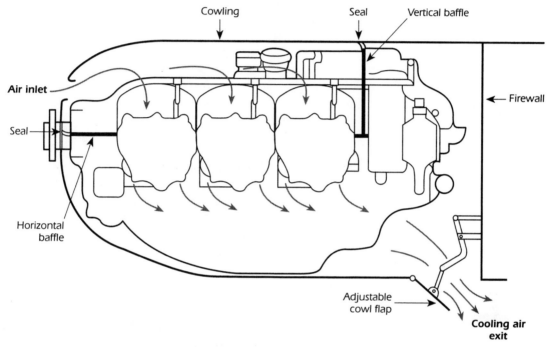

Figure 147. Pressure cooling system for a horizontally-opposed engine

Section 17
Propellers

Chapter 56 **Propeller Aerodynamics**

Aircraft propellers do not get nearly the attention they deserve because they normally give us very little trouble. But they are extremely important as they are the component that converts the torque of the engine into thrust to move the airplane forward.

A propeller is a special type of airfoil that is turned by the engine to produce an aerodynamic force in much the same way a wing produces lift. The cross-sectional shape of a propeller blade resembles that of a wing with a thick section near the hub set at a high angle and the sections getting progressively thinner, the angle less steep as the blade progresses toward the tip.

Figure 148 illustrates some of the terms used with a propeller blade. The flat side of the blade, the side that strikes the air first, is the face of the blade and the curved side that resembles the upper surface of a wing is called the back. The angle between the chord line of the blade and the plane of rotation is the blade angle.

Since the blade angle varies along the blade, it is specified at a particular blade station measured in inches from the centerline of the hub, or in percent of the blade length.

Rather than specifying the blade angle in degrees, many propellers are rated according to their geometric pitch which is the distance a propeller would advance in one revolution if it were turning in a solid. For example, a propeller with a 50-inch pitch would advance 50 inches for each revolution if there were no slippage.

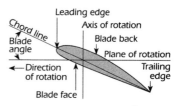

Figure 148. Airfoil section of a propeller blade

blade station. A reference position on a propeller blade that is a specified number of inches from the center of the propeller hub.

Angle of Attack

The amount of thrust produced by a propeller is determined by the angle of attack of the blades; this angle is not the same as the blade angle. The blade angle is fixed for any blade station, but the angle of attack for any blade angle varies with the forward speed of the airplane and the RPM of the engine.

When the engine is turning at takeoff RPM before the airplane begins to move, the angle of attack is the highest and the thrust is maximum. As the airplane picks up speed, the angle of attack becomes smaller and the thrust decreases.

angle of attack. The acute angle between the chord line of a wing, helicopter rotor blade, or propeller blade and the relative wind.

Forces Acting on a Propeller

There are five important forces that act on a propeller: centrifugal force, thrust bending force, torque bending force, aerodynamic twisting force, and centrifugal twisting force.

The first three forces serve no useful purpose but require the propeller to be made strong to withstand them.

Centrifugal force is the strongest force that acts on a propeller and it tries to pull the blades out of the hub. For example, a 25-pound propeller blade turning at 2,700 RPM exerts a force of approximately 50 tons on the blade root.

When a propeller is producing thrust, the thrust bending force tries to bend the tips forward. This is opposed by centrifugal force which tries to pull the blade straight (Figure 149).

Torque is a force that tries to cause rotation, and torque bending force tries to bend the propeller blade in its plane of rotation in a direction opposite to its rotation.

The two twisting forces are used in controlling the pitch of a constant-speed propeller. Aerodynamic twisting force tries to twist the blade to a higher pitch angle and centrifugal twisting force tries to twist them to a lower pitch angle. Some constant-speed propellers have counterweights clamped to the blade roots to alter the effect of the twisting forces.

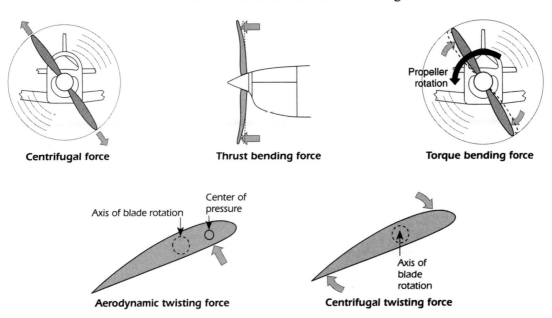

Figure 149. The five forces that act on a propeller

Chapter 57 **Types of Propellers**

The simplest propellers have a fixed pitch (*see* Figure 150). The blade angle is a compromise and is chosen to either produce the maximum thrust at a low speed for takeoff and climb, or at high speed in cruise flight. A low blade angle (low pitch) puts the least strain on the engine and allows it to turn up at its maximum RPM and produce its maximum power. A fixed-pitch propeller with a low pitch angle is called a climb propeller. When high cruising speed is more important than a short takeoff distance, a cruise propeller is chosen. This has a higher pitch angle and loads the engine more than a climb propeller, but it advances through the air a greater distance each revolution.

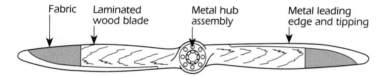

Fabric   Laminated   Metal hub   Metal leading
         wood blade   assembly   edge and tipping

Figure 150. A fixed-pitch wooden propeller

An adjustable-pitch propeller allows a technician to change the pitch angle of the blades when the engine is not operating. Adjustable-pitch propellers are only found on some antique airplanes (*see* Figure 151).

A controllable-pitch propeller allows the pilot to change the pitch with the engine running. A low pitch angle is used for takeoff and a high pitch is used for cruise flight. This type of propeller is a step in the right direction, but by controlling the pitch angle with a flyweight-type governor rather than a simple valve or switch, a controllable-pitch propeller may be made into a constant-speed propeller. (See examples of these illustrated in Chapter 58, where their construction is discussed.)

Constant-speed propellers are found on all medium- and high-performance airplanes. They give the pilot the best control over the power produced and the efficient operation of the engine. With a constant-speed propeller, the propeller pitch control determines the engine RPM and the throttle determines the engine manifold pressure.

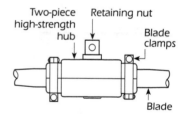

Two-piece   Retaining nut
high-strength
hub   Blade
             clamps

             Blade

Figure 151. A ground-adjustable metal propeller

Constant-speed propellers use a flyweight-type governor driven by the engine to sense the speed of the engine. Moving the propeller pitch control changes the compression of a speeder spring inside the governor to adjust the engine RPM. If the nose drops and the engine speeds up, the governor senses this and causes the pitch of the propeller to increase and bring the RPM back to that set by the pilot. If the nose should pitch up and the RPM decreases, the governor senses this change and decreases the pitch of the blades causing the engine to come back to the desired RPM.

Note: When increasing the power on an engine equipped with a constant-speed propeller, increase the RPM first, then the manifold pressure. This spreads the power increase over more RPM. When decreasing power, decrease manifold pressure first, then the RPM. When setting up the RPM and MP, always use the combinations recommended in the POH.

---

windmilling propeller. A propeller that is being turned by air flowing through it rather than by the engine.

feathering propeller. A propeller with blades that can be moved to an extremely high-pitch angle of approximately 90° so they face directly into the airstream and produce no aerodynamic forces.

A windmilling propeller creates a tremendous amount of drag, and a failed engine may be seriously damaged if the propeller causes it to continue to rotate. Most multiengine airplanes are equipped with feathering propellers. The blades of a feathering propeller can be turned so they are almost parallel with the relative wind and there is no force causing them to turn. With this blade angle the drag is minimum.

Turboprop engines operate over a very limited range of RPM and varying the propeller pitch controls the thrust. These propellers have a wide range of blade angle travel. They can be set at a very flat pitch to produce the minimum drag for starting, they can be set to a negative pitch to produce a reverse thrust, and they can move beyond the high-pitch range to a feather angle.

Chapter 58 **Propeller Construction**

Propellers for most light airplanes have, in the past, had two fixed-pitch blades and have been made of laminated birch wood. During World War II some propellers were made with hollow steel blades, but almost all modern propellers have blades made of forged aluminum alloy. Propellers for turboprop engines are usually made of composite materials such as polyurethane foam, Kevlar™, graphite, and glass fibers held in an epoxy matrix.

Any time the tip speed of a propeller is allowed to reach the speed of sound, excessive noise and vibration result. For there to be enough blade area to absorb the torque and get the required thrust, and at the same time keep the propeller diameter down to limit tip speed, many propellers have three or more blades. Some modern propellers have five or six blades and Propfan™ and Unducted Fan™ propellers have as many as 12 blades.

Pitch Change Mechanism

There have been a number of methods used to change the pitch of a propeller. Some have used electric motors in the hub to change the pitch and some have used a hand crank to change the pitch through a series of worm gears. The most efficient pitch change method is the hydraulic cylinder inside the dome. This is used on almost all modern constant-speed propellers.

There are two types of hydraulically controlled constant-speed propellers found on modern airplanes: the counterweight-type propeller and the noncounterweight type.

Counterweight-Type Constant-Speed Propeller

Some constant-speed propellers have a heavy counterweight clamped tightly around the root of each blade. They are positioned in such a way that centrifugal force tries to move the counterweights into the plane of rotation and increase the blade pitch angle. Figure 152 (on the next page) shows such a propeller, and Figures 153 and 154 show the way the pitch angle is changed.

The blade pitch angle is controlled by a flyweight-type governor that directs oil into the propeller to decrease the pitch

Propfan engine. The trade name registered by Hamilton Standard for an ultrahigh-bypass turbine engine.

Unducted Fan engine. The trade name registered by General Electric for a type of ultrahigh-bypass turbofan engine that drives one or more propellers which have between 8 and 12 blades. These blades which are not enclosed in a duct or shroud, are very thin, have wide chords, and are highly swept back with a scimitar shape.

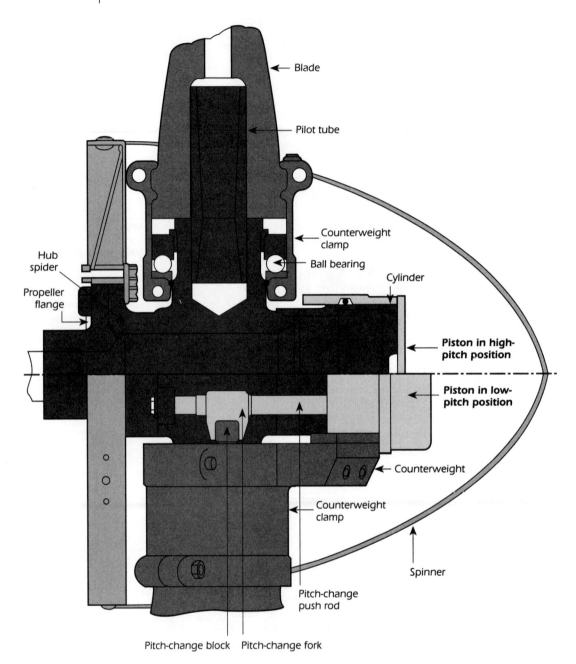

Figure 152. Counterweight-type constant-speed propeller

and allows oil to drain from the propeller to increase the pitch. Figure 153 shows that when the governor indicates that the engine RPM is slower than that called for by the pilot, an underspeed condition, engine oil boosted in pressure by a pump inside the governor is directed into the propeller. This oil pushes the piston forward and the pitch-change push rods rotate the blades to a lower pitch angle against the force of the counterweights. The lower pitch angle allows the engine speed to increase to the RPM called for by the governor.

When the RPM is higher than that called for by the governor, an overspeed condition, oil is drained out of the propeller and centrifugal force acting on the counterweights pulls the piston back and rotates the blades to a higher pitch angle. This loads the engine and decreases the RPM to the value set by the governor. *See* Figure 154.

Noncounterweight-Type Constant-Speed Propeller

The other type of constant-speed propeller used on general aviation airplanes does not use a counterweight to help control the pitch, but uses a combination of aerodynamic twisting force and oil pressure to increase the pitch and centrifugal twisting force and the force from an internal spring to decrease the pitch. *See* Figure 155 on the next page.

The governor used with a noncounterweight propeller is similar to that used with a counterweight propeller, but directs oil in the opposite way. When the engine is operating in an underspeed condition, the governor drains oil from the propeller. When it is in an overspeed condition, oil is sent into the propeller.

When oil is drained from a noncounterweight propeller the combination of centrifugal twisting force and the force of the low-pitch spring moves the piston forward and the blades into a lower pitch angle. The load on the engine is thus reduced and it speeds up until the RPM is that called for by the governor. The governor then shuts off the flow of return oil from the propeller. *See* Figure 156.

When the engine RPM is higher than that set by the governor, a passage inside the governor sends engine oil, boosted in pressure by the pump inside the governor, into the propeller. This oil acts on the forward side of the piston and moves it back, compressing the low-pitch spring and moving the blades to a higher pitch angle. This increases the air load on the engine and brings the RPM back to the speed called for by the governor. *See* Figure 157.

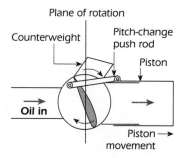

Figure 153. The pitch is decreased when oil from the governor moves the piston forward.

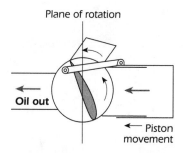

Figure 154. When oil is drained from the propeller, the counterweights move toward the plane of rotation and increase the pitch angle.

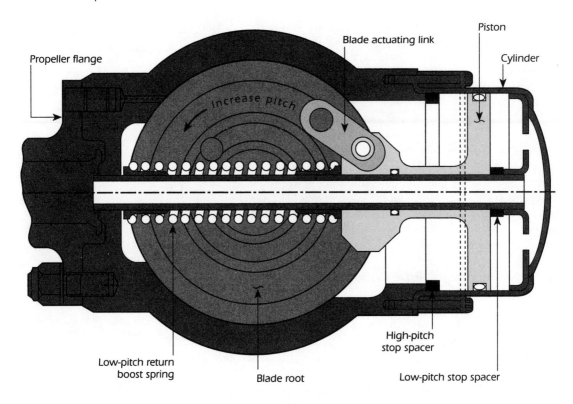

Figure 155. Noncounterweight constant-speed propeller

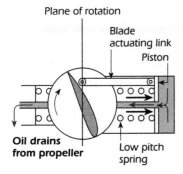

Figure 156. When oil is drained from a noncounterweight propeller the blades move to a lower pitch angle.

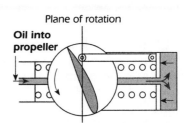

Figure 157. When oil is directed into a noncounterweight propeller the blades move to a higher pitch angle.

Chapter 59 **Feathering Propellers**

If an engine on a twin-engine airplane fails, it is important to immediately stop its propeller from rotating. This minimizes the damage to the engine and greatly reduces the drag caused by the windmilling propeller. This minimizes the damage to the engine and greatly reduces the drag caused by the windmilling propeller.

Just as there are two popular types of nonfeathering constant-speed propellers, there are two popular types of feathering constant-speed propellers: one made by Hartzell and one by McCauley.

Hartzell Constant-Speed Feathering Propeller

The Hartzell feathering propeller operates on the same basic principles as the nonfeathering counterweight propeller but includes two additional features: a feathering spring and a centrifugally actuated high-pitch stop. *See* Figure 158 on the next page.

When the engine is operating in its normal constant-speed range, the governor directs oil into the propeller cylinder to move the blades to a lower pitch angle to increase the RPM, and allows oil to drain out of the propeller to increase the pitch angle.

To feather the propeller, move the propeller pitch control to its full aft position. This opens a passage in the governor that allows the oil in the propeller cylinder to drain back into the engine oil sump. Centrifugal force acting on the counterweights and the force from the feathering spring move the blades into their full-feathered position which is a pitch angle of between 80° and 85°.

If the engine loses oil pressure, the counterweights and the feather spring automatically move the blades into their full feather position. To prevent the propeller from feathering each time the engine is shut down on the ground, a high-pitch stop plate on each blade root contacts a spring loaded high-pitch stop pin in the hub. This pin prevents the blades from moving into the feathered position when the engine is not rotating. If oil pressure is lost in flight, the propeller will windmill fast enough that centrifugal force will hold the stop pin back against the force of the spring and allow the blades to move into their full feather position.

windmilling propeller. A propeller that is being turned by air flowing through it rather than by the engine.

feathering propeller. A propeller with blades that can be moved to an extremely high-pitch angle of approximately 90° so they face directly into the airstream and produce no aerodynamic forces.

Mnemonic aid for feathering the correct propeller: dead foot, dead engine—i.e., you should feather the propeller connected to the engine that requires no rudder pressure to maintain straight ahead. Pull back the corresponding throttle and if you see no apparent change, you have verified the correct failed engine and can proceed feathering the propeller on that engine. Identify, verify, feather.

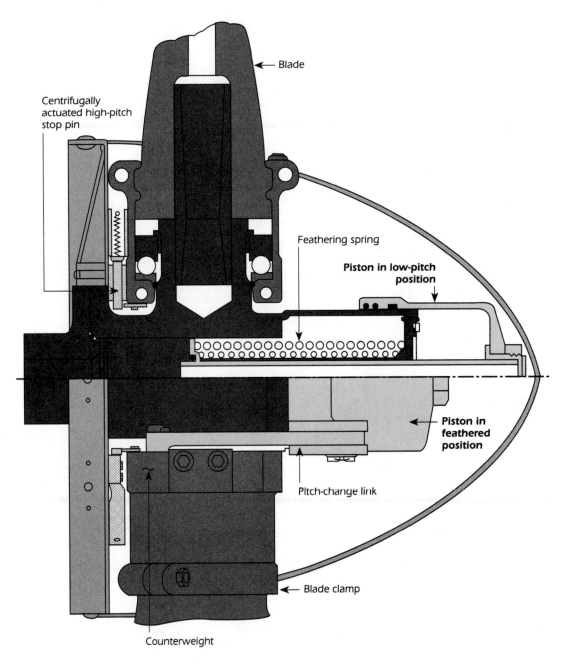

Centrifugally
actuated high-pitch
stop pin

Blade

Feathering spring

**Piston in low-pitch
position**

**Piston in
feathered
position**

Pitch-change link

Blade clamp

Counterweight

Figure 158. Hartzell feathering propeller

To unfeather this propeller, the propeller pitch control is moved to its normal range and the engine is started. As soon as the engine oil pump begins to move oil through the engine and into the propeller cylinder, the piston moves forward and the blades move into their low-pitch angle.

Some Hartzell feathering propellers use an accumulator to hasten the unfeathering process. In normal operation, the accumulator charges with engine oil boosted in pressure by the pump inside the governor. When the propeller pitch control is moved into its full aft position, a valve traps this oil in the accumulator. When the pitch control is returned to its normal range to unfeather the propeller, the oil is released from the accumulator and flows into the propeller cylinder to hasten the unfeathering.

accumulator. A component in a feathering propeller control system that holds engine oil trapped under pressure created by compressed air. To unfeather the propeller, this oil is directed into the propeller cylinder.

McCauley Constant-Speed Feathering Propeller

This propeller operates similar to the noncounterweight propeller but it has counterweights around the blade shanks and uses a spring to aid in feathering. *See* Figure 159 (on the next page).

For normal operation engine oil boosted in pressure by the pump inside the governor is sent into the cylinder to move the piston rearward and the blades into low pitch. As the piston moves rearward, it compresses the feathering spring.

When the propeller pitch control is moved to its full aft position in flight, a valve inside the governor is opened which allows oil in the propeller cylinder to flow back into the engine sump. Centrifugal force holds the high-pitch blade latches disengaged so the combined forces of the counterweights and the feathering spring can move the piston forward and rotate the blades into their feathered position.

When the engine is shut down on the ground there is no centrifugal force to hold the blade latches out and they stop the blades in their normal high pitch position.

Some McCauley propellers use an accumulator to supply oil under pressure to speed up the unfeathering process.

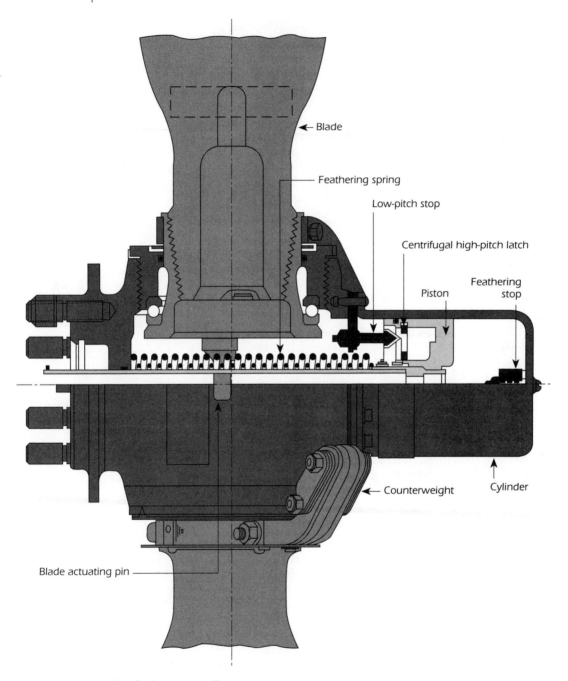

Figure 159. McCauley feathering propeller

Chapter 60 **Turboprop Propellers**

There are two basic types of turboprop engines and they require different types of propellers. The single-shaft turbine
engine drives the propeller through a series of reduction gears
from the same shaft that drives the compressor. A free-turbine
engine has a separate power turbine that drives the propeller
through a set of reduction gears. Both types of engines operate
at a relatively constant speed and the propeller thrust is
changed by controlling the blade pitch angle.

Turboprop engines have two operating modes: the alpha
mode and the beta mode. The beta mode is the ground operation mode which includes start, taxi, and reverse operations.
The alpha mode is the flight mode and includes all operations
from takeoff through landing.

The propeller pitch control is integrated with the engine
fuel control in such a way that when the power lever is

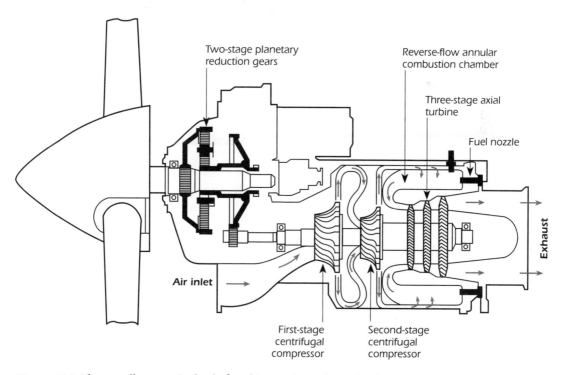

Figure 160. The propeller on a single-shaft turbine engine is driven by the same turbines that drive
the compressor.

advanced, the propeller blades move into a higher pitch and the fuel control meters more fuel into the engine. When the power lever is moved all the way to its aft stop, the propeller blades move to a preset negative angle to produce reverse thrust.

The propeller may be feathered in flight by manually opening the feathering valve or automatically by a negative torque sensor that senses the loss of positive torque.

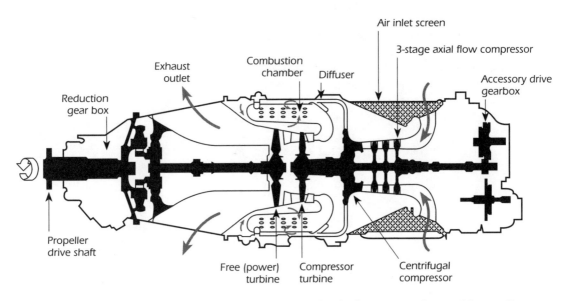

Figure 161. The propeller on a free-turbine engine is driven by the free power turbine and has no direct connection to the turbine that drives the compressor.

Chapter 61 **Propeller Servicing**

Because the propeller is such a highly stressed component, the FAA requires that all major repairs or major alterations be done by the propeller manufacturer or by a certificated repair station that is approved for the specific operation.

A powerplant technician is limited to removing and installing propellers, lubricating them, and performing minor repairs or minor alterations. The most important minor repair is smoothing out pits and roughness in the leading edges caused by running the engine in an area where dirt and loose gravel can be sucked into the whirling blades. Any pit in a propeller blade should be referred to a technician because they can cause stress risers that can lead to the loss of a portion of a blade and thus serious damage to the engine.

Propeller Vibration

Any roughness of an aircraft engine is a cause for concern, and it is possible that this could be caused by the propeller. There are two things that can cause propeller induced vibrations: the propeller being out of track and being out of balance.

Propeller Track

Before touching the propeller, be sure that the ignition switch is OFF, and even when it is in the OFF position, treat the propeller as though it were ON. There is always the possibility that an ignition switch P-lead may be disconnected or broken which would make the magneto "hot," or active.

Set the parking brake or chock the wheels and position the propeller so one blade is straight down. Place a box or some other device on the ground below the propeller blade with a piece of paper on a flat board so the blade tip just touches it. Pull forward on the end of the blade to take any play out of the blade and make a mark on the paper where the blade touches it. Very carefully rotate the propeller until the other blade is straight down and repeat the process. If the two marks are more than 1/16 inch apart the blades are out of track and an AMT should be consulted to determine the reason.

stress riser. A location on a structure where the cross-sectional area changes drastically. Stresses concentrate at such a location and are likely to cause failure. A scratch, pit, or gouge in the surface of a propeller blade can develop into a stress riser.

Propeller Balance

When a propeller is new or when it has been repaired at an FAA-approved repair station, it has been balanced but any damage to a blade or to the spinner could throw it out of balance.

Almost all modern airplanes have the propeller enclosed in a spinner that makes the airplane more attractive and streamlined, but of more importance, it directs the cooling air into the cowling in the way the designers have intended. When a spinner is included in the required equipment, the airplane must not be flown without it.

An improperly repaired spinner or spinner bulkhead can cause an out of balance condition that must be corrected. A technician can use an electronic balancer (Figure 162) that when properly operated can show the amount of out-of-balance and the location and amount of weight to be attached to the spinner bulkhead to bring the propeller into acceptable balance.

Propeller Synchronizing

When the two propellers of a twin-engine airplane are not turning at exactly the same speed, a very annoying low frequency vibration is set up in the aircraft. Mechanical tachometers are normally not sensitive enough to synchronize the engines, so it is best done by tweaking one of the propeller pitch controls until the vibration disappears.

Some twin-engine airplanes are equipped with an automatic synchronizer system that adjusts the governor of one engine (the slave engine) to maintain the same RPM as that of the other engine (the master engine).

Propeller Deicing System

An airplane that is approved for flight into known icing conditions normally is required to have a propeller deicing system. This consists of a set of electrically conductive rubber boots bonded to the leading edge of the blades.

An important part of a preflight inspection before any flight into known or suspect icing conditions is to determine that the propeller deicing system is working properly. Turn the system ON in the AUTOMATIC mode and watch the propeller ammeter. It should indicate a flow of current each time one of the heater elements draws current. After the system is turned OFF, feel all the boots to be sure they are equally warm.

Figure 162. An electronic balancer shows the AMT the amount a propeller is out of balance and the location to place balance weights on the spinner bulkhead to bring the propeller back into an acceptable state of balance.

Glossary

absolute pressure. Pressure referenced from zero pressure or a vacuum. Absolute pressure is normally measured in inches of mercury (in. Hg.).

accumulator. A component in a feathering propeller control system that holds engine oil trapped under pressure created by compressed air. To unfeather the propeller, this oil is directed into the propeller cylinder.

advancing blade. The blade of a helicopter rotor that is moving in the same direction as the helicopter is moving.

adverse yaw. A flight condition at the beginning of a turn in which the nose of an airplane starts to move in the direction opposite the direction the turn is being made. Adverse yaw is caused by the induced drag produced by the downward-deflected aileron holding the wing back as it begins to rise.

alternating current (AC). Electricity in which the electrons continually change their amount of flow and periodically reverse their direction of flow.

alternator field current. A small flow of current from the battery through the voltage regulator to the coil in the alternator rotor. Varying this small current controls the alternator output voltage. When the alternator side of the master switch is turned OFF, the field current stops and turns the alternator off.

altimeter setting. Station barometric pressure corrected for the height of the station above mean sea level.

aluminum alloy. Aluminum to which has been added one or more other chemical elements. These alloying elements increase the hardness, toughness, resistance to fatigue, or durability of the aluminum. Aluminum alloys are the primary metals used in the construction of aircraft and other structures that require high strength and light weight.

amplitude modulation (AM). A system of changing the voltage of a radio-frequency (RF) carrier to allow it to carry information. The amplitude of the carrier is changed (modulated) by superimposing the information-carrying audio frequency (AF) signal on it. The amplitude of the modulated carrier varies in the same way as the amplitude of the audio-frequency information wave.

AMT. Aviation Maintenance Technician

angle of attack. The acute angle between the chord line of a wing, helicopter rotor blade, or propeller blade and the relative wind.

anti-icing system. A system that prevents the formation of ice on an aircraft structure.

arm. The horizontal distance, in inches from the reference datum, to the center of gravity (CG) of an item. A positive (+) arm is behind the datum and a negative (–) arm is ahead of the datum.

ATC. Air traffic control

antitorque pedals. Foot pedals used by the pilot to control the pitch of the antitorque rotor on the tail of a single-rotor helicopter.

audio frequency (AF). The frequency of vibrations that can be detected by the normal human ear. They are considered to be between 15 and 20,000 hertz.

autogiro. A heavier-than-air rotary-wing aircraft that is sustained in the air by rotors turned by aerodynamic forces rather than by engine power. When the name Autogiro is spelled with a capital A, it refers to a specific series of machines built by Juan de la Cierva or his followers. The FAA-sanctioned name for this type of machine is a gyroplane.

aviation gasoline (Avgas). A highly refined hydrocarbon fuel obtained by fractional distillation of crude petroleum. Its important characteristics are purity, volatility, and antidetonation qualities.

axial-flow compressor. A type of compressor used in gas turbine engines in which the air passes through the compressor in essentially a straight line, parallel to the axis of the compressor. The compressor is made of a number of stages of rotating compressor blades between stages of stationary stator vanes. The compression ratio is determined by the number of stages of compression.

battery contactor. A heavy-duty magnetically operated switch that carries current from the battery to the alternator bus. The contactor is controlled by current from the battery half of the split-rocker master switch.

Bernoulli's principle. When the total energy in a column of moving fluid remains constant, any increase in the kinetic energy of the fluid (its velocity) results in a corresponding decrease in its potential energy (its pressure).

bezel. The rim around an instrument case that holds the glass cover.

blade station. A reference position on a propeller blade that is a specified number of inches from the center of the propeller hub.

bleeding of the brakes. The maintenance procedure of removing air entrapped in hydraulic fluid in the brakes. Fluid is bled from the brake system until fluid with no bubbles flows out.

Brayton cycle. The constant-pressure cycle of energy release used in a gas turbine engine. Fuel is added to the air passing through the engine and burned. Heat from the burning fuel expands the air, and since the air is not confined, it accelerates as it moves through the engine.

The events: intake, compression, ignition, combustion, expansion, and exhaust all take place at the same time, but at different locations within the engine.

bungee cord. An elastic cord made up of a series of small strips of rubber or rubber bands encased in a loosely braided cloth cover.

bus. A common point in an aircraft electrical system from which power from the alternator and battery supply current to all of the components in the electrical system.

calibrated orifice. A hole of specific diameter used to delay the pressure change in the case of a vertical speed indicator.

carburetor air heater. A sheet metal jacket surrounding part of the engine exhaust system through which air from inside the engine nacelle or compartment flows and picks up heat. When the air temperature is low or the humidity is high, heated air can be directed through the carburetor heat valve into the carburetor. Air that flows through the carburetor air heater is not filtered.

carburetor ice. Ice that forms inside the throat of a carburetor installed on an aircraft reciprocating engine. When air flows through the carburetor venturi, it speeds up, and both its pressure and temperature drop. When liquid fuel is discharged into the throat of the venturi, it vaporizes, and this change of state drops its temperature. When the temperature of the air is low enough, moisture in the air condenses out and freezes. It is possible for carburetor ice to build up inside the venturi and restrict the air flowing into the engine enough to cause the engine to stop. Carburetor ice is normally prevented by heating the air before it enters the carburetor.

circuit breaker. An electrical component that automatically opens the circuit any time an excess of current flows. Most popped circuit breakers can be closed in flight to restore an opened circuit.

coaxial cable. A type of two-conductor electrical cable in which the center conductor is held rigidly in the center of a braided shield which serves as the outer conductor. Coaxial cable, commonly called coax, is used to connect radio receivers and transmitters to their antenna.

collective pitch control. The helicopter control that changes the pitch of all of the rotor blades at the same time. Movements of this control increases or decreases the lift produced by the entire rotor disk.

combustor. The section of a gas turbine engine in which the fuel is injected, mixed with air and burned. The intense heat from the combustion expands the air flowing through the combustor and directs it out through the turbine.

combustible mixture. An air-fuel mixture of between 8 pounds of air to 1 pound of gasoline to 18 pounds of air to 1 pound of gasoline.

composite structure. A type of aircraft structure made of plastic resins reinforced with strong, lightweight filaments. Fiberglass, carbon, Kevlar, and boron are materials used for composite structure. Composite materials combine high strength and rigidity with light weight.

coning angle. The upward flapping angle formed by helicopter rotor blades as they are producing lift.

cowl flaps. Moveable flaps located at the exit of the cowling that houses an air-cooled aircraft engine. Opening or closing the cowl flaps controls the amount of air flowing through the cowling and this in turn controls the amount of heat removed from the engine cylinders.

crankcase. The housing of a reciprocating engine which encloses the crankshaft, camshaft,

and many of the accessory drive gears. The cylinders mount on the crankcase, and the engine is attached to the airframe by the crankcase.

corrosion. An electrochemical action that takes place inside a metal or on its surface. The metal reacts with an electrolyte, and part of the metal is changed into a salt, which is the corrosion. Corrosion is dry and powdery and has no physical strength.

critical angle of attack. The highest angle of attack at which air passes over an airfoil in a smooth flow. At angles greater than the critical angle, the air burbles or flows in a disturbed pattern and lift is lost.

critical altitude. The maximum altitude at which a turbocharged aircraft engine can produce its rated takeoff power.

current. The flow of electrons. Current is measured in amperes (amps).

cyclic pitch control. The helicopter control that allows the pilot to change the pitch of the rotor blades individually, at a specific point in their rotation. It allows the pilot to tilt the plane of rotation of the rotor disk to change the direction of lift produced by the rotor.

cylinder. The component in a reciprocating engine that houses the piston and valves; they form the combustion chambers of the engine.

datum. An imaginary vertical reference plane or line chosen by the aircraft manufacturer from which all arms used for weight and balance computation are measured.

deicer. A system or component used to remove ice from a surface after it has formed; not to be confused with anti-icers that prevent the formation of ice.

density altitude. Pressure altitude corrected for nonstandard temperature. Density altitude is used for computing the performance of an aircraft and its engines.

detector. The circuit in a radio receiver that converts the received radio-frequency signal to an audio-frequency signal that can be heard.

detonation. An explosion or uncontrolled burning inside the cylinder of a reciprocating engine. Detonation occurs when the pressure and temperature inside the cylinder become higher than the critical pressure and temperature of the fuel, and may be caused by using fuel that has a lower octane rating or performance number than is specified for the engine. Detonation can destroy an engine.

deviation. A magnetic compass error caused by local magnetic fields within the aircraft. Deviation error is different on each heading.

differential pressure. A single pressure which is the difference between two opposing pressures.

diffuser. A duct installed in the compressor outlet of a turbine engine to reduce the velocity of the air leaving the compressor and to increase its pressure before it enters the combustor.

diode. An electronic component that acts as an electron check valve. Current can flow through it in one direction but is blocked in the opposite direction. ——▶▌——

direct current (DC). Electricity in which the electrons move through the system in one direction only.

divergent oscillation. Oscillations whose amplitude increases with time.

double gimbal. A type of support, similar to a universal joint, that allows a gyroscope to remain in an upright condition as the aircraft rolls or pitches.

electromagnet. A device that is magnetized by current flowing through a coil of wire inside or around an iron pole piece. The strength of the magnet is determined by the amount of current flowing through the coil and the number of turns of wire in the coil.

elevators. The horizontal movable control surface in the tail section, or empennage of an airplane.

encoding altimeter. A sensitive altimeter that sends signals to the ATC transponder, showing the pressure altitude the aircraft is flying.

EWCG (Empty Weight Center of Gravity). The center of gravity of an aircraft when it contains only the items specified in the aircraft empty weight.

feathering propeller. A propeller with blades that can be moved to an extremely high-pitch angle of approximately 90° so they face directly into the airstream and produce no aerodynamic forces.

Fowler flap. A flap mounted on rollers that ride in grooves in the flap bracket. When the flap is lowered, it moves down and aft increasing both the wing camber and area.

free turbine. A turbine or stage of turbines in a gas turbine engine that is independent of the turbine used to drive the compressor in the gas-generator section of the engine. A free turbine may be used to drive the reduction gears for the propeller in a turboprop engine, or the transmission of a helicopter. Free turbines are also used in industrial turbine engines to drive pumps or generators. Sometimes referred to as free power turbines.

frequency modulation (FM). A method of putting an audio-frequency signal on a radio-frequency carrier. The AF signal changes the frequency of the carrier by an amount determined by the amplitude of the audio voltage. The amplitude of the FM carrier is clipped so static caused by electrical interference produces a minimum of distortion.

front and rear ends of an engine. The front end of an engine is the end that has the propeller even though it may be mounted as a pusher. The technical name for the rear end of the engine is the antipropeller end.

FSS. Flight service station

gage pressure. Pressure referenced from the existing barometric pressure. In engine oil pressure it is the pressure that is produced by the oil pump.

global positioning system (GPS). Navigation system that uses satellite rather than ground-based transmitters for location information.

ground effect. The increase in lift produced by an airfoil (or in the lift of a helicopter) when flying near the ground. The additional lift comes from an effective increase in the angle of attack without the accompanying increase in induced drag; this is caused by the deflection of the downwashed air. Ground effect disappears when flying about a half wing span (or, half-rotor span) above the surface.

ground symbol. A symbol in the diagram of a single-wire electrical system that shows where the device is grounded (connected to the aircraft or engine structure).

gyroplane. A type of rotorcraft whose main rotors are not connected to the engine except for the initial spin-up. Aerodynamic forces cause the main rotor to spin during normal flight. An autogiro is a form of gyroplane.

Heli-Coil insert. A patented stainless steel coil of wire having a diamond-shaped cross section. It is screwed into the spark plug hole in a cast aluminum alloy cylinder head to form wear-resistant threads.

helicopter. A heavier-than-air flying machine that is supported in the air by aerodynamic lift produced by an engine-driven rotor. Since the rotor is engine driven, a helicopter does not need forward motion through the air for the rotor to produce lift.

hydraulic system. A fluid power system that transmits a force from one location to another through an incompressible fluid. A pneumatic system does the same thing but uses a compressible fluid such as air.

IFR. Instrument flight rules

jackscrew. A hardened steel rod with strong threads cut into it. A jackscrew is rotated by a motor or by hand to apply a force to move the leading edge of an adjustable stabilizer.

Kollsman window. A barometric scale window of a sensitive altimeter used to adjust the altitude for the altimeter setting.

lags or leads (compass error). When starting a turn from a northerly heading, the compass lags behind the turn. When starting a turn from a southerly heading, the compass leads the turn.

latitude. The angular north–south measurement of location on the surface of the Earth, north and south of the equator. Latitude is measured in degrees, minutes, and seconds (or degrees, minutes and hundredths of a minute). Parallels of latitude cut the Earth in a series of imaginary parallel slices. The equator is 0° latitude, the north pole is 90° north latitude and the south pole is 90° south latitude.

lean mixture. An air-fuel mixture that contains more than 15 parts of air to 1 part of fuel, by weight.

loading graph. A graph of load weight and load moment indexes; diagonal lines for each item relate the weight to the moment index without having to use mathematics.

loading schedule. A method and procedure used to show that an aircraft is properly loaded and will not exceed approved weight and balance limitations during operation.

longitude. The angular east–west measurement of location on the Earth's surface. The surface of the Earth is divided by 360 meridians, or lines of longitude that pass through both the north and south poles. The meridian passing through the Royal Observatory in Greenwich, near London, England is 0° longitude and is called the prime meridian. On the opposite side of the Earth is the 180° meridian which is called the international date line. Longitude east of the prime meridian is called east longitude and that west of the prime meridian is west longitude.

magneto. A small, self-contained electrical generator and a step-up transformer for ignition. A set of breaker points, timed to the crankshaft, interrupts the flow of current in the primary winding. This interruption induces a high voltage in the secondary winding at the proper time for a spark to occur at the spark plug inside the cylinder. If the aircraft electrical system fails completely, the engine will continue to run.

manifold pressure. The absolute pressure inside the intake manifold that forces the fuel-air charge into the cylinders.

matrix. The material used in composite construction to bond the fibers together and to transmit the forces into the fibers. Resins are the most widely used matrix materials.

MIL standards. A group of standard specifications used by the United States military services to describe the products they buy. MIL standards are known and used by most manufacturers to keep parts standardized and interchangeable.

moment. The product of the weight of an item in pounds multiplied by its arm in inches. Moment is stated in pound-inches (lb.-in.).

moment index. The moment (weight times arm) divided by a reduction factor such as 100 or 1,000 to make the number smaller and reduce the number of digits.

momentum. The product of a mass times its velocity.

monocoque structure. A single-shell type of aircraft structure in which all flight loads are carried in its outer skin. The skins are formed into compound curves and fastened together into a structure resembling an eggshell.

MSL. The elevation above mean sea level.

naturally aspirated engine. A reciprocating engine that uses atmospheric pressure to force the charge of fuel-air mixture into the cylinders. A naturally aspirated engine differs from a supercharged engine that uses a mechanical air compressor to increase the pressure of the air and force the fuel-air mixture into the cylinders.

Newton's third law of motion. States that every action (or force) gives rise to a reaction (or opposing force) of equal strength but of opposite direction.

nonprecision approach. An instrument approach to an airport that does not incorporate the use of a glide slope.

null. The position of an ADF loop antenna when the signal being received is cancelled in the two sides of the loop and the signal strength is weakest.

octane rating. A rating of the antidetonation characteristics of a reciprocating engine fuel, based on the performance of the fuel in a special test engine. The higher the number the better the fuel resists detonation.

P-lead. The primary lead, or the wire that connects the primary circuit of a magneto to ground when the magneto is OFF.

plain bearings. Bearings made of a material such as lead or babbit that has a low coefficient of friction.

planetary gears. A system of gears that reduces the speed of the propeller shaft without changing its direction of rotation as is done with a simple spur gear system.

plenum chamber. An enclosed chamber in which air can be held at a pressure slightly higher than that of the surrounding air. A plenum chamber allows the air pressure to stabilize before it enters the compressor of a gas turbine engine.

POH. Pilot's Operating Handbook

position error. The error in the indication of flight instruments connected to the static air system. This error is caused by the air at the entrance of the static system not being absolutely still. Position error is normally greatest at low airspeeds where the angle of attack is highest.

power. The amount of work in foot-pounds divided by the time in seconds or minutes used to do the work. One horsepower is equal to 33,000 foot-pounds of work done in one minute or 550 foot-pounds of work done in one second.

power (electrical). The ability of an electrical system to do work. Power is measured in watts, and is the product of current and voltage (power = current x voltage).

precession. The characteristic of a gyroscope that causes an applied force to be felt, not at the point the force is applied, but at a point 90° in the direction of rotation from that point.

pressure altitude. Altitude above the standard reference plane of 29.92" Hg or 1013.2 mb.

primary winding. The winding made of heavy wire in the step-up transformer inside a magneto. Current is induced into the primary winding by the rotating magnet.

primer (finishing system). A component in a finishing system that provides a good bond between the surface and the material used for the topcoats.

primer (engine starting component). A small, hand-operated pump, used to spray gasoline into the induction system of a reciprocating engine for starting.

propeller anti-icer. A system that spreads a mixture of alcohol and glycerin along the propeller blades when the aircraft is flying in icing conditions. The alcohol and glycerin prevent water reaching the metal of the propeller blade and freezing on it.

Propfan engine. The trade name registered by Hamilton Standard for an ultrahigh-bypass turbine engine.

radial. A line of radio bearing radiating outward from a VOR navigation facility. There are 360 radials radiating out from each VOR and each radial is named for the number of degrees clockwise from magnetic north that the radial leaves the facility.

radio frequency (RF). The frequency of electromagnetic energy that is high enough that it will radiate from any conductor through which it flows. This is normally considered to be from 150 kilohertz (kHz) all the way up into the infrared range.

reciprocating engine. A form of heat engine that changes chemical energy into mechanical energy. A mixture of fuel and air is drawn into a cylinder as a close-fitting piston moves inward. The valve through which the fuel-air mixture entered the cylinder then closes, and the piston moves outward, compressing the mixture. As the piston nears the outward end of its stroke, the compressed fuel-air mixture is ignited by an electric spark, and it burns. The burning gases heat the air in the cylinder, and as it expands, its pressure forces the piston inward, producing mechanical work. The reciprocating motion of the piston is converted into rotary motion of the crankshaft by a connecting rod that connects the piston to one of the throws of the crankshaft.

rectifier. An electrical device that allows electrons to travel in one direction but blocks their travel in the opposite direction.

reduction factor (weight and balance). A number, usually 100 or 1,000 by which a moment is divided to produce a smaller number that is less likely to cause mathematical errors when computing the center of gravity.

reduction gears (turbine engines). A gear arrangement in which the output shaft turns more slowly than the input shaft, used to increase the torque produced by the rotor of a turbine engine.

resistance. The friction caused when electrons move in a circuit. Resistance is measured in ohms.

retread. The replacement of the tread rubber on an aircraft tire.

retreating blade. The blade of a helicopter rotor that is moving in the direction opposite to the direction the helicopter is moving.

rich mixture. An air-fuel mixture that contains less than 15 parts of air to 1 part of fuel, by weight.

rigidity in space. The characteristic of a gyroscope that prevents its axis of rotation tilting as the Earth rotates. This characteristic is used in attitude gyro instruments.

ruddervator. The control surfaces on an airplane that combine the function of the rudder and the elevators. Ruddervators are the movable surfaces in a V-tail empennage.

SAE (Society of Automotive Engineers). A professional organization that formulates standards for the automotive and aviation industries.

secondary winding. The winding made of many turns of fine wire in the step-up transformer inside a magneto. When the breaker points interrupt the flow of current in the primary winding, its magnetic field collapses and induces a very high voltage in the secondary winding.

semimonocoque structure. A form of stressed-skin aircraft structure in which the outer skin is supported by a substructure of formers and stringers that gives the skin its shape and increases its rigidity.

shimmy. Abnormal and often violent vibration of the nose wheel of an airplane.

shock cooling. Rapid cooling of a piston engine by suddenly retarding the throttle while the engine is hot and the outside air is cold. Shock cooling causes the cylinders to shrink around the pistons and cause serious cylinder wall scuffing.

shock wave. A pressure wave formed when an aircraft passes through the air at a speed greater than the speed of sound. Pressure disturbances cannot move out ahead of the aircraft and they build up in the form of a shock, or pressure, wave.

side slip. A flight maneuver in which an airplane is banked while the rudder keeps it on a straight heading. This crossed-control condition causes the airplane to move sideways toward the low wing.

specific weight. The ratio of the weight of an aircraft engine to the brake horsepower it produces.

spin. A maneuver in which one wing is stalled while the other continues to produce lift. The airplane descends slowly in a steep nose-down rotating attitude.

split-rocker master switch. The master switch used on many modern airplanes. One side of the switch controls the alternator and the other side controls the battery contactor which connects the battery to the alternator bus. The battery side can be turned ON without turning on the alternator but the alternator side cannot be turned ON without turning on the battery side. The alternator side can be turned OFF without affecting the battery side.

spur gear. A gear wheel with teeth radiating outward from its periphery.

squat switch. A safety switch on one of the main landing gear shock struts actuated by the torque links when weight is on the landing gear. A squat switch may be used to prevent the landing gear handle from being moved to the UP position when weight is on the landing gear, or to prevent the cabin from being pressurized when on the ground.

stabilator. A single-piece movable horizontal tail surface on an airplane that serves the dual purpose of the horizontal stabilizer and the elevators.

stall. An aerodynamic condition in which the angle of attack becomes excessive and the air no longer flows smoothly over an airfoil. When an airfoil stalls, it no longer produces lift.

strain. A deformation, or physical change, in a material caused by a stress.

stress. A force within an object that tries to prevent an outside force from changing its shape.

stress riser. A location on a structure where the cross-sectional area changes drastically. Stresses concentrate at such a location and are likely to cause failure. A scratch, pit, or gouge in the surface of a propeller blade can develop into a stress riser.

supercharger. An air pump used to increase the pressure of the air taken into the cylinders of a reciprocating engine. The amount of power a reciprocating engine can develop is determined by the mass, or weight, of the fuel-air mixture taken into the cylinders. By compressing the air before it enters the cylinders, a greater mass of air can be used, and more power can be developed by the engine.

supercooled water. Water in its liquid state at a temperature below its normal freezing temperature. When supercooled water is disturbed, it immediately freezes.

superstructure. The framework of formers and stringers attached to the main truss of a truss-type aircraft fuselage to give it its streamline and attractive shape.

TBO. A period of time specified by the manufacturer of an aircraft engine as the maximum length of time the engine should be run between overhauls without normal wear causing parts of the engine to be worn beyond safe limits.

thermocouple. An electrical generating device consisting of wires of two dissimilar metals connected to form two junctions. An electrical current is generated in the wires that is proportional to the temperature difference between the two junctions.

thrust. The forward aerodynamic force produced by a propeller, fan, or turbojet engine as it forces a mass of air to the rear, behind the airplane.

tire bead. The high-strength carbon-steel wire bundles that give an aircraft tire its strength and stiffness where it mounts on the wheel. The beads are encased in rubber-impregnated fabric.

torque. A force that produces, or tries to produce, rotation.

torsional vibration. A twisting vibration in a crankshaft caused by the power impulses transmitted from the pistons into the crankshaft.

total pressure. The pressure a moving mass of fluid would have if it were stopped. Total pressure is the sum of the static pressure and the pressure caused by the ram effect.

transceiver. A piece of radio communications equipment in which all of the circuits for the transmitter and receiver are contained in the same housing.

transformer. An electrical device that changes the values of current and voltage in an AC circuit. When voltage is increased, current is decreased in the same proportion.

transformer-rectifier. An electrical device that reduces the value of the AC to that suitable for the battery and changes the AC into DC to keep the aircraft batteries charged.

transonic flight. Flight in which an aircraft transitions from subsonic to supersonic flight. Some air flowing over the aircraft is slower than the speed of sound and other is supersonic.

transponder. The airborne portion of the ATC radar beacon system.

truss structure. A type of structure made of longitudinal beams and cross braces. Compression loads between the main beams are carried by rigid cross braces called compression struts. Tension loads are carried by stays or wires that go from one main beam to the other and cross between the compression struts.

turboprop engine. A form of gas turbine engine that uses one or more stages of turbines to drive a set of reduction gears, which in turn drives a propeller. Most of the heat energy in the exhaust gases is converted into torque, rather than into a stream of high-velocity exhaust gases, as is done in a turbojet engine.

Unducted Fan engine. The trade name registered by General Electric for a type of ultrahigh-bypass turbofan engine that drives one or more propellers which have between 8 and 12 blades. These blades which are not enclosed in a duct or shroud, are very thin, have wide chords, and are highly swept back with a scimitar shape.

unidirectional fabric. Fabric in which all of the threads run in the same direction. These threads are often bound with a few fibers run at right angles, just enough to hold the yarns together and prevent their bunching.

UTC time (Universal Time Coordinated). Universal time corrected for seasonal variations in the Earth's rotation. It is the same as Greenwich Mean Time (GMT) which is the time at the Royal Observatory in Greenwich, England. It is also known as Zulu time.

variation. The compass error caused by the difference in the physical locations of the magnetic north pole and the geographic north pole.

venturi. A specially shaped restriction in an air passage that is designed to speed up the flow of air. As the air speeds up its pressure drops.

voltage. The electrical pressure that forces electrons to flow in a circuit. This pressure is measured in volts.

waste gate. A controllable butterfly valve in the exhaust pipe of a reciprocating engine equipped with an exhaust-driven turbocharger. When the waste gate is open, the exhaust gases leave the engine through the exhaust pipe; but when closed, the gases must pass through the turbine that drives the turbocharger compressor. By controlling the opening of the waste gate, the speed of the turbocharger can be controlled, and this speed determines the manifold pressure in the engine.

waypoint. A pseudo-location to which a VORTAC station has been electronically moved by an RNAV system. It is established either by its radial and DME distance from an existing VORTAC station, or by its latitude and longitude. Navigation equipment can direct flight to a waypoint in the same way it can to an actual radio facility.

windmilling propeller. A propeller that is being turned by air flowing through it rather than by the engine.

work. A physical measurement of force used to produce movement; the product of force times distance. When one pound of force causes an object to move one foot, one foot-pound of work has been done.

yaw. A flight condition in which an airplane rotates about its vertical axis. Yawing is not the same as turning because an airplane can be yawed while continuing in straight flight.

Index

Notes

Notes

Notes